WORTHY IS THE WORLD:
The Hindu Philosophy
of
Sri Aurobindo

Sri Aurobindo

WORTHY IS THE WORLD:
The Hindu Philosophy
of
Sri Aurobindo

Beatrice Bruteau

Rutherford • **Madison** • **Teaneck**
FAIRLEIGH DICKINSON UNIVERSITY PRESS

© 1971 by Associated University Presses, Inc.
Library of Congress Catalogue Card Number: 73-144091

Associated University Presses, Inc.
Cranbury, New Jersey 08512

ISBN: 0-8386-7872-6
Printed in the United States of America

Contents

Foreword

By Robert T. Francoeur*

During the high Middle Ages Western man attained a magnificent panoramic vision of himself and his place in the cosmos. The substance of philosophy, theology, mysticism, legal and political thought, the arts, and the science of the day were forged into a masterful diorama by Dante, Aquinas, Bonaventure, Anselm, Bernard of Clairvaux, Abelard, Siger of Brabant, Robert Grosseteste, Roger Bacon, and other synthesizing minds. The genius of Greek science and philosophy, the mysticism of the Neoplatonists and the Arabians, the spirituality of Augustine, and the thought of earlier Jewish thinkers were distilled into a Weltanschauung of unparalleled harmony of conviction.

For a few decades, perhaps a century or two, that vision endured as a meaningful and relevant image of man and the cosmos. But soon the industrial revolution, nominalism,

* Dr. Francoeur, Associate Professor of Experimental Embryology and Interdisciplinary Studies at Fairleigh Dickinson University, is probably the leading exponent in the United States of the thought of Teilhard de Chardin. Author of *The World of Teilhard, Perspectives in Evolution, Utopian Motherhood: New Trends in Human Reproduction,* and *Evolving World; Converging Man,* he is one of the founders of the American Teilhard de Chardin Association and until 1971 served as Chairman of its Executive Committee.

the advent of the printing press and the consequent de-
mands of in-depth study based on the exploding wealth of
ideas of earlier thinkers forced Western man into com-
partmentalized thinking and specialization. The world of
Dante shattered into antiquated fragments. But nothing
emerged to replace this panoramic vision of man and the
cosmos. Fragmentation only increased the anguish of Western man, confronted now with the disturbing mobility and
rapid changes of the industrial and technological culture.

Even in its earliest days Darwinian evolution appeared
to many thinkers in a variety of traditions to be a possible
keystone in the development of a new Weltanschauung for
modern man. Thus we have observed the fascination of
cosmogenesis triggered by the synthesizing vision of the
French Jesuit paleontologist, Pierre Teilhard de Chardin,
author of *The Phenomenon of Man.* On a less popular but
likely more scientifically profound level has been the growing relevance of Ludwig von Bertalanffy's integration of
general system theory—the basis of computers and information theory—with evolutionary science and developmental
biology. Teilhard and Bertalanffy have independently
fashioned modern world views that are incredibly comple-
mentary and blessed with a marvelous interfertility.

Despite their partial success neither Bertalanffy nor Teilhard would lay claim to more than having sketched an
outline for a new synthesized vision of man and cosmos.
No rational man would today think of essaying a complete
diorama which remains true to our present state of knowledge as well as the sum of mankind's past experience. Man
today experiences a compelling, anguished hope that soon
we will have such a complete diorama, on the basis of
which we can live with hope. In their own way, both
Teilhard and Bertalanffy have given substance to this hope

for Western man. Their creative and often mystical insights have been tightly woven into a fabric along with the practicalities of modern science. But however compelling and pregnant their outlines, neither synthesis has drawn to any extent on the richness of the Eastern mind.

For this reason I would like to suggest that the outline proposed in depth by Sri Aurobindo and here ably elucidated by Dr. Bruteau may very well complete a seminal triad of Eastern and Western minds, a pregnant combination of minds from quite diverse roots that can provide from their integration a modern sequel to the medieval Weltanschauung of Dante and Aquinas.

Aurobindo's appeal for Western man in the last quarter of the twentieth century can not be traced simply to some passing fascination with Eastern mysticism. Aurobindo's importance goes far deeper, because his view embraces a strongly positive, hopeful, and inspiring vision of mankind's future, which Western man craves provided it not be a rosy-hued illusion. He furnishes a wide-ranging integration of scientific, political, moral, and spiritual questions, a view of reality rooted in an evolutionary perspective, and, perhaps most important, the sound relevance of a vision based on thoughtful experience and the prophetic insights of a true mystic who has immersed himself in the hard realities of this world and has not sought to escape them. The thought of Aurobindo represents a totally new image of the Eastern mind, an image desperately needed to complement and fill out the as yet impatiently incomplete outlines commonly known in the West.

Acknowledgments

I wish to thank Professor Thomas Berry of Fordham University, Dr. Judith Tyberg of the East-West Cultural Center of Los Angeles, and Professor Haridas Chaudhuri of the California Institute of Asian Studies for the hours of consultation they generously gave me in the course of my research and for the many helpful suggestions they offered. I also wish to thank Mr. Fred L. Burkel of Visual Metaphor, Inc., New York, for executing the art work on the diagrams and designing the dust jacket.

Grateful acknowledgment is also made to the following publishers for permission to quote from the publications indicated:

Dover Publications, Inc., New York: *The Vedanta Sutras of Badarayana,* with the commentary by Sankara, translated by George Thibaut, 1962.

Sri Aurobindo Ashram Press, Pondicherry: Sri Aurobindo, *The Life Divine,* 1960.

Sri Aurobindo Library, Madras: T. V. Kapali Sastry, *Lights on the Fundamentals,* 1950.

The Sri Aurobindo Library, New York: Sri Aurobindo, *Essays on the Gita,* 1950.

11

Introduction

THE FACT THAT AUROBINDO WROTE HIS MAJOR WORKS IN
English has undoubtedly been an important factor in
stimulating worldwide interest in his thought. Had he
written in Bengali or Hindi the very same message would
probably have taken several generations before reaching a
wider audience. Not only did he write easily in English,
but he understood the West. Although aware of its short-
comings, he thoroughly appreciated the importance of its
energy and creative drive. In attempting to evaluate the
special genius of Sri Aurobindo, Sorokin concludes after
a long study of his works:

> From a scientific and philosophical standpoint, the works of
> Sri Aurobindo are a sound antidote to the pseudo-scientific
> psychology, psychiatry, and educational art of the West. Sri
> Aurobindo's *The Life Divine* and other Yoga treatises are
> among the most important works of our time in philosophy,
> ethics, and humanities. Sri Aurobindo himself is one of the
> greatest living sages of our time; the most eminent moral
> leader.[1]

---

1. Professor Pitirim A. Sorokin's remarks were contained in an address
delivered at the Sri Aurobindo birthday celebration in New York in 1949.
Cf. Sisirkumar Mitra, *Sri Aurobindo and the New World* (Pondicherry:
Sri Aurobindo Ashram Press, 1957), p. 49.

There are not a few who rank Aurobindo among the outstanding figures of the modern world. He has been compared with Bergson, with Hegel, and with Bradley. Among his fellow countrymen, he is consistently classed with Radhakrishnan as a philosopher, with Tagore and Gandhi as a leader of modern India, and with Sri Ramakrishna and Sri Ramana Maharshi as a yogi and a saint.

It was Tagore who said of him: "India will speak to the world through your voice."[2] His death at the age of seventy-nine was a signal for national mourning, led by Dr. Rajendra Prashed, then President of the Republic, who foresaw that Aurobindo's message would "continue to inspire generations as yet unborn, not only in this land but also in the world at large."[3]

The world at large has not remained ignorant of Sri Aurobindo, who lived from 1872 to 1950. Aside from the fact that since his death he has figured prominently in international congresses of philosophy in Europe and the New World,[4] his passing has been commemorated in anniversary symposia at Columbia University in New York, at the Sorbonne, at the Italian Institute for the Middle and Far East, and at the University of Marburg in Germany. Translations of his works are available in French, Spanish, German, and Chinese, as well as in the Indian languages of Bengali, Guzrati, and Hindi. Aurobindo Centers have been set up in India and the United States. In Africa there are six establishments—in Nairobi, Mombassa, Mampala, Dar-es-Salaam, Bikoba, and Livingstone. Among

---

2. Mitra, p. 59. Tagore's reverence for Aurobindo dates back to the turn of the century, when the latter was still in his thirties. On September 8, 1907, Tagore published an Ode to Aurobindo in *Bande Mataram*, available in English from the Sri Aurobindo Ashram.

3. Cf. R. R. Diwakar, *Mahayogi Sri Aurobindo* (Bombay: Bharatiya Vidya Bhavan, 1962), p. 99.

4. Notably at Brussels in 1953 and at São Paolo in 1954.

his leading commentators outside India are Judith Tyberg, Haridas Chaudhuri, and Frederic Spiegelberg in this country, Sir Francis Younghusband in England, Jean Filliozat and F. Challaye in France, Ernst Benz and O. Wolff in Germany, G. Tucci in Italy, Hugo Bergmann and T. Obvanger in Israel, and Tan-Yun-Shan of China. Indian commentators and adherents include A. B. Purani, Kapali Sastry, Sisirkumar Mitra, S. K. Maitra, R. R. Diwakar, and K. D. Sethna.

Why this worldwide interest? It is owing, I believe, to the fact that in an age when metaphysics is somewhat under a cloud, Aurobindo stands for a new and revitalized technical and practical approach to the traditional problems. As Professor Frederic Spiegelberg of Stanford University puts it:

> I am very grateful that I came into contact with Sri Aurobindo so late in life, for after having wrestled with the ultimate problems of existence for years, I am now in a position to appreciate his solutions to them. . . . I have never known a philosopher so all-embracing in his metaphysical structure as Sri Aurobindo, none before him had the same vision.[5]

Charles A. Moore, in his Introduction to the selections from Aurobindo's works in *A Source Book on Indian Philosophy*, coedited by him and Sarvepalli Radhakrishnan, is especially attracted by Aurobindo's ability to transform Indian thought and show its global import:

> Sri Aurobindo formulates a philosophy which—like the ra-

5. From an interview published in *Mother India* (Bombay); cf. Mitra, *The Vision of India* (New York: Laico, 1949), p. 218. After visiting the Sri Aurobindo Ashram, Spiegelberg introduced Aurobindo's *Essays on the Gita* to his students at Stanford University. Later, in collaboration with Professor Haridas Chaudhuri, he coedited a commemorative symposium volume entitled *The Integral Philosophy of Sri Aurobindo* (London: Allen and Unwin, 1960).

tionally grounded philosophy of Radkahrishnan—eliminates the alleged negativism and illusionism of traditional Indian philosophy and thus prepares the way for a more positive way of life for the Indian people and which makes possible a much greater mutual philosophical understanding of India and the West, and eventually—possibly—a significant synthesis of Eastern and Western thought.[6]

It would be tedious to list the names, statements, and activities of noted French, German, British, and American philosophers who have assumed the task of introducing Aurobindo's thought to Western audiences and readers through lectures, seminars, books, and articles. The enthusiasm with which some have regarded him is apparent in these two evaluations from England, one appearing in the London *Times Literary Supplement* in 1944 and the other in the *World Review* in 1949:

> Of all modern Indian writers Aurobindo—successively poet, critic, scholar, thinker, nationalist, humanist—is the most significant and perhaps the most interesting. . . . He has crystallised the mellow wisdom of a lifetime into a luminous prose in *The Life Divine,* which, it is not too much to say, is one of the masterworks of our age. The book has length, breadth, and height. In a real sense, it enriches our experience.[7]

> It is not surprising that, while to many of his countrymen he is the greatest single influence in the recovery of the great soul and spirit . . . of India . . . his originality is, at the same time, seen to lie in the way in which he has created a synthesis between her past spiritual achievement and modern European thought, so that the future spiritual destiny of India and the future destiny of Europe are inescapably the same destiny. . . . We are at the turning-point in the spiritual history of man. Aurobindo is the embodiment of a revolution in human life

6. S. Radhakrishnan and C. A. Moore, eds., *A Source Book in Indian Philosophy* (Princeton, N. J.: Princeton University Press, 1957), p. 576.
7. Sir Francis Younghusband, Review of *The Life Divine,* by Sri Aurobindo, *Times Literary Supplement* (London), July 8, 1944.

which new knowledge, new powers, new capacities, are creating at this hour.[8]

These samples of opinions from various sources may serve to suggest that the work of Sri Aurobindo is a challenging subject for serious study. Along with scholars and students in Israel, China, Latin America, Europe, and the United States, I have assumed the task of exploring one aspect of his global vision and of estimating its importance at this juncture of international understanding.

In setting forth Sri Aurobindo's philosophical system, particularly his doctrine on the reality, value, and capacity for transformation of the world, I have followed the traditional Indian approach, first studying the man's life and spiritual experience, so far as these can become available to a mind other than his own, then considering his philosophical system as an organized expression of his inner vision. After surveying the whole structure of his metaphysics, I have narrowed the discussion to the point I especially wish to emphasize: Aurobindo's rejection of illusionism and escapism in philosophy and spiritual life. This rejection is made possible by a specific metaphysical construction which enables him to propose a different set of answers to the traditional questions of what is real and valuable.

The conclusion will consider whether he has been successful in giving a new turn to the old problems and whether his fundamental orientation is apt to generate further useful philosophical thought.

---

8. E. F. F. Hill, "An Indian Philosopher: Sri Aurobindo," *World Review* (London), October, 1949, pp. 67–69.

WORTHY IS THE WORLD:
The Hindu Philosophy
of
Sri Aurobindo

1
Aurobindo's Life and Spiritual Experiences

INDIAN PHILOSOPHY IS TRADITIONALLY BASED ON SPIRITUAL experience. It hears as witnesses in its court not only sensory observation and rational argumentation but those spiritual perceptions obtained in higher states of consciousness which seldom enter into our Western philosophical productions. It is on the basis of such perceptions that certain systems of Indian philosophy have raised the question, "Is the world real?" There are, the Indian yogi-philosophers report, states of consciousness in which one "realizes" the unreality of the world. This experience is, to be sure, only the beginning of their philosophizing, which goes on, with careful logic and perceptive psychological analyses, to build intricate metaphysical structures. Nevertheless, when there is debate between two points of view in Indian philosophy, logic does not give the final judgment. Ultimately appeal must be made to the spiritual experience on which the argument is based and one must decide whether one type of experience is "higher" and therefore "truer" than another.

Behind this criterion is the position, basic to all Indian philosophies, that Reality is Value as well as Existence. Only that may be called "real" in the truest sense of the term which confers the highest value.[1] This broader attitude toward philosophy is expressed in the Indian's word for this discipline, darśana.[2] It is derived from the verbal root dṛiś, to see, meaning to have intuitive experience of the object, in fact, to realize it by becoming one with it.[3] The discovery of truth must come by direct experience, even though the explanation of truth will afterwards take place by means of reason. Only those "explanations" are respected in India which come from those who have "seen." A man's life, his spiritual history, testifies to his authority as a teacher.[4]

When Aurobindo, therefore, claims that he had only to set down in terms of the intellect his spiritual experiences and the philosophy was there,[5] he is speaking from the

---

1. S. K. Maitra, *The Meeting of the East and the West in the Philosophy of Sri Aurobindo* (Pondicherry: Sri Aurobindo Ashram, 1956), p. 9. Cf. his Presidential Address at the Twenty-third Session of the Indian Philosophical Congress, Bombay, 1948.

2. Sanskrit words occurring in the text will be given with their correct spelling, including diacritical marks, when they appear for the first time. In subsequent usage, however, they will for typographical convenience assume the more common anglicized forms.

3. S. Radhakrishnan and C. A. Moore, eds., *A Source Book in Indian Philosophy* (Princeton, N. J.: Princeton University Press, 1957), pp. xxv–xxvi.

4. Cf. T. V. Kapali Sastry, *Sri Aurobindo: Lights on the Teachings* (Madras: Sri Aurobindo Library, 1948), p. 10: "Sri Aurobindo, like the great spiritual teachers before him in India, is first a Yogin; next comes his philosophy giving an account of the ultimate truths envisaged by Yogic vision. The metaphysical basis of his system is secure, because it is related at every turn to experiences of spiritual life, to truths that are verified and verifiable by Yogic knowledge."

5. "I knew precious little about philosophy before I did the Yoga and came to Pondicherry—I was a poet and a politician, not a philosopher. How I managed to do it and why? First, because Paul Richard proposed to me to cooperate in a philosophical review—and as my theory was that a Yogi ought to be able to turn his hand to anything, I could not very well refuse; and then he had to go to the war and left me in the lurch with sixty-four pages a month of philosophy all to write by my lonely

mainstream of the Indian darshana tradition. That the terms of his intellect proved to include a meticulous sense of order and a powerful capacity for synthesis is our good fortune. But the vision which was so ordered and so synthesized, Aurobindo would tell us, came by the grace of God.

YOGA

There are four distinct spiritual experiences in Aurobindo's life on which the intellectual exposition of his philosophy is based. The first of these occurred a number of years after his return to India from England, where he had been from the age of seven. He served for a time as Principal (President) of Baroda College, but his interest in politics led him to resign. He set himself to fight the appalling poverty and other social evils of his homeland by every means available. He became deeply involved in the Indian independence movement, and it was this eagerness for moral and mental power to uplift the masses of the people and set them free that first led him to take up yoga.[6] His study of the lives and teachings of Sri Rama-

---

self. Secondly, because I had only to write down in the terms of the intellect all that I had observed and come to know in practising Yoga daily and the philosophy was there automatically." Letter of Sri Aurobindo to Dilip Kumar Roy, *Sri Aurobindo on Himself* (Pondicherry: Sri Aurobindo Ashram, 1953), p. 348.

Since most of the books referred to in this work have been published by the Sri Aurobindo Ashram in Pondicherry, citations hereafter will use only the initials S.A.A.

6. When someone first proposed to Aurobindo that he practice yoga, he refused: "A yoga which requires me to give up the world is not for me." A. B. Purani, *The Life of Sri Aurobindo* (S.A.A., 2nd ed., 1960), p. 102. "A solitary salvation leaving the world to its fate was . . . distasteful." *Sri Aurobindo on Himself*, p. 26. Yet shortly after his refusal he witnessed the extraordinary healing of his brother Barin, ill of a serious fever, by the ministrations of a passing naga-sannyasin. Reluctantly Aurobindo conceded, ". . . there must be a mighty truth somewhere in this yoga. . . . The agnostic was in me, the atheist was in me, the

krishna and Swami Vivekananda seems to have been responsible for decisive action in this matter. Through these
two outstanding figures in modern Indian spirituality
Aurobindo came to appreciate the significance of yoga in
relation to the life of action, and also the importance of
India's message for the whole world.[7]

Aurobindo's spiritual development is unusual in several
respects. First of all, one ordinarily expects to find that
childhood experiences and early training set the course for
mature life. But Aurobindo apparently defied both environment and education. As Diwakar, one of his biographers, says of him:

> It is not easy to conceive how Sri Aurobindo, who was
> almost a stranger to India and to Indian culture up to the
> age of twenty-one, should have eventually taken to the In-
> dian way of spiritual discipline. It would not have been so
> strange if he had become a Christian or if he had adopted
> the Brahmo form of worship. But he followed, for a great
> length of time, almost the orthodox type of Sadhana.[8]

However, Aurobindo did not quite perform sadhana
in the orthodox manner. For one thing, it is usual for a
spiritual aspirant to seek a guru under whom he will be
trained. But Aurobindo could not find a guru suitable for
him. He learned yoga as he had learned languages—on his

---

sceptic was in me and I was not absolutely sure that there was a God
at all. . . . So when I turned to the yoga and resolved to practice it and
find out if my idea was right, I did it in this spirit and with this prayer
to Him, 'If Thou art, then Thou knowest my heart. Thou knowest that
I do not ask for Mukti (liberation), I do not ask for anything which
others ask for. I ask only for strength to uplift this nation, I ask only to
be allowed to live and work for this people whom I love.'" *Speeches and
Writings* (S.A.A., 1952), p. 62.

7. R. R. Diwakar, *Mahayogi Sri Aurobindo* (Bombay: Bharatiya Vidya
Bhavan, 1962), p. 53.

8. Diwakar, p. 128. The Brahmo Samaj is a Hindu "church" conducted
very much like a Unitarian Church in the West. *Sādhanā* is a course of
spiritual discipline.

own, checking with teachers only at a few critical points. It is said that he learned *prāṇāyama*[9] from an engineer who was a disciple of Sri Sadguru Brahmananda at Chandod, and it is known that Sri Vishnu Bhaskar Lele of Gwalior was of great help to him at two important stages in his development.[10] Otherwise, he learned by study of the Hindu scriptures and by his own experiments.[11] Those who follow him can say that it is fortunate that he did so, because in this way he found a new type of yoga, one suited to the problems of the twentieth century and available to a humanity caught up in the necessity of action in governing a complex world.

For Aurobindo political life and spiritual life were one. A yoga which would bring about the revitalization of India could not be a dreaming about the past or an escape into another world, or an apathetic resignation before the forces of life. This sadhana was not for the sake of individual salvation or for attaining supreme peace. Every activity of individual and nation must be transformed and

---

9. Pranayama: control of the generalized vital force, mainly by means of controlling the breath. Frequently a preliminary yogic practice but not indispensable. Aurobindo valued it for sharpening the mind and improving the memory.

10. Diwakar, p. 55.

11. "I began my Yoga in 1904 without a Guru; in 1908 I received important help from a Mahratta yogi [Lele] and discovered the foundations of my sadhana; but from that time till the Mother [Mira Richard] came to India I received no spiritual help from anyone else. My sadhana before and afterwards was not founded upon books but upon personal experiences that crowded in on me from within. But in the jail [a political imprisonment in 1908] I had the Gita and the Upanishads with me, practiced the yoga of the Gita and meditated with the help of the Upanishads; these were the only books from which I found guidance; the Veda which I first began to read long afterwards in Pondicherry rather confirmed what experiences I already had than was any guide to my sadhana. I sometimes turned to the Gita for light when there was a question or a difficulty and usually received help or an answer from it." Letter quoted in *Sri Aurobindo and His Ashram*, official publication of the Sri Aurobindo Ashram, 1964, p. 35.

elevated to a spiritual level, put at the service of God for any action that might be the Lord's will.[12]

NIRVANA

After several years of practicing pranayama, hours of solitary meditation in the midst of a life of ceaseless activity, distraction, and involvement in the world, Aurobindo felt the need to consult an authority on yoga. It was December, 1907. He was again in Baroda at the time and called Lele to visit him.

This meeting was a landmark in Aurobindo's life. After hearing Aurobindo's account of his spiritual practices and his experiences up to this point, Lele retired with him to meditate for three days, during which he instructed Aurobindo to make a supreme effort to empty his mind completely of all that could be called "mind-stuff"[13] in order that the Divine might enter and take possession.

"Sit in meditation [Lele said to Aurobindo], but do not think, look only at your mind; you will see thoughts coming into it; before they can enter throw these away from your mind till your mind is capable of entire silence." . . . We sat together and I followed with an absolute fidelity what he instructed me to do, not myself in the least understanding

12. Cf. a letter written at this time, quoted in Diwakar, pp. 150–53, expressing Aurobindo's belief that individual gifts belong to the Lord and are to be used in His service for the benefit of humanity, his determination to save India through the strength given him by God, and his intense desire for the direct experience of God.

13. "Mind-stuff": Sanskrit, *citta*. According to Patanjali, chitta is made up of three components, *mānas, buddhi,* and *ahamkāra.* Manas is the recording faculty which receives impressions gathered by the senses. Buddhi is the discriminative faculty which classifies these impressions and reacts to them. Ahamkara is the ego-sense which claims these impressions for its own and stores them up as individual knowledge. Cf. Swami Prabhavananda and Christopher Isherwood, trs., *How to Know God,* The Yoga Aphorisms of Patanjali (Hollywood, Calif.: Vedanta Press, 1953) , pp. 15–16, commentary on sutra I.2.

where he was leading me or where I was myself going. The first result was a series of tremendously powerful experiences and radical changes of consciousness which he had never intended—for they were Advaitic and Vedantic and he was against Advaita Vedanta (being a Bhakta) [14]—and which were quite contrary to my own ideas, for they made me see with a stupendous intensity the world as a cinematographic play of vacant forms in the impersonal universality of the Absolute Brahman.[15]

A supreme calm descended upon Aurobindo and was permanently established within him. This was the *samādhi*,[16] the experience in which the whole of creation disappears, often taken for the climax of the spiritual quest. But it is only the negative side of the realization of God. As Sri Ramana Maharshi has said, spiritual life begins after samadhi. The lower consciousness being stilled and focused, one becomes an instrument for the Divine Will.

Another name for this experience is *Nirvāna*: that in which the ordinary sensory and rational experience of the world is "blown out" like a candle. On *that* level of consciousness there is then a "void." It is a valid experience in Aurobindo's eyes, and he accepts the philosophical conclusions which follow from it. However, he sees it as only the beginning of the discovery of the spiritual world and the complete truth about Being. The stilling of the lower

---

14. *Bhaktā*: one who practises *bhakti-yoga*, union with the personal God through love. He would naturally tend to be opposed to the Advaita Vedanta, which holds that the Reality is One without a second and does not allow for that duality which makes love possible.

15. Letter of Aurobindo to Dilip Kumar Roy, quoted in Diwakar, pp. 167–68.

16. Cf. Diwakar, p. 159: "The Upanishads speak of the supraconscious stage (*Prajñāna*) in which all ordinary experiences are transcended and there is one great, limitless, homogeneous experience without duality. This is the stage of the non-conceptual intuition of the self where knower, knowledge, and known merge into one. It is a totality of simple and undifferentiated experience, the bedrock of all our ordinary consciousness and knowledge. It is at once the essence of our individual self and the highest principle of the universe, the Brahman."

level of consciousness is but the prerequisite to the activation of higher levels.[17]

THE VISION OF KRISHNA

The next important event in Aurobindo's sadhana came
in 1908 in Calcutta. The independence movement had developed into a revolutionary movement and Aurobindo
was its acknowledged leader. However, not everything
done by the young revolutionaries was under Aurobindo's control, and a number of incidents of violence occurred. One of these tragic incidents involved Aurobindo's brother, Barin, and both he and Aurobindo were
arrested. Aurobindo was confined in the Alipore jail, for
the most part in solitude, from May 4, 1908, until May 6,
1909, when he was acquitted.

This year was one of the most important in Aurobindo's
life, a period of great deepening of his spiritual sense and
a radical shift and expansion of his vocation. Up to this
time his concentration had been mainly on freeing India
from foreign rule, and he had pursued his sadhana for that

---

17. A practical example can be given. This is not to be taken as
typical of what is meant by activation of higher levels, for that will
appear in the three following significant moments of Aurobindo's life,
but it is interesting in its own right, especially as it casts some light on
the composition of Aurobindo's philosophical works. Immediately after
his experience of Nirvana, Aurobindo began to have difficulty in his
political life, for when he was expected to address an audience, his mind
would often go blank. Lele therefore advised him to empty his mind
deliberately, place himself in the presence of God, and wait for the words
to come of themselves. This proved to have such a powerful effect on his
audiences that Aurobindo thereafter used this method not only for public
speaking but for all his spiritual and philosophical writing as well. "I
have made no endeavour in writing, I have simply left the higher Power
to work. . . . When I was writing the *Arya* [the periodical version in
which all his philosophical works first appeared] . . . I never [used to]
think. . . . It is out of a silent mind that I write whatever comes ready-
shaped from above." Letter quoted by Dilip Kumar Roy, *Sri Aurobindo
Came to Me* (S.A.A., n.d.) , p. 247.

purpose specifically. Now he resolved to dedicate himself entirely to the spiritual quest; instead of the sadhana subserving his political aims, his political duties became part of his sadhana. Also, he became much more explicitly conscious of his mission to the whole world, not to India alone, and of the significance of his work for the future of humanity.[18]

In prison, Sri Aurobindo spent almost all of his time in meditation. He had the Upanishads and Bhagavad-Gita with him. He studied these thoroughly and practiced yoga according to the instruction he found there. He says of this time:

> I had had many doubts before. I was brought up in England amongst foreign ideas and an atmosphere entirely foreign. About many things in Hinduism I had once been inclined to believe that they were imaginations, that there was much of dream in it, much that was delusion and Maya. But now, day after day, I realised in the mind, I realised in the heart, I realised in the body the truth of the Hindu religion. They became living experiences to me, and things were opened to me which no material science could explain.[19]

The outstanding and overwhelming event of this year was his vision of Sri Krishna as the all-pervading Lord of

---

18. Cf. Purani, p. 138.
19. The Uttarpara Speech, published as a pamphlet by the Ashram; this passage is also found in Purani, p. 132. On "Hinduism," cf. the following passage by a French disciple of Sri Aurobindo: "The so-called 'Hinduism' is an invention of the West; the Indian speaks only of 'the eternal law,' *sanātāna dhārma*, which he knows is not an Indian monopoly but is also for the Mussulman, the Negro, the Christian and even the Anabaptist. That which seems to be the most important part of a religion for the Westerner, the structure which *distinguishes* it from all other religions and which says that a man is not a catholic or a protestant unless he thinks in this way or in this other and subscribes to such and such an article of faith, this is the least important part for the Indian, who instinctively seeks to remove all outward differences in order to find the whole world at a central point where all things communicate." Satprem, *Sri Aurobindo, or The Adventure of Consciousness* (New York: India Library Society, 1964), pp. 22–23.

creation.[20] Sri Aurobindo has described this vision in his Uttarpara speech, delivered in a suburb of Calcutta after his release. It was the first occasion on which he had made any public statement of his spiritual experiences.

> I looked at the jail that secluded me from men and it was no longer by its high walls that I was imprisoned; no, it was Vasudeva who surrounded me. I walked under the branches of the tree in front of my cell, but it was not the tree, I knew it was Vasudeva, it was Sri Krishna whom I saw standing there and holding over me His shade. I looked at the bars of my cell, the very grating that did duty for a door, and again I saw Vasudeva. It was Narayana who was guarding and standing sentry over me. As I lay on the coarse blankets that were given me for a couch, I felt the arms of Sri Krishna around me, the arms of my Friend and Lover. This was the first use of the deeper vision He gave me. I looked at the prisoners in jail, the thieves, the murderers, the swindlers, and as I looked at them, I saw Vasudeva, it was Narayana whom I found in those darkened souls and misused bodies.[21]

This second milestone in Sri Aurobindo's pilgrimage is characterized in the first place by its being a vision of the personal God. It is no longer the unutterable, the time-less, spaceless, vacant infinite of Brahman, but the living Lord, to whose will he surrenders his whole being.[22] The

---

20. Sri Krishna: The absolute, infinite Reality, insofar as it creates and preserves the world, is called Vishnu, the divine Lord. Hindus believe that Vishnu becomes incarnate on the earth as a man from time to time when the human condition has fallen to a low ebb and men are in need of salvation. One of these incarnations was as Krishna, a cowherd of Vrindaban who later served as charioteer to Arjuna in the famous battle of Kurukshetra which is recorded in the Bhagavad-Gita. Hindus take many attitudes towards God: as father, mother, child, friend, teacher, spouse, sweetheart. Sri Krishna is usually regarded as the divine lover of mankind and his cult is a form of bhakti-yoga, union with God by love.

21. *Speeches and Writings*, p. 90. *Vasudeva:* the all-pervading God, a name of Vishnu. *Narayāna:* the Primeval Cosmic Man, the first being, the source of the universe, a name of Vishnu.

22. "I am not master of myself. I shall have to go wherever Bhagawan [the Lord] leads me like a robot in his hands." Letter to Mrinalini, quoted in Diwakar, p. 160.

experience is characterized secondly by the fact that it comes, not by personal effort, but sheerly by the grace of God. Sri Aurobindo's recognition of this shows in a letter he wrote to a close relative:

> I hope in the meanwhile, that the Lord, out of His infinite mercy, will bless you with the same light with which He has endowed me. But that entirely depends upon His abundant grace.[23]

While in the jail, Aurobindo had had intimations of the planes above the conscious mind, above even the highest level attained by the traditional yoga. His aim now was to realize these "overhead planes," and eventually to bring down the power of a superior consciousness to transform the lower levels of ordinary mind, life, and matter into fit instruments of the divine action.

For this purpose he withdrew from the active political life of Bengal, spent a brief period at Chandernagore, and took up residence in the French territory of Pondicherry, about eighty miles south of Madras on the east coast.

THE MULTIFORM UNITY

The third great illumination was, in a way, a synthesis of the two preceding, the realization of the formless absolute and the vision of the all-pervading Lord. It was a vision of the supreme Reality as a multiform Unity, simultaneously static and dynamic, characterized by silence and expression, emptiness and creativity, infinite and yet composed of manifold forms.[24] This experience was the foundation for Aurobindo's unique distinction between the

---

23. Diwakar, p. 161.
24. Cf. Haridas Chaudhuri, *Sri Aurobindo: The Prophet of Life Divine* (2nd ed.; S.A.A., 1960), p. 14.

"Higher, or divine, Maya" and the "Lower, or undivine, Maya," a distinction which Haridas Chaudhuri calls one of his major contributions to the history of Indian philosophy and spirituality.[25]

This vision occurred while Aurobindo was in Chandernagore in 1910. At that time he was investigating what he sometimes called the dark half of truth. "Human knowledge throws a shadow that conceals half the globe of truth from its own sunlight,"[26] he felt, by the too-impatient rejection of what is bad or false without waiting to discover the grains of truth and goodness in even the worst error and evil. But, Aurobindo argued, if we follow Swami Vivekananda in holding that we advance not from error to truth, but from less complete truth to more complete truth, and if we take care to include, not cut off, each step successively transcended, then the darker half of reality can be gradually illumined, the abysses as well as the heights of truth be seen.

Satprem, a French disciple of Sri Aurobindo, gives a dramatic description of the type of experience undergone by Aurobindo at Chandernagore.[27] He begins by remarking that one's greatest vice is often an indication of the direction in which lies one's greatest potential virtue. As we descend into the acknowledgment of our weaknesses and miseries, he says, we experience the growing intensity of the need for light and healing. Both the lower limit and the upper limit of consciousness are extended, balancing one another: as the dark levels of the subconscious become visible to our sight, so equally do the planes of light above the ordinary consciousness. The contrast sharpens, the

---

25. *Ibid.*, p. 26.
26. *Thoughts and Aphorisms,* sayings of Sri Aurobindo, compiled and edited by the Ashram staff (S.A.A., 1959) , p. 88.
27. *Sri Aurobindo, or The Adventure of Consciousness,* pp. 227–34.

sense of evil below and of healing light above deepens. Everything seems to center on one single obstacle which must be overcome.

As one descends from rational consciousness, one finds first the consciousness of the body by which the organs, the tissues, and the cells are wonderfully organized, each knowing what to choose, receive, or reject. Below this level is a physical subconsciousness which is a vestige from our long evolutionary past. Here there are still traces of the ancient habits of living things, the reflexes, the fears, the defences—habits of hiding, running away, deception, habits of hardening one's outer covering, of fixed repetition of activities, of self-dooming specialization. Below this again is the vast inorganic in which life itself is embedded, but which also appears as its very opposite, something which life and the values of life cannot penetrate. Meaning seems not to be there, care is not there, only inexorable universal law. The Vedic rishis (if we accept Aurobindo's interpretation of their obscure utterances) spoke of it as "the infinite rock." Aurobindo himself called it the Inconscient, and experienced it as a blind rejection of Life's upward thrust.[28]

The aim of Aurobindo's yoga in this context was to transmute the negatives of every level, down to the very bottom of existence. Moral evils, mental evils, diseases of life, obstacles of matter—all must receive the transforming light descending from above and be brought into a harmonious single pattern. The realization he had on this occasion, descending in his meditation into the depths of the physical subconscious, is described by Satprem:

. . . at one bound, without transition, at the bottom of this

28. *Ibid.*, pp. 227–28.

"inconscient" Matter and in the dark cells of this body, without falling into ecstatic trance, without the loss of the individual, without cosmic dissolution, and with eyes wide open, Sri Aurobindo found himself precipitated into the supreme Light. . . . Night, Evil, Death are a mask. . . . There is only That One, *tad ekam*. . . . The supreme divine consciousness . . . was there at the very heart of Matter. The step above the overmind is not "above," it is here and in all things. . . . God-Spirit meets God-Matter and this is the divine life in a body.[29]

In this experience we find the rooting of Aurobindo's affirmation of the Divine in the world and the setting of his goal as the transformation of the mental, the vital, and the material into fully worthy instrumentalities of the Divine. Instead of turning away from the earth in order to be holy, instead of fighting the flesh with its spiritual opposite, Aurobindo proposed to utilize the very qualities of the earth and the flesh themselves. God is already there; He does not need to be brought in but only to be liberated.

This is the key of the Transformation, the key of victory over the laws of Matter by the Consciousness in Matter—the Consciousness above is the Consciousness below. . . . For surely the earth is our salvation, the earth is the place of the Victory and the perfect accomplishment, nothing needs to escape into the heavens, all is there and totally there in a body . . . if we have the courage to open our eyes and go down.[30]

It was through this experience also that Aurobindo found what he believed to be the lost secret meaning of the Veda Samhita, which, if verified, would be a significant contribution to Indian, and world, philosophy. Having had the mystic experience himself, he felt he was able to recognize it under the symbols of the scriptures. Basing

29. *Ibid.*, p. 232.
30. *Ibid.*

himself on this interpretation of the Hymns, an interpretation which he also applied to the Upanishads, he claimed that his world-affirming position was perfectly orthodox, being in conformity with the Vedas.

THE DAY OF SIDDHI

The crowning experience of Aurobindo's sadhana came on November 24, 1926. It is called "the Day of Siddhi," *siddhi* being the attainment of that for which *sadhana* strives. But before we can describe it a certain amount of explanatory background must be given.

Since 1910 Aurobindo had been living in the ashram which he founded in Pondicherry. In 1920 Mira Richard, afterward known simply as the Mother, joined him, and in 1926 he turned over to her the administration of the whole ashram and withdrew into seclusion.[31]

It is important to remember that Aurobindo's seclusion did not mean that he had lost touch with the world of action. On the contrary, he made a point of keeping abreast of important events. He took a great number of newspapers from several countries, periodicals of various sorts, and continued his lifelong habit of reading books of all types in half a dozen languages. In addition, he carried on an extensive correspondence. His seclusion was devoted to the effort to transform the lower levels of being by the descent of the higher planes of consciousness, an activity

---

31. Now past ninety, the Mother still supervises every aspect of the Ashram's life. The Ashram itself has 1500 members, of whom 600 are children, and there are many thousands of devotees throughout India and the world. A large establishment is maintained in Pondicherry, with modern and beautiful buildings, many types of industries and crafts, and all levels of education. In February, 1968, the Mother dedicated a new city near Pondicherry. Designed by the Mother, in collaboration with architects and engineers from various countries, Auroville is intended to embody Sri Aurobindo's teachings on every level of its civic life.

which was, in his view, most practical and relevant to the
problems of the world. He believed that it was only by
gaining understanding and mastery in this invisible world
that one would be able to act effectively on the planes of
physical, social, and political life.

From the time of his confinement at Alipore, Aurobindo
had been aware of planes of consciousness above the ordinary mind. Later on he gave names to these: Higher Mind,
Illumined Mind, Intuitive Mind, Overmind. These are
only so many graded approaches to the real source of Consciousness-Force, or energy-substance, the Supermind.[32]
They are not ways of knowing or faculties of the mind;
they are realms of being, fields of existence. When a man
ascends to one of them—or equivalently, its power descends into him—it is not only his knowledge which is affected but his entire being, in all its states and activities,
including even his body. "Each stage of this ascent is therefore a general, if not a total, conversion of the being into
a new light and power of a greater existence." (LD, 1117)

Important extensions of consciousness take place in all
of the levels above the mind, but the ascent to the Overmind requires the introduction of a new dimension: the
centralizing individual ego-sense must be replaced by a
totalizing cosmic sense. Interior experiences formerly perceived as originating from the ego are now seen as coming
from the universal knowledge. The sense of the separate
self operating in knowledge is lost; it becomes a specialized
"point of view" within the cosmic consciousness. In the
Overmind one can know through any "point of view" as

32. Sri Aurobindo, *The Life Divine* (Sri Aurobindo International Centre
of Education Collection, vol. III; S.A.A., 1960), p. 1116. References to
The Life Divine hereafter will be entered directly in the text as "LD,"
followed by a page number.

readily as through any other, and one's concern likewise is as much for any other being as for one's own self. The sense of selfhood is itself expanded; one "identifies" with every other being. (LD, 1130-31)

Each ascending stage brings about an integrating transformation in the person and a closer unity in the human community. The sense of quiet, peace, light, unity within oneself, harmony with others, being awake and clear, the sense of being in touch with reality, of being in communion with the divine, increases from level to level. The intellectual, the affective, and the volitional powers are multiplied in intensity and effectiveness. Nevertheless, the lower levels of nature resist the transformation and cling to their fixed habits of operating within their limited worlds. This is a persistence which they were obliged to develop in order to hold their ground in the process of evolution. (LD, 1122) But, now, for the same reason, that is, in order that evolution may advance, they must give way and allow themselves to be caught up into greater configurations, to become specifics within a more generalized whole.

The key to the transformation lies in bringing down into the lower planes of being the power of the original creative consciousness, which is unity by nature. Even the Overmind, exalted though it is in its sense of *universe,* of the oneness of all beings, has not this power of transformation, for it has built its sense of unity out of the play of multiplicity. A truly integral transformation must come from the original unity itself, the unity which precedes and grounds all possible diversity. Such a level of reality is what Aurobindo calls the supramental. Even it is still an intermediate formulation, referring both to a term above itself, the unitarian and indivisible Absolute, and to a term below itself, the analytic and dividing levels of Mind. (LD, 148)

On all the levels of Mind, up to and including the Overmind, whatever degree of unity is present nevertheless presupposes diversity, whereas on the level of the supramental, diversity presupposes unity. Supermind contains within its unity the differentiation into all the many facets which on the level of the Overmind become active potencies for separate beings, and descending through the lower grades of Mind to our ordinary consciousness, become actual separated beings.

Now, since Consciousness and Force are twin aspects of Existence, knowledge and will are the forms under which this Power creates the world of space and time.

> The Supermind then is Being moving out into a determinative self-knowledge which perceives certain truths of itself and wills to realise them in a temporal and spatial extension of its own timeless and spaceless existence. Whatever is in its own being, takes form as self-knowledge, . . . and that self-knowledge, being also self-force, fulfils or realises itself inevitably in Time and Space. (LD, 172)

That is why the "realization" (Siddhi) of the Supermind is effective through all the layers of being, down to the least particle of matter, and why it alone can bring to pass the transformation to which Sri Aurobindo aspired, the transformation of the whole of the mental, vital, and material world into a perfect medium of expression of the Divine Spirit.

This is the unique feature of Sri Aurobindo's yoga and is a principle which is at the heart of his whole philosophy. He lays great stress on the importance of matter and on the cooperation of the human body in the achievement of the divine life. In doing this he separates himself from those yogis who preach sannyasa, or renunciation of the body and worldly activity. His affirmation is strong: "The body is full of consciousness; it is a manifestation of God."[33]

> The mind cannot be transformed unless the vital being is transformed. . . . The whole change of the vital being cannot be effected unless the physical being also is open and changed, for the divine vital cannot realise itself in an unfitting environmental life. . . . In the process of Yoga, there is a whole totality and each part depends upon the other. Therefore, to stop short may be a preparation for another life but it is not the victory.[34]

The final victory, the descent of the Supermind, was not attained even on the Day of Siddhi, but the descent of the Overmind was experienced and this was felt to be a promise of the descent of the Supermind at a later date. The internal content of the experience cannot be described, but the externals of the event are set forth by Purani, who was present on the occasion.[35] It was an evening meditation at which Aurobindo, the Mother, and their disciples were present. It was silent and without action except that the disciples came forward one by one to salute and be blessed by the Mother. Nevertheless, everyone present had the distinct experience of the presence of a Higher Consciousness and of a significance extending beyond their immediate circle. Sri Aurobindo himself identified the event as the descent of Krishna into the physical:

The 24th of November, 1926, was the descent of Krishna

33. Letter to Barin, quoted in Diwakar, p. 195.
34. Birthday speech of Sri Aurobindo, August 15, 1926, quoted in Diwakar, p. 204. Cf. also this remark: "I have no intention of giving my sanction to a new edition of the old fiasco, a partial and transient spiritual opening within, with no true and radical change in the law of the external nature." *On Yoga II, Tome Two* (S.A.A., 1958), p. 406.
35. Purani, pp. 245–47.

into the physical. Krishna is not the supramental Light.
The descent of Krishna would mean the descent of the Overmind Godhead preparing, though not itself actually, the
descent of Supermind and Ananda. Krishna . . . supports
the evolution through the Overmind leading it towards his
Ananda.[36]

YOGA AND PHILOSOPHY

Through these yogic realizations, Aurobindo was able to
propose "in the terms of the intellect" new solutions to
basic and vexing philosophical problems, especially the
reconciliation of the one (infinite) and the many (finite),
and the problems of human action which derive from it.
He was particularly concerned with the question: Is the
world of individuality and multiplicity real? Is it valuable?
Shall we human beings devote our energies to trying to
improve it? Or shall we use it temporarily, then abandon
it? Or struggle to escape from it? Or deny it? The question of the reality of the world is the question of the value
and the direction of human action.

Not only has this been a perennial human problem,
stimulating the greatest philosophers in every age, but it
is the basic problem of the real, grounded in obvious but
apparently contrary human experiences. On the one hand
is the sense of evil and material limitation in contrast to
the intuition of infinite spiritual perfection, and on the
other hand the undeniable presence of quasi-divine capacities for intelligence and love in man and his insistent
need to find every phase of his life meaningful.

If the world is not worthwhile—and its evils and limitations urge us to so judge it—then we would do better to
devote ourselves to spiritual exercises which will take us

---

36. Statement written in October, 1935, quoted by Purani, p. 247.
Ananda: bliss, an attribute of the Absolute.

out of it safely, into another world which *is* worthwhile, perhaps perfect. But an already perfect world would have no need of our action to bring it to its destiny. In that case, what should be the role of human creativity? If we cannot use it seriously on earth—for who will invest the most precious energies of his soul in a work which has no permanent value?—and need not use it at all in Heaven, what can be the significance of this image of the divine power and love in ourselves? But if, on the other hand, the Divine whom we seek is *here,* in the world, and the world itself is intrinsically capable of transformation, then an entirely different outlook and program of life become possible. The problem of the reality of the world is not as esoteric game for yogis and other strange philosophers. It confronts us subliminally—and often explicitly—in every action we undertake.

Aurobindo is vigorously on the side of the argument which finds the divine presence in the world. But this is not to be understood as if there were no quality of transcendence in his conception of God. The great merit of his contribution consists precisely in the way in which he is able to exhibit, both theoretically and practically, a philosophy which recognizes the natural complementarity, or in his word, integrality, of the transcendent and the incarnate aspects of God.

He calls his philosophy *Purnadvaita,* from *Pūrna,* whole, total, integral, and *Advaita,* non-dualism. Indian philosophers speak of "non-dualism" rather than of "monism" in order to emphasize the note of transcendence of all substantial categories. Any "one" thing of which reality consisted could be conceived only in distinction from some other thing. "Non-dualism" implies that the nature of the ultimate reality (of which all manifest beings are projections) is inconceivable and noncategorizable. The reality is neither matter nor thought; both are later than the ultimate being.

Aurobindo's modification of his Advaita as "Purna" is said with reference to the two great systems in the Indian philosophical tradition: that of Śankara (Advaita simply, regarding the world as relatively unreal) and that of Ramanuja (Vishishtadvaita, or "complex whole," in which the world is regarded as the body of God, real but totally dependent). "Purna" connotes a stronger intrinsic value vested in the world than does Vishishta but no degree of separation from God.

The Real, in Aurobindo's view, is one, but it is a oneness of totality, not of exclusion. It is free from the duality of division and separation, but it is not a simplistic oneness or a unity achieved by denying everything which is not itself. It is, says Aurobindo, the deeper unity of wholeness, which embraces all and finds every being to be its own self.

The metaphysical structures based on this insight are rather complex and will be examined in some detail in the following chapters. With this preparation, we will take up Aurobindo's polemic against the view which would deny or escape the world. The negative arguments will be balanced by a positive presentation of his vision of the integral human being in harmony with a real but spiritualized world. We hope to show that Aurobindo has found a way of holding together, in intellectual vision and in concrete action, the extremes of man's experience, the utterly transcendent Godhead and the creative possibilities of matter.

2
Brahman and Maya

WE HAVE SUMMARIZED THE INSIGHTS WHICH AUROBINDO
gained through his practice of yoga in four major realizations: 1) realization of the Absolute Reality as utterly
transcendent with respect to all form; 2) realization of the
Absolute Reality as a personal God, the creative and all-
pervasive Lord of the universe; 3) realization of the Absolute Reality as simultaneously unmoving and moving,
formless and possessing form, beyond the world and fully
in the world, essentially indeterminable but manifesting
endless determinations; 4) realization of the various planes
of being, linked in graded continuity from the lowest
matter to the highest spirit, an integral non-dual Reality.

To show the close connection between spiritual experience and metaphysical formulation in Aurobindo, it will
be useful to consult his major works, reorganizing the material in such a way as to expose it as a series of "conclusions" drawn from his yogic realizations.

The first three conclusions, for instance, which are
treated in this chapter, derive successively from the four
realizations, taken in order, and deal with the two basic

terms of Indian philosophy, Brahman and Maya. These terms have traditionally represented the extreme poles in any metaphysical structure. Aurobindo proposes to revise this relation radically by holding: 1) that matter (Maya pole) is as real as spirit (Brahman pole), 2) that Brahman itself is cosmic and individual (Maya) as well as transcendent (Brahman), and 3) that Maya should be regarded as having a higher sphere (Brahman) and a lower sphere (Maya).

Aurobindo's masterwork is *The Life Divine,* and the following exposition will lean heavily on it. However, it is lengthy, literary, and intricately reasoned. The present organization of Aurobindo's basic themes represents an attempt to outline, condense, and clarify the main argument.

FIRST CONCLUSION: MATTER AND SPIRIT ARE EQUALLY REAL

There are, in Aurobindo's mind, two extremes to be avoided. He calls them the two Negations: materialism and spiritualism, each holding that its principle alone is the true reality, the other being only an appearance or epiphenomenon of this basic substance. Both alike lead to the devaluation of cosmic existence and of the individual human life. Neither can offer us any motive for striving to perfect the world or ourselves in the world. According to materialism, the material universe will outlive our meaningless moment of organic activity. According to spiritualism, the world is a mirage, or at best a temporary abode doomed to eventual destruction.

If we separate matter and spirit, says Aurobindo, we must choose between them; this is clear from the history of thought. Materialism he regards as obviously untenable since it can be demonstrated that there are realms of being inaccessible to the senses. Even sense knowledge transcends the senses, for it is a reconstruction of sensations by the higher powers of the mind. (LD, 74) On the other hand, Aurobindo acknowledges that materialism has served a worthy philosophical purpose by emphasizing the genuine reality of the material world.

Materialism, for Aurobindo, is a relatively easily rectified error. He is much more concerned about "the refusal of the ascetic." It is, he says, "more complete, more final, more perilous in its effects on the individuals or collectivities that hear its potent call to the wilderness" than the denial of the spiritual by the materialist. (LD, 28) Materialism is capable of correcting itself. Its own zeal for knowledge of the world will eventually force it beyond the limits it had set for itself. But the revolt of spirit against matter can paralyze a culture for centuries, as has happened in India from the time of the Buddha up to the present. Such a spiritualism can undercut all cultural progress by preaching salvation as liberation from life in this world or as attainment of one's final goal in another world. But whether man arrives at a heaven of loving union with the personal God or at a nirvana in which all separate existence is lost in the Void, he equally deserts the still evolving world and declares by implication, if not directly, that individual and collective life in this growing world has no ultimate value. (LD, 28–29)

Nevertheless, in justice to the ascetic ideal, it must be admitted, Aurobindo grants, that it has performed a great service in orienting the minds of men toward the quest of union with God. Even if it has framed that quest and its goal in terms too narrow to be the whole truth, those terms do constitute part of the truth. Like the materialist, the ascetic has built up his position from an undeniable

perception: that very experience of the transcendent Brahman which Aurobindo himself had known during the
three days' meditation with Lele. His description of it in
The Life Divine is drawn from that personal knowledge:

> For at the gates of the Transcendent stands that mere and
> perfect Spirit described in the Upanishads, luminous, pure,
> sustaining the world but inactive in it, without sinews of
> energy, free from all appearance of relation and of multi-
> plicity,—the pure Self of the Adwaitins, the inactive Brahman,
> the transcendent Silence. And the mind when it passes those
> gates suddenly, without intermediate transitions, receives a
> sense of the unreality of the world and the sole reality of
> the Silence which is one of the most powerful and convincing
> experiences of which the human mind is capable. (LD, 28)

Aurobindo, in his own yogic development, corrected
this powerful experience by his other realization, that the
Absolute as the personal Lord is immanent in every least
particle of the universe and active in all its motions. Neither
experience caused him to reject the other. He did not
read the duality of his experiences as a call to make a
choice between them but as a call to find the larger framework of understanding which would reconcile them. Materialism and spiritualism contain each a serious error and
a precious truth. Both find an unexpected vindication in
Aurobindo's system.

This was always Aurobindo's way when facing an apparent contradiction. He observed that Nature advances by
oppositions and by movement from discord to harmony.
Nature's own method for bringing about the resolution
is not to reduce one pole of an opposition to the other, nor
even to modify both so as to avoid the clash, but rather to
expand the whole theater of their operations by building
a more complex unity. Man's mind, itself a part of Nature,

should therefore also proceed by seeking wider and more complex universes of understanding which can contain and reconcile elements that are contradictory in smaller contexts. (Cf. LD, 2–3)

Aurobindo can even claim that this is a more orthodox position, closer to the teaching of the Vedas. Replying to the Advaitins' argument from scripture that the Reality is "One without a second," he points out that another scripture says, "All this is the Brahman." Each formula epitomizes the profound experience of an inspired seer. Somehow both of these truths must be affirmed within a broader context. (LD, 30)

SECOND CONCLUSION: THERE ARE THREE POISES OF BRAHMAN

Aurobindo found a larger and more complete affirmation of both insights in his theory of the "three poises" of Brahman. If it is true that the supreme reality is both "One without a second" and yet "all this," then Brahman must be both transcendent and immanent. But the immanence has two aspects, says Aurobindo, and here the mark of the twentieth century shows plainly in his thought: the Godhead is immanent not only in a cosmic sense but in an individual sense as well. These three, the transcendent, the cosmic, and the individual, are equal in reality and value, but the primacy remains with the transcendent. "World lives by That; That does not live by the world." (LD, 27)

In the experience of the silent void, when one is raised above all form and activity, there is realization of the transcendent poise of Brahman. Nevertheless, Aurobindo claims, it is precisely *in* the experience of the silence, if one enters deeply enough, that one finds energies pouring out into activities in the universe. (LD, 33) The silence is experienced as the basis both of activity and of withdrawal from activity. (LD, 34) It is called "being" insofar as it is the ground of all cosmic existence; it is called "non-being" to indicate its freedom from any particular form of actual existence. (LD, 35–36)

The second, or cosmic, poise is also called Cosmic Consciousness. It is an intelligence and power immanent in all of Nature, "the Witness of cosmic existence and its Lord." (LD, 26) In this poise the transcendent Spirit exercises its power of self-determination and acts as Creator, Governor, and Destroyer of the universe.[1] The Cosmic Consciousness creates and is aware of Matter as a single existence and of bodies as the formations into which that one existence divides itself. It projects and knows Life and Mind in a similar fashion, as vast unities including within themselves all possible multiplicities. (LD, 26) The cosmic creation is not separate from the cosmic consciousness but is itself "a Conscious Energy one with Being that creates it." (LD, 27) This is the foundation of the world's reality.

The notion of Conscious Energy is fundamental to Aurobindo's whole system. It comes from a union of the traditional concepts of divine consciousness (*Chit*) and divine creative energy (*Śakti*). On the one hand, consciousness or intelligence is not powerless, and on the other hand, the force at work in Nature is not blind. One of the outstanding features of Aurobindo's work is the prominence which he gives to the principle of Shakti. Shakti is energy, power, strength, force, activity; it is related to the concrete, the manifest, the dynamic, and is distin-

---

1. Cf. Haridas Chaudhuri, *The Philosophy of Integralism* (Calcutta: Sri Aurobindo Pathamandir, 1954), p. 124.

guished from *Śiva*, the principle of transcendence.[2] By affirming the union of divine consciousness with Shakti, Aurobindo is protected against falling into idealism when he declares that "the world is real precisely because it exists only in consciousness." (LD, 27) The consciousness in which the world exists is identical with the infinitely determinable energy which becomes all grades and all species of finite beings. If the first poise of Brahman is Being, the second is Power-to-be, or Becoming.

The third poise is also Becoming, but manifest now as the multitude of individual beings in whom the universal appears separated and divided. Aurobindo lays great stress on the individual, his reality, his value, his persistence. He insists that even when fully united with both the cosmos and the transcendent Deity, the individual continues to possess and to enjoy his own individuality, though not as a divisive egoism which negates other beings in order to establish its own identity. (Cf. LD, 437 and 442)

The consciousness of man can enter into all three poises:

> The individual consciousness can see itself as limited and separate, but can also put off its limitations and know itself as universal and again as transcendent of the universe; this is because there is in all these states or positions or underlying them the same triune consciousness in a triple status. (LD, 405; cf. LD, 412, 787)

Aurobindo's ideal man would realize a perfect harmony of the three poises:

> The true Person is not an isolated entity, his individuality is universal; for he individualises the universe; it is at the same time divinely emergent in a spiritual air of transcen-

2. In India the Shakti principle is regarded as feminine and is worshiped as the Divine Mother under various aspects. The tantric tradition especially has developed this cult, and there are strong resemblances between its tenets and those of Aurobindo.

dental infinity, like a high cloud-surpassing summit; for he individualises the divine Transcendence. (LD, 1157)

As the person can realize his being in each of the three states, so he can have three different orientations toward his own eternal and temporal existence. He can know himself as eternal, as comprehending past, present, and future simultaneously, and as moving in time.

> The Being can have three different states of its consciousness with regard to its own eternity. The first is that in which there is the immobile status of the Self in its essential existence, self-absorbed . . . without development of consciousness in . . . happening; this is . . . its timeless eternity. The second is its whole-consciousness of the successive relations of all things belonging to . . . an actually proceeding manifestation, in which what we call past, present and future stand together . . . viewed as a whole; . . . this is the stable status or simultaneous integrality of Time. . . . The third status is that of a processive movement of Consciousness-Force and its successive working out of what has been seen by it in the static vision of the Eternal; this is the Time movement. But it is in one and the same Eternity that this triple status exists and the movement takes place. (LD, 430–31)

The relation of time to eternity is particularly pertinent to the question of the value of this world. It brings out graphically the images under which we customarily view our sphere of existence, images formed on that level of consciousness which Aurobindo calls Mind, a level which sees the world as made up of separate items unambiguously distinguished from each other. To Mind time appears to be one thing and eternity quite another. But on a higher level of consciousness, Aurobindo says, the distinction is overcome.

There are not really two eternities, one an eternity of status,

another an eternity of movement, but there are different
statuses or positions taken by Consciousness with regard
to the one Eternity. (LD, 431)

Aurobindo admits that it is necessary to invoke a higher
level of consciousness in order to make such statements,
for a metaphysics of three coequal phases of the one Brahman cannot be readily acceptable to ordinary consciousness
and conceptual logic. The normal mind can be expected
to avow that it knows perfectly well what the Absolute is
—namely, that in which there are no relations. And consequently, any attempt to unite the Absolute and the relative is obviously self-contradictory and preposterous. One
who speaks from the Indian philosophical tradition might
further argue (depending on his particular school of
thought) either that the undifferentiated unity of the reality precludes cosmos and individual, or that cosmos and
individual can attain their goal of union with the transcendent only by ceasing to be cosmic and individual.

Answering this objection, Aurobindo points out that
the motive underlying the objection is the choice to put
the contradiction in the Eternal and cry "Mystery!" rather
than to absorb the opposition in one's own mind and
struggle to grow big enough to sustain it. The objector's
attitude is "clear, lucid . . . involving no extraordinary
gymnastics of the reason trying to exceed itself and losing
itself in shadows . . . of mysticism." (LD, 445) Nevertheless, Aurobindo charges, it contains a threefold error:

> . . . the error of making an unbridgeable gulf between the
> Absolute and the relative, the error of making too simple
> and rigid and extending too far the law of contradictions,
> and the error of conceiving in terms of Time the genesis of
> things which have their origin and first habitat in the
> Eternal. (LD, 446)

The law of contradiction and the mode of temporal conceptualization apply only to separated entities within a homogeneous universe of discourse. Our spiritual experience, says Aurobindo, teaches us that the whole range of reality cannot be so characterized. Yet we are so habituated to reasoning in terms of beings defined by their mutual exclusion of one another's qualities that we unthinkingly apply this logic in areas in which it is not appropriate. Even the Absolute, which is in one breath admitted to be ineffable, is in the next qualified as if it too stood in the realm of opposites. Thus it is irreconcilably divided from its own opposite, the world of the relative. It is this "false step of our logic" that leads us into the dead-end of illusionism, the doctrine that the Absolute alone is finally real and that all beings possessing form are projections of Maya. (Cf. LD, 447)

If we could only loosen a little the tendons of our logic-bound minds, urges Aurobindo, so that we could without prejudice consider the facts of our experience, we would be able to make an intelligent ordering of all factors, though not according to the paradigms of conceptual logic. For instance, "individual," as said of man, does not mean just one limited being, as though our ego, identified by its repulsion of all other egos, were the center of existence. (Cf. LD, 87)

> There is a true individual who is not the ego and still has an eternal relation with all other individuals which is not egoistic or self-separative, but of which the essential character is practical mutuality founded in essential unity. (LD, 442)

In fact, the individual being, as we abstractly define it—as something that separates itself from everything else and stands apart—never has existed in the concrete world. In reality, every being is intricately involved with other beings. Its very being is constituted by dynamic relations with beings on every level of its own existence, whether physical, vital, or mental. (Cf. LD, 97) Our definition of individual is what a mathematical physicist would call an idealization for theoretical purposes. But we tend to forget this. Because we argue from the definition rather than from the reality, we find the individual a priori incapable of union with any other being.

If we turn now to our own experience, we discover that the individual man always exists in relation to his total experience of world-being, that in fact he "comes to embrace the whole world and all other beings in a sort of conscious extension" of himself, but he "still individualises and it is still he who exists and embraces this wider consciousness while he individualises." (LD, 437, 438) Furthermore, he is "aware of all other individuals as selves of himself." (LD, 439) The world-material of experience now is no longer seen as a great field outside himself in which he is embedded and under which he is passive. It appears equally as contained within the consciousness of the individual. Both as individual within the cosmos and as individual expanded to embrace the cosmos, he stands affirmed in the full reality of his being. The individual then realizes that since he can be conscious of himself in either of these ways, he is essentially above them both. He is ultimately "one in being with the Transcendence and seated and dwelling within it." (LD, 438)

Weighing these experiences, Aurobindo describes the individual as "a conscious being who is for our valuations of existence a being of the Eternal in his power of individualising self-experience." (LD, 443) Individual being

—and cosmic and transcendent being, also—are more complex realities than ordinary logic can handle.

> Not only am I in the world and the world in me, but God is in me and I am in God; by which yet it is not meant that God depends for His existence on man, but that He manifests Himself in that which He manifests within Himself; the individual exists in the Transcendent, but the Transcendent is there concealed in the individual. Further I am one with God in my being and yet I can have relations with Him in my experience. I, the liberated individual, can enjoy the Divine in His transcendence, unified with Him, and enjoy at the same time the Divine in other individuals and in His cosmic being. (LD, 443–44)

The rules of structure governing this grasp of our experience, what Aurobindo calls "the logic of the infinite," are quite unlike the laws of identity and contradiction which govern the structure of abstract concepts. For instance, the great divisions of Being, infinite and finite, unconditioned and conditioned, do not really represent oppositions. We have named the *in*finite and the *un*conditioned from the finite and the conditioned by negation, because the latter are more familiar to us. But in reality that which we call the non-finite contains within itself the whole of the finite; therefore infinite and finite are not even separate, much less opposed. And in the next order of division, where we distinguish transcendent and cosmic, universal and individual, each member of the pair is contained in its contrary. (Cf. LD, 449) The universal becomes particular in the individual, the individual bears all the characteristics of the universal. The universal, or cosmic, consciousness is fulfilled by diversifying itself in numerous individuals, while each individual fulfills himself by expanding into universal sympathy and identifying with the entire cosmos. The cosmos contains in itself, both

as universal and in each individual within it, the full immanence of the transcendent. The transcendent, for its
part, contains all, manifests all, and constitutes all. (Cf.
LD, 450)

The doctrine of the three poises of Brahman is the basic
insight of Aurobindo's philosophy. He sees it as the necessary theoretical grounding for the concrete enterprise
of promoting the evolution of a divine life on earth.

> Brahman preserves always Its two terms of liberty within
> and of formation without, of expression and of freedom from
> the expression. We also, being That, can attain to the same
> divine self-possession. The harmony of the two tendencies
> is the condition of all life that aims at being really divine.
> Liberty pursued by exclusion of the thing exceeded leads
> along the path of negation to the refusal of that which God
> has accepted. Activity pursued by absorption in the act and
> the energy leads to an inferior affirmation and the denial of
> the Highest. But what God combines and synthesises, where-
> fore should man insist on divorcing? To be perfect as He is
> perfect is the condition of His integral attainment. (LD, 50)

THIRD CONCLUSION: THERE ARE A HIGHER MAYA
AND A LOWER MAYA

The first conclusion was drawn from the union of the
first two of Sri Aurobindo's spiritual realizations, that of
the transcendent Absolute and that of the all-pervading
Creator-God. The second conclusion was the result of ad-
joining to these the third realization, that of the coexistence of the opposites. In the third conclusion we may
integrate all with the fourth realization, that of the continuity of the levels of being, and obtain a complete—
though, for the moment, static—picture of Aurobindo's
universe.

Aurobindo inherited a philosophical tradition which

spoke of the Reality itself, Brahman, and of its manifestation, *Māyā*. Although he insists that both are real and cannot be separated from one another, thus distinguishing
himself from Sankara, who introduced the term maya in
its philosophical sense, Aurobindo continues to use this
terminology. But he gives it a completely new significance.

Maya has ordinarily designated a world of mere appearance, something insubstantial even though vivid to the
senses, a deception to be seen through, a snare to be
escaped. It was at best a low-level semi-reality in terms of
which we worked out our salvation and from which we
graduated to higher realms. Aurobindo introduces into
this tradition a distinction between what he calls a higher,
or divine maya and a lower, or undivine maya.

The divine maya is not insubstantial, not a deception or
snare. It is creative power. A principle of selective manifestation, it stands between the unitary Absolute and the
world of multiple forms. A mediator is needed, because
the infinite action of an infinite being would produce only
an infinite world. A world incarnating a certain order of
finite relations implies the operation of "a selective faculty
of knowledge commissioned to shape finite appearance out
of the infinite Reality." (LD, 137) This was the meaning
of maya for the ancient Vedic seers, according to Aurobindo.

> Maya meant for them the power of infinite consciousness
> to comprehend, contain in itself and measure out, that is to
> say, to form—for form is delimitation—Name and Shape out
> of the vast illimitable Truth of infinite existence. It is by
> Maya that static truth of essential being becomes ordered
> truth of active being. (LD, 137)

The transcendent poise of the Absolute is strictly indescribable, unspeakable. If we attempt to attach any predi-

cate to it, we falsify it. However, that which *can* be correctly characterized by the highest, least limiting, and most powerful properties we know is the divine maya. The first truth which we can enunciate of the divine maya is that "It is," "It exists." Aurobindo calls this highest level of the divine maya the "Pure Existent." He says that "pure being is the affirmation by the Unknowable of Itself as the free base of all cosmic existence." (LD, 35) It is something which, being known, all is known, as the Upanishad says. (LD, 678)

Our first perception of the world reveals it to us as "a boundless energy of infinite existence" which "dwells equally in all existences." It "is indivisible and gives, not an equal part of itself, but its whole self at one and the same time to the solar system and to the ant-hill." (LD, 85, 86) But behind this energy in action there must be an energy abstaining from action, an absolute energy which is simply and purely absolute existence. (Cf. LD, 90) It is infinite, "timeless, spaceless . . . immutable, inexhaustible and unexpended, not acting though containing all that acts, not energy, but pure existence." (LD, 88) It is not a phenomenon. "If all forms were to disappear, that would remain." (LD, 90) It is what the scriptures and the tradition call *Sat*, reality, being, existence.

This is the argument from reason for the Pure Existent. But to establish firmly that he is speaking of "a fact and no mere concept," (LD, 93) Aurobindo also brings an argument from experience.

> So long as the intuition fixes itself only upon that which we become, we see ourselves as a continual progression of movement and change in consciousness in the eternal succession of Time. . . . But there is a supreme experience and supreme intuition by which we go back behind our surface

self and find that this becoming, change, succession are only
a mode of our being and that there is that in us which is not
involved at all in the becoming. Not only can we have the
intuition of this that is stable and eternal in us, not only
can we have the glimpse of it in experience behind the veil
of continually fleeting becomings, but we can draw back into
it and live in it entirely, so effecting an entire change in our
external life. (LD, 92–93)

But the becoming is also a fact. "Stability and movement
. . . are only our psychological representations of the Absolute, even as are oneness and multitude." (LD, 93) Being
and becoming are a double fact; both must be accepted,
but we may investigate the relations between them. Becoming appears in the world as a Force. Is it an intelligent
Force? Does it whirl blindly around the stably poised
Being, throwing out forms at random, or is it a creative
self-consciousness? This is a crucial question, of course, for
on its answer depends the validity of Aurobindo's position
that the world has a value, a value worth working for, a
supreme value which may be attained.

To prove his case, Aurobindo begins by showing that
two of the historically most prominent opposing positions
are untenable. The *Sankhya* system in Indian philosophy
spoke of the creative energy as *Prakriti* and held it to be
totally unconscious. All consciousness was vested in a separate principle, *Purusha,* which acted on Prakriti in order
to manifest the world. But the theory failed to account for
sensation, the transmutation of unconscious vibrations of
force into consciousness. Modern materialism, which re-
sembles it, has a similar difficulty. Beginning from unconscious force, it is never possible to derive conscious being.
The investigations of science itself increasingly show that
the capacity of our consciousness always exceeds that of
our nervous system. That theoretical position which holds

that consciousness uses the brain seems more true to the facts than that which maintains that the brain produces consciousness. (LD, 102) However, both Sankhya and materialism are correct insofar as they assert that "the principle of things is a formative movement of energies," (LD, 97) a view which is confirmed "when we examine from within our own experience" and find that "all our actions are the play of . . . knowledge-force, desire-force, action-force, and all these prove to be really three streams of one original and identical Power." (LD, 98)

Embarking on the positive part of his argument, Aurobindo then raises two questions: how does the movement arise, and why? The first he answers by accepting the position of the ancient Indian tradition, that Force is inherent in Existence: Brahman and Shakti are one. The inherent Force may be either at rest or in motion, but it is not alien to, not even separate from, the infinite Existence. (LD, 98) But why ever move? Why not always rest? If both the Force and the Existence in which it inheres are unconscious, the question is meaningless. There can be no purpose, no "why." If the existence is conscious but the Force unconscious, manifesting without any reason, then it would impose its random movement on the Existence, bring it into manifestation willy-nilly. But an absolute Existence dominated by its own Shakti would not be the supreme infinite Existence we supposed. An absolute conscious Existence must be free to manifest or not to manifest. But this is equivalent to saying that the manifestation is conscious and meaningful, that the moving Force is intelligent.

Here again, as in the case of the image of the individual, Sri Aurobindo posts a warning. We must not uncritically assume our usual image of "consciousness" when we say that the fundamental energy of the universe is conscious.

The usual image is drawn from our ordinary mental waking consciousness, and such a consciousness, far from characterizing the whole world, is a very particular qualification of only certain beings in the universe. To limit ourselves to such a narrow image when we are trying to investigate the most general unity of the world is so primitive that Aurobindo does not hesitate to declare that it "must now definitely disappear out of philosophical thinking." (LD, 101) Waking consciousness is not even an adequate image for the whole of human consciousness, which includes also dream consciousness, the subconscious, and the deep unconscious. Since there are associated with the complex structure of the human nervous system at least several levels of consciousness, some lower, others higher than ordinary consciousness, would it not be reasonable to ask whether there are other levels of consciousness similarly associated with other structures of matter?

> Are there not in us and in the world forms of consciousness which are submental, to which we can give the name of vital and physical consciousness? If so, we must suppose in the plant and the metal also a force to which we can give the name of consciousness although it is not the human or animal mentality for which we have hitherto preserved the monopoly of that description. Not only is this probable but, if we will consider things dispassionately, it is certain. (LD, 103)

Aurobindo also believes that we are entitled to see in this universal consciousness a universal purpose, and he adduces the marvels of instinctual skill in animals and the delicately balanced complex operations of inanimate Nature as evidence. (LD, 105–6) He refers briefly to the fact of waste as an argument against purposefulness in Nature, but dismisses it by saying that we do not see the whole picture of Nature's work and what appears to us as waste may not be so in the overall plan. (LD, 106)

The "universal consciousness" must be thought of as "a self-aware force of existence" (LD, 105) which occurs as a spectrum of various levels, as Aurobindo saw it in his fourth great realization. Our ordinary mentality appears about midway, having below it the grades of vital and physical consciousness and above it the planes of the superconscient. (LD, 105) This conception of consciousness is what the Indian tradition has called *Chit,* the conscious-energy which creates the worlds. It is the second word which may be spoken of the divine maya.

Chit, as noted above, is united by the tradition and by Aurobindo with Shakti, or the Divine Mother.[3]

> In the unending revolutions of the world, as the wheel of the Eternal turns mightily in its courses, the Infinite Energy, which streams forth from the Eternal and sets the wheel to work, looms up in the vision of man in various aspects and infinite forms. Each aspect creates and marks an age. Sometimes She is Love, sometimes She is Knowledge, sometimes She is Renunciation, sometimes She is Pity. This Infinite Energy is Bhawani, She is also Durga, She is Kali, She is Radha the Beloved, She is Lakshmi, She is our Mother and the Creatress of us all.[4]

This conception of the Divine Mother is an important part of Aurobindo's thought, and we can see from the above discussion why this should be so. It is She who is the source of all energy, all power, in whom dwells the

---

3. Cf. S. Chatterjee, "Mind and Supermind in Sri Aurobindo's Integralism," in H. Chaudhuri and Fr. Spiegelberg, eds., *The Integral Philosophy of Sri Aurobindo* (London: Allen & Unwin, 1960), pp. 38–39.
4. "Bhawani Mandir," written by Sri Aurobindo and circulated during the Bengal-partition days in the early years of this century. Reproduced in full in A. B. Purani, *The Life of Sri Aurobindo* (S.A.A., 2nd ed., 1960), pp. 84 ff.

universal purpose, the Force behind evolution—in short, the potency of this world and of man to grow and to attain a supreme value. By religious surrender to Her, man's will becomes "free from a mechanical determination by . . . the drive of . . . inferior nature." (LD, 1103)

> The energy of the liberated individual would be no longer the limited energy of mind, life and body, with which it started; the being would emerge into and put on—even as there would emerge in him and descend into him, assuming him into it—a greater light of Consciousness and a greater action of Force: his natural existence would be the instrumentation of a superior Power, an overmental and supramental Consciousness-Force, the power of the original Divine Shakti, . . . the omnipotent and omniscient World-Mother raising the being into herself, into her supernature. (LD, 1103–4)

But why should the Mother give birth to these many beings, Aurobindo asks himself, "why should Brahman, perfect, absolute, infinite, needing nothing, desiring nothing, at all throw out force of consciousness to create in itself these worlds of forms?" And he answers, "It can be only for one reason, for delight." (LD, 108) The eternal existence is not a bare existence, it is a conscious existence; but neither is it a valueless conscious-existence, "it is a conscious existence the very term of whose being, the very term of whose consciousness is bliss," a reveling in "the infinite flux and mutability of itself." (LD, 109) As the very nature of the divine maya is consciousness, so is it bliss, *Ananda*. It is the third word that can be spoken of the divine maya.

Immediately we confront the problem of evil. It is all very well to say theoretically that the nature of being is bliss, but our daily experience confronts us with the reality of physical pain and moral evil, which flatly contradicts the theory. Or at least it seems to do so. To maintain the position he has thus far taken, Aurobindo will have to put on a very strong defense, and to this end he will again invoke the method of looking at the problem in a larger and more complex context. It is probably the most difficult problem which Aurobindo's method of expanded complexity will attempt to resolve.

Aurobindo begins his defense by pointing out several false ways of putting the problem. In the first place, it is not a preponderance of evil that has to be accounted for. Actually, the sum of pleasure in life far exceeds the sum of pain, but we ordinarily do not notice the pleasure because it is so habitually present and normal. We notice only extraordinary things which stand out against the background of usual experience. (LD 110–11) Second, the problem is often complicated by a false issue arising from the idea of a personal extra-cosmic God whose power and responsibility have to be taken into account. If such an extra-cosmic deity is assumed, the explanation of evil and suffering is impossible, Aurobindo declares. (LD, 112) It is also a false framing of the question to ask how the Absolute, whose nature is free and conscious and must therefore be all-good, does not reject evil and prevent it from existing. This version of the problem has allowed to slip into its formulation an image from the dualistic world: the image of goodness, based on the relation of creature to creature. (LD, 113) It is putting things in reverse order. We must first see what goodness means on the level of the Absolute, where all is one; then we may make an application to the world of duality.

Thus, rising above the human point of view, we must first of all recognize that we do not live in an ethical world. (LD, 114) Aurobindo says very strongly that "the attempt of human thought to force an ethical meaning into the whole of Nature is one of those acts of wilful and obstinate self-confusion . . . which most effectively prevent [the human being] from arriving at real knowledge and complete sight." (LD, 114) There is no ethical situation below the level of humanity. There is recoil of any nature from that which injures it and attraction for what benefits it, and this is the primitive root of the eventual ethical distinction. But only with self-consciousness and consequent self-blame—or recoil of self from oneself—does the ethical dimension proper enter. (LD, 114) Even then the line of continuity from the crude attraction-repulsion dipole is traceable. Nature on any level seeks self-expansion, self-expression, fulfillment of the form in which it finds itself, and advancement to a freer and more encompassing form. Whatever promotes this achievement is "good"; whatever hinders it is "evil." This basis of judgment is still operating when we reach the ethical man whose conception of what constitutes his fulfillment has now exceeded his own ego to embrace at first a few other persons, then all men, ultimately the totality of the universe.

Returning now to the blissfulness of the Absolute, we cannot call in question its "goodness" by referring to repulsions which we experience. Clearly we are able to experience such repulsions only to the degree that we also experience ourselves as separated from that which repels us. Inasmuch as the division of being into apparently separate items is only one aspect of reality and, in terms of evolution, a temporary phase of the evolutionary process, our basis of judgment of good and evil can be only partial and temporary.

Hence we must now enlarge our notion of "delight." It is not limited to our familiar sensory and emotional pleasures. It is rather something which is common to all levels of being: the satisfaction of the Conscious-Force when it achieves the development it seeks. And it does achieve it, but on the way there occurs this phenomenon of conflict and repulsion, as well as the phenomenon of attraction and union. "Delight of becoming . . . takes different forms of movement of which pleasure and pain are positive and negative currents." (LD, 117) As Becoming struggles up out of the realm of separateness and sharp opposition toward the greater sympathy and communion of the higher planes of consciousness, conflict and repulsion will disappear. Pain, like self-centered individuality, is a device of Nature with a temporary purpose in the upward thrust of evolution, to protect the fragile and complex structures of separated beings until they can be reunited in a higher level of harmony that will preserve within its unity the beauty of their diversity.

The same is true, says Aurobindo, of those actions which we now call "unethical." Ethics is a discipline of the turning point at which energy fixed in the patterns of self-protective egoism is being converted to self-forgetful union. As all moral goodness is summed up in the one virtue of love, or union with the other person, so "if and when Mind in man becomes capable of being free, unegoistic, in harmony with all other beings and with the play of the universal forces, the use and office of suffering" will diminish. (LD, 128)

Even now, insofar as we consider that "we" are not separated from or opposed to other beings but in reality united with them, they will not be able to do "us" any injury. We simply alter our sense of identification to coincide with the greater whole. After all, we had already established that behind the medley of forms thrown out by the Divine Mother there is the root of all existence in the Infinite Absolute. So we must consider that "behind all our experiences supporting them by its inalienable delight and effecting by its movement the variations of pleasure, pain and neutral indifference," (LD, 123) is the one indivisible conscious being, and "that is our real self." (LD, 123) The mental being, subject to the triple vibration of pleasure, pain, and indifference, is only a representation of this real self, "put in front for the purposes of that sensational experience of things which is the first rhythm of our divided consciousness in its response and reaction to the multiple contacts of the universe." (LD, 123) Behind this superficial experience is our profound consciousness—which takes delight in all experiences.

This is a tremendous claim, but again Aurobindo can present the experiential side of his argument as well as the theoretical side.

> If we learn to live within, we infallibly awaken to this presence within us which is our more real self, a presence profound, calm, joyous . . . a presence which, if it is not the Lord Himself, is the radiation of the Lord within. We are aware of it within supporting and helping the apparent and superficial self and smiling at its pleasures and pains as at the error and passion of a little child. And if we can go back into ourselves and identify ourselves, not with our superficial experience, but with that radiant penumbra of the Divine, we can live in that attitude towards the contact of the world and, standing back in our entire consciousness from the pleasures and pains of the body, vital being and mind, possess them as experiences whose nature being superficial does not touch or impose itself on our core and real being.[5]

---

5. LD, 124–25. It was such an ability which enabled Gandhi, after half an hour's preparation in meditation to so fix his consciousness in the profound self as to undergo an appendectomy without anesthesia. Cf. also Aurobindo's testimony that his personal experience of this interchangeability of pain and pleasure "began . . . in the Alipore Jail

It is only habit, he teaches, that keeps us in bondage to pain now.

> It is within our competence to return quite the opposite response, pleasure where we used to have pain, pain where we used to have pleasure. It is equally within our competence to accustom the superficial being to return instead of the mechanical reactions of pleasure, pain and indifference that free reply of inalienable delight which is the constant experience of the true and vast Bliss-Self within us. (LD, 125)

Sat, Chit, Ananda—Existence, Conscious-Force, and Bliss—the divine maya now stands before us, first expression of the ineffable Absolute, revealed as the traditional Sachchidananda[6] of the scriptures.

> The self of things is an infinite indivisible existence; of that existence the essential nature or power is an infinite imperishable force of self-conscious being; and of that self-consciousness the essential nature or knowledge of itself is, again, an infinite inalienable delight of being. (LD, 119)

Sachchidananda is the form of our fundamental cognition of the Absolute. To the ordinary mind it is known as three discrete self-existent aspects, but the higher consciousness (the Supermind) realizes them as three that are one, although each is distinct. (LD, 373–74) It is a conscious unity in differentiation. (LD, 244)

> Saccidananda is not Existence plus Knowledge plus Bliss, but is pure Existence which is at the same time pure Knowledge, and is pure Knowledge which is at the same time pure Bliss.[7]

---

when I got bitten in my cell by some very red and ferocious looking warrior ants and found to my surprise that pain and pleasure are conventions of our senses." *Sri Aurobindo on Himself and on The Mother* (S.A.A., 1953), p. 316.

6. Alternate spelling, saccidananda. The consonant *t* is modified when it immediately precedes certain other letters.

7. Haridas Chaudhuri, *Sri Aurobindo: The Prophet of Life Divine* (2nd ed.; S.A.A., 1960), pp. 33–34.

This is the supreme affirmation of the Vedanta;[8] all its
other tenets rest on this. The hope of all betterment of
life is grounded in this view, says Aurobindo, for it proposes that the essence of all life is a divine and immortal
existence, the essence of all thought is a radiation of a
universal truth, the essence of all action is the advancement of a self-achieving good, and the essence of all sensation is the play of absolute delight in being. (LD, 69)
This hope is rooted in the ultimate ground itself, not in a
floating representation of it. Although Sachchidananda is a
manifestation of Brahman, it is not an accidental projection of its being, a trinity of determinations which cease
to exist in the Absolute itself, but they are eternal inherent
truths of the Supreme Being itself.

> The Absolute is not a mystery of infinite blankness nor a
> supreme sum of negations; nothing can manifest that is not
> justified by some self-power of the original and omnipresent
> Reality. (LD, 381)

And in the evolution of the world this real Sachchidananda can be expected to emerge in its full glory. Man,
though an individual, will live as a universal being; his
mental consciousness will expand to a superconscious
vision of the whole; his restricted affectivity will be dilated
to the dimensions of a universal love. Even his vital being
will be elastic under the shocks of all other creatures on
it, and his very physical being will experience itself as
one with the flux of all physical energy. "His whole nature
has to reproduce in the individual the unity, the harmony,

---

8. The Vedanta: "the end of the Veda," interpreted sometimes as
meaning the Upanishads, the final portions of the Vedas, sometimes as
meaning the goal or purpose of the Vedas. It is also the name of one of
the six principal darshanas, or ways of looking at the world, one which
probably characterizes the thinking of most modern Hindus. In this
context the word seems to be used as a summary of the most widely
accepted teachings of the Hindu tradition.

the oneness-in-all of the supreme Existence—Consciousness-Bliss." (LD, 132; cf. LD, 1111)

The higher maya is a manifestation of Brahman in the realm of Knowledge or Truth (*Vidyā*). The lower maya is also a manifestation of Brahman, even a reflection of the higher maya, but now in Ignorance (Avidyā). Aurobindo's doctrine of the Ignorance[9] is one of the most original topics in his system, and we will discuss it in detail presently. For the moment, however, we want only to show the two hemispheres of Aurobindo's world: Existence, Consciousness, Bliss above, and Mind, Life, and Matter below.

The lower hemisphere is no more unreal than the upper, but it does in a certain sense possess the qualities of being a snare and a delusion. It is a delusion as long as we believe that our true nature is characterized by these levels of being in their present stage of development, and it is a snare when we restrict our aspirations either to getting the most out of this lower world or to jettisoning it altogether in favor of a quite independent upper world. Aurobindo advocates a middle way: "The lower, present and deluding mental Maya has first to be embraced, then to be overcome." (LD, 137) His program for the lower world is to give full acceptance to its true nature and thereby to elevate it to the perfection which is naturally inherent in it and which it can attain under the influence of the higher world. Its role is not temporary; its destiny, including its transformation, is eternal.

Discussion of the lower hemisphere involves a principle which must wait for its full development in the section on involution and evolution: it is the principle of division,

---

9. Aurobindo uses the expression "the Ignorance." Perhaps the definite article is intended to strengthen the connotation of a realm of being, not merely a condition of knowledge.

a power of the Ignorance by which the essential unity of the higher world is made to appear as an aggregate of separate beings here below. This division begins with Mind, is expressed in Life, and reaches its limit in Matter. Although subject to transformation, Mind—and its sequents in this order, Life and Matter—is indispensable for cosmic being, for Mind is the faculty which measures and limits, establishes particular viewpoints in terms of which the cosmic movement can be oriented and give rise to specific concrete formations.

> [If there is not a being] capable of fixing himself normally in his own firm standpoint for certain purposes of the divine activity, if there is only the universal self-diffusion or only infinite centres without some determining or freely limiting action for each, then there is no cosmos. (LD, 320)

The work of "fixed development, measurement and inter-action of relations" requires the presence of Mind. (LD, 320) It is "an interpreter between the universal Reality and the manifestations of its creative Consciousness-Force." (LD, 769)

We have seen that the fullness of being requires both unity and multiplicity. The multiple is manifestation of the one. But since this unitary being is of the nature of consciousness, manifestation of the multiple means that the unitary consciousness must become a multiple consciousness. It might be an essentially unitary consciousness which nevertheless recognizes within itself a certain differentiation in multiplicity, and such is the Supermind. Or it might be a multiple consciousness still held within the embrace of the fundamental unitary consciousness, and such is the Overmind. But there is also the possibility of a consciousness which has so concentrated on multiplicity alone as to forget unity altogether, and this type of consciousness is Mind.[10]

Mind can be described as a "development by limitation" from a primal Will to vision and to production (LD, 145), for its work of measurement and separation is not a creation by power and yet it is an instrumentality of such a creative power. It must see objects as separate and fixed in order to have some firm basis for establishing individual existence and building relations—its role in the ascending evolution. But it does not thoroughly understand the objects it perceives in this way, and it possesses no sovereign control over them; it can only channel their forces by first obeying them.

> The nature of Mind as we know it is an Ignorance seeking for knowledge; it is a knower of fractions and worker of divisions striving to arrive at a sum, to piece together a whole,—it is not possessed of the essence of things or their totality. (LD, 769)

Mind in the Ignorance comes into being when consciousness regards the world from one viewpoint exclusively, identifying completely with that viewpoint and refusing to be united to others, which it negates as opposed to itself. (LD, 199) Yet this is a distortion of the truth of individualization for the sake of which Mind is required in the universe.

> [The true function of Mind is] to hold forms apart from each other by a phenomenal, a purely formal delimitation of their activity behind which the governing universality of the being remains conscious and untouched. It has to receive the truth of things and distribute it according to the unerring perception of a supreme and universal Eye and Will. It has

10. Cf. Chaudhuri, *Prophet,* p. 37. Mind does synthesize, but that is an artificially constructed union, founded on separation, not a unitary type of consciousness.

to uphold an individualisation of active consciousness, delight, force, substance which derives all its power, reality and joy from an inalienable universality behind. It has to turn the multiplicity of the One into an apparent division by which relations are defined and held off against each other so as to meet again and join. It has to establish the delight of separation and contact in the midst of an eternal unity and intermiscence. It has to enable the One to behave as if He were an individual dealing with other individuals but always in His own unity, and this is what the world really is. (LD, 203)

But the separation of Mind from the higher unitary consciousness is only the beginning of a chain of separations which form the world of our ordinary experience. Once Mind exists, Life must follow, for "life is simply the determination of force and action, of relation and inter-action of energy from many fixed centres of consciousness." (LD, 321) This "essence of life," so to speak—not necessarily life as we know it in the plants and animals of Earth—is what the ancient Indian philosophers called *Prāṇa*, "the substantial will and energy in the cosmos working out into determined form and action and conscious dynamics of being." (LD, 321)

The work of Prana tends to emphasize the aggregation of forces as well as their division, although it presupposes such division. Its first accomplishment is to construct the chemical atom, "the first aggregate" and "the first basis of aggregate unities." (LD, 240) Its second task is the organization of energies which we recognize as vitality. On this level both unification and dissolution are in operation, the net result being the building up of a unified world of subunits which constantly surrender their unity to one another. "Interchange, intermixture and fusion of being with being, is the very process of life." (LD, 240)

Here, on the level of Life, we can see very graphically

the whole problem of our world and the concern that is at the heart of Aurobindo's thought. There are two forces at work, one which constructs and protects individuals in their separation from each other, and one which unites individuals with one another.

> In the physical world [Nature] lays much stress on the former impulse; for she needs to create stable separate forms, since it is her first and really her most difficult problem to create and maintain any such thing as a separative survival of individuality and a stable form for it in the incessant flux and motion of Energy and in the unity of the infinite. . . .
>
> But as soon as Nature has secured a sufficient firmness in this respect for the safe conduct of her ulterior operations, she reverses the process; the individual form perishes and the aggregate life profits by the elements of the form that is thus dissolved.
>
> This, however, cannot be the last stage; that can only be reached when the two principles are harmonised, when the individual is able to persist in the consciousness of his individuality and yet fuse himself with others without disturbance of preservative equilibrium and interruption of survival.[11]

The problem is only intensified on the level of human life, where mental and moral forces are added to the vital ones. The community tends to absorb the individual and the individual resists the community and other individuals in order to preserve his identity. All of man's effort through law and through love to order these two forces to each other is only a rephrasing of Nature's fundamental problem. (LD, 245) In order for this concrete "problem of the one and the many" to be resolved, the lower maya must be transformed by the higher maya. Then it will no longer be a snare and a delusion.

Meanwhile, however, the problem persists in the lower hemisphere, where the foundation and the all-conditioning

---

11. LD, 241 (broken into paragraphs for emphasis).

status of things is Matter, expressing the maximum degree of separation in our world. Life and Mind are evolved in Matter and, while they modify it greatly, they are also limited by it. Neither of them succeeds in transforming it altogether. This is the characteristic of the lower maya, the maya in Avidya, or Ignorance; it does not possess the power of creation. (LD, 840)

The first thing Aurobindo says about Matter is that in a certain sense it *is* unreal, that is to say, our conceptions of it are unreal. (LD, 279) We do not yet know its true nature, but this much we know, that every time we learn a little more about the nature of matter, it always turns out that our naïve image of it had been quite inadequate. In this century science has dissolved the solidity of phenomenal matter into a mist of electrical forces and then evaporated these into a pattern of probabilities. That science should reduce matter to energy, Aurobindo applauds as a first approach to the truth (LD, 280), and when philosophy further reduces both to phenomena of the spiritual consciousness which alone is the root reality, he feels that we are drawing even nearer. But this still does not account for the phenomenal presence of matter, which must serve some useful purpose of Spirit.

Matter must be the unconscious, the inert, the maximally discrete in order for the characteristic divisiveness of Mind to be carried to its furthest limit. Separateness, lack of communion, is precisely the condition of unconsciousness or inertia. Lacking such movement, or dynamic interchange of energies, in its own right, Matter necessarily appears as passive, that is to say, in our perception, as solid, stable, massive, enduring.

This attitude of our ordinary consciousness towards Matter

is a symbol of the essential object for which Matter has been created. Substance passes into the material status in order that it may present to the consciousness which has to deal with it durable, firmly seizable images on which the mind can rest and base its operations and which the Life can handle with at least a relative surety of permanence in the form upon which it works. (LD, 302)

Matter must therefore be pure substance as "form in its utmost possible development of concentration, resistance, durably gross image, mutual impenetrability,—the culminating point of distinction, separation and division." (LD, 302)

Contemporary science may tell us that matter, far from being a solid mass in space, is a vibrant network of dynamic patterns, but this is not the way our senses, under the influence of Mind, perceive it. (LD, 284–85) Sense perception of Matter is the last deduction from Mind's first premise of separation in being, and the senses will continue to see a gross and solid world until the Mind itself is transformed by the Supermind.

The transformation can be confidently expected. "Matter . . . is form and body of Spirit and would never have been created if it could not be made a basis for the self-expression of the Spirit." (LD, 766) Corroborating the speculative argument, as usual, by concrete experience, Aurobindo offers his own testimony in answer to the question, What happens when the human consciousness is replaced by the divine?:

One feels perpetual calm, perpetual strength, is aware of Infinity, lives in Eternity. Everything becomes a manifestation of the Brahman. For instance, as I look round the room I see everything as the Brahman—it is not thinking, it is a concrete experience, even the wall, the book is Brahman. I see you not as X but as a divine being in the Divine. It is a wonderful experience.[12]

The reality underlying Matter, Aurobindo holds, is an extension of substance which is not itself discrete (atomic) and therefore not an aggregation. It is a coexistence which is not a contemporaneous distribution in space. Division and aggregation, the characteristics of our ordinary conception of Matter, are only modes through which the forces of the lower world represent the continuous underlying reality.

> Therefore we arrive at this truth of Matter that there is a conceptive self-extension of being which works itself out in the universe as substance or object of consciousness and which cosmic Mind and Life in their creative action represent through atomic division and aggregation as the thing we call Matter. (LD, 285)

But this "truth of Matter" is the reality as perceived by the higher consciousness, not the work of the dividing Mind in its quasi-creative operation.

Fortunately, however, these powers of the lower hemisphere have a natural predisposition to be transformed by the principles of the upper hemisphere, for they are actually instrumentalities or reflections of that higher world. In the Absolute itself all is all without any barrier of separative consciousness. In the divine maya "all is in each and each is in all for the play of existence with existence, consciousness with consciousness, force with force, delight with delight." But in the undivine maya, under the influence of Mind, each individual is persuaded that "he is in all but not all in him and that he is in all as a separated being not as a being always inseparably one with the rest of existence." (LD, 137)

---

12. Passage written January 1, 1939, quoted in Purani, p. 225.

The theory of the two mayas is the instrument by which Sri Aurobindo expects to refute his great enemy in the philosophical realm, Illusionism.

> This distinction between the lower and the higher Maya is the link in thought and in cosmic Fact which the pessimistic and illusionist philosophies miss or neglect. To them the mental Maya . . . is the creatrix of the world, and a world created by mental Maya would indeed be an inexplicable paradox and a . . . nightmare . . . which could neither be classed as an illusion nor as a reality. (LD, 138)

The clue is to grasp the whole range of the levels of consciousness, from the lowest Mind, involved in the material world, through the ascending series to the Supermind, the true creator of the manifest world. Furthermore, the process of involution and evolution must be seen as a deliberate action of the Absolute itself for the sheer delight of the play of forms. It can then be seen that this world as it presently exists is not to be taken as definitive. It is in process, it is a temporary stage in the descending and ascending movement of the Divine Shakti. Therefore it is to be embraced, assented to,—and transformed.

3

Supermind and Evolution

SACHCHIDANANDA ABOVE AND MATTER, LIFE, AND MIND below constitute the beginning of a static picture of Aurobindo's universe. But a few more pieces must be added before even this is complete. The most important of these is the Supermind. I have referred to the Supermind several times already, because it is almost impossible to discuss anything in Aurobindo's system without mentioning it. But, on the other hand, just why it is needed and what its significant role is cannot be understood until these other aspects have been established to form a frame for it. The Supermind is essentially a mediator between the upper and lower worlds. (LD, 275)

From this point on, the "conclusions" being used as a scheme of organization for this presentation will be drawn successively from the sum of all that has gone before.

FOURTH CONCLUSION: SUPERMIND MEDIATES BETWEEN THE TWO MAYAS

When we have posed the unity of Sachchidananda on the one hand and the divided world of Matter, Life, and Mind on the other, we have set up two poles of being in opposition to one another. If we are to attain to the transcendence of Sachchidananda, we would seem obliged to abandon the world of Matter, Life, and Mind. But this would be the destruction of all our hopes: "If we must abolish the consciousness of mind, life, and body in order to reach the one Existence, Consciousness, and Bliss, then a divine life here is impossible." (LD, 170)

> From this solution there is no escape unless there be an intermediate link between the two which can explain them to each other and establish between them such a relation as will make it possible for us to realise the one Existence, Consciousness, Delight in the mould of the mind, life and body. (LD, 170–71)

But, asserts Sri Aurobindo, the intermediate link exists. It is called "Supermind" because it is a principle superior to ordinary mentality, and it is called "Truth-Consciousness" because it operates in terms of the fundamental truth of things, which is unity, rather than in terms of the diversity which Mind sees. (LD, 171)

In discussing the higher maya, we say that being itself is of the nature of consciousness-force, producing forms for the sheer delight of the self-manifestation. It is consciousness-force, then, or a limitation of that absolute being as knowledge-will, which is governing the origination and interrelation of forms in the Matter-Life-Mind world. If it is knowledge-will, could it not simply be Mind itself? But Mind, that level of consciousness immediately available to us, is a receiver and interpreter—even, as we have seen, a distorter—of truth, not the inventor thereof. "Earth-existence cannot be the result of the human mind which is itself the result of earth-existence." (LD, 281) The consciousness which has formed the world must be superior to it. Multiplicity can be understood within the context of unity, but unity can never be referred to multiplicity as its ground of being. The principle which governs the manifold world and holds it together as a universe "must be in possession of the unity of things and must out of it manifest their multiplicity." (LD, 171) But Mind does not possess this unity. It is precisely the principle of division which ignores unity. Therefore the creating and governing principle must be a Supermind. (LD, 209)

That a power above Mind is needed as the operating principle in the world is shown also by Mind's inadequacy in both knowledge and force, the two qualities of the divine Chit which account for manifestation in form. In Aurobindo's terminology, Mind is not a faculty of knowledge at all. (LD, 140) It uses knowledge but it does not acquire knowledge. The norm of knowledge is what he calls knowledge by identity, in which the separation of knower, knowledge, and the thing known is transcended. Mental knowing, by this standard, is very crude indeed. Because it is subject to this sense of separation from the objects of knowledge, Aurobindo holds, the mind cannot properly be said to "possess" knowledge. (LD, 140) It only seizes on this or that aspect of truth, distorted through the lens of its own assigned function in the created world of establishing and protecting individuality, and applies it for the accomplishment of its purposes as defined by this mandate.

> The utmost mission of Mind is to train our obscure consciousness which has emerged out of the dark prison of Matter, to enlighten its blind instincts, random intuitions, vague perceptions till it shall become capable of this greater light and this higher ascension. (LD, 151)

Therefore Mind cannot be the principle from which the reality of the created relations originated.

Mind is also deficient in power. For each new unfolding in the evolution of the world there must be a foundation in the preceding level that makes the new development possible. And when the new development takes place, it both modifies the matrix from which it grew and is modified by it. But it cannot be said that the new stage or form of being is itself the principle energizing and directing the development, unless it succeeds in perfectly transforming the parent matrix. (LD, 840) By this criterion, neither Life nor Mind can qualify as the creative principle of the world. So there must be "a secret Consciousness greater than Life-consciousness or Mind-consciousness . . . a supramental consciousness-force . . . the power of that which is the supreme essence and substance of all things, a power of the Spirit." (LD, 841)

Even if we were to imagine a Mind endowed with power to bring an unlimited number of new forms into existence, but limited by the deficiencies of knowledge and power we have just described, we would not have the cosmos we see we do have. Such a Mind, restricted to a recombination of the forms it was able to observe through its lens of individuation, would simply multiply the variety of beings on this plane of existence. Since it would be unable to rise above this plane, unable to produce a hierarchy of existence, unable to initiate true development, all its activity would fall into meaninglessness, and the world it produced could justly be called neither wholly unreal nor wholly real. And the philosopher who began with such an image of the principle governing the world would inevitably construct a philosophy of Illusionism, if not Nihilism. (LD, 141)

Here we see that it is by the combined force of the doctrine of the two mayas and of the Supermind that

Aurobindo can propose a world-view to conquer the defeatist position of Illusionism. Want of imagination, concluding too soon that the only way the world can be is the way we see it at this moment, not taking the dynamic principle of existence seriously as a source of heirarchical evolution—these are some of the faults that lead to such a negative philosophy. Indeed, if Mind were all we had to work with, we might well take a very negative outlook on life.

> The reasoning mind with its logical practicality has no other way of getting the better of Nature's ambiguous and complex movements than a regulation and mechanisation of mind and life. If that is done, the soul of humanity will either have to recover its freedom and growth by a revolt and a destruction of the machine into whose grip it has been cast or escape by a withdrawal into itself and a rejection of life. (LD, 1257–58)

If the dividing Mind were the first principle of creation, then it would also be the ultimate attainment possible. It might impose form on Life and Matter for a while but would finally be overpowered by them. (LD, 298) But man will not settle for this. Finite though his mind is, as long as he can sense a greater finite above, or the infinite above all, his aspiration will not be satisfied until he reaches it. (LD, 296) Only if there is a power superior to Mind, one which can operate a hierarchical evolution, one which can ground ultimate unity, can this aspiration be satisfied.

Leaving aside divine union, man cannot attain even the human community he so ardently desires unless there is a principle active in him of a higher order than the dividing Mind. The sympathy engendered by merely mental knowledge of one another will always be subject to denial by the unexpected appearance of the dark forces of indi-

vidualization. In order to have a genuine union, we must
enter into that in which we are actually one with each
member of the community. But "the lower conscious
nature is bound down to ego in all its activities, chained
triply to the stake of differentiated individuality. The
Supermind alone commands unity in diversity." (LD, 255)

The fact that we do strive for such unity and harmony
bears witness to the presence in us already of the unifying
Supermind. (LD, 341) But as long as we are restricted to
perception through mental processes alone, we can only
know of the existence of the Supermind by inference or
by a vague intuition. Order in the universe implies a
"knowledge inherent in the existence which is expressing
itself," and observed progress implies a "divinely seen
goal." (LD, 143) As we watch the efforts of our reason
to dominate the manifold movements of matter, life, and
our own minds, we come to realize that reason itself is
only a representative of a more powerful consciousness
behind. And the consciousness which governs our minds
and the consciousness which governs the laws of the material universe must be the same consciousness.

> But it is only when we cease to reason and go deep into
> ourselves, into that secrecy where the activity of mind is
> stilled, that this other consciousness becomes really manifest
> to us—however inperfectly owing to our long habit of mental
> reaction and mental limitation. Then we can know surely in
> an increasing illumination that which we had uncertainly
> conceived by the pale and flickering light of Reason. (LD,
> 143)

The Vedic seers called this "other consciousness" *rtam
bṛhat,* the Truth, the Vast.[1] According to S. K. Maitra,
the term means "the consciousness of essential truth of

---

1. Rig Veda (hereafter, RV) I.1.8. Cf. Aurobindo, *On the Veda* (S.A.A.,
1964), p. 68.

being (satyam) , of ordered truth of active being (ritam)
and the vast self-awareness (brihat) in which alone this
consciousness is possible."[2] In the Veda this truth-consciousness is called the god Agni's "own home."[3] (Agni per-
sonifies divine Fire (Energy) and is represented as having
two aspects, Force and Light.) [4] The Vedic seers further
considered that the high drama of creation, the emergence
of the divine light out of the sea of unconsciousness,[5] the
rising up of immortality from the rule of death,[6] the
liberation of all the riches of the upper world from the
lower, in which they lie concealed as treasure buried in
the earth, takes place in Man.[7]

> This was, in their view . . . the sense and justification of
> man's actual existence and his conscious or unconscious
> Godward effort, his conception so paradoxical at first sight
> in a world which seems its very opposite, his aspiration so
> impossible . . . towards a plenitude of immortality, knowl-
> edge, power, bliss. (LD, 574–75)

The existence of a Supermind, above our ordinary mentality but still accessible to our highest aspirations, thus
seems to be attested by both scripture and personal spiritual
experience. Guided by this double illumination, it becomes possible, even on the level of Mind, for one to speak
—by contrast and analogy, with an admittedly very inade-

2. S. K. Maitra, *An Introduction to the Philosophy of Sri Aurobindo*
(Calcutta: Culture, 1941) , p. 25.
3. RV I.75.5. Cf. Aurobindo, *On the Veda* (S.A.A., 1964) , pp. 73, 75, 81.
4. *On the Veda*, p. 70.
5. RV IV.16.4; III.39.4–5; VII.76.4. Cf. *On the Veda*, pp. 160, 138.
6. RV V.30.14.
7. "Our fathers found out the hidden light, by the truth in their
thoughts they brought to birth the Dawn." RV VII.76.4. Cf. *On the Veda*,
p. 138.
"Human beings slaying the Coverer have crossed beyond both earth
and heaven and made the wide world for their dwelling place." RV I.36.8.
Cf. *On the Veda*, p. 162.
See also *On the Veda*, pp. 81, 83–84, 204, for the expansion of the
divine truth-consciousness in man through the help of the gods.

quate language—of the Supermind. (LD, 146) First of all,
we need to limit somewhat the meaning of this ambiguous
term, "Supermind." It is fairly clear from the above discussion that it does not mean the same sort of consciousness
as Mind, only in a supereminent degree. It is indeed an
entirely different level of the conscious-energy.[8] But it
should be equally clear that it does not so far transcend
Mind as to be out of touch with it altogether. Supermind
is the mediator between the Absolute and the mental-
material world and has a certain identity of being with
both—as it must in a non-dual world. At the top we have
the indivisible One, all being and energy perfectly concentrated; at the bottom we have Mind's conception of the
universe, an apparent disintegration of this reality. In the
midst stands the Supermind.

> [It is a] firm self-extension in the Truth-consciousness which
> contains and upholds the diffusion and prevents it from being
> a real disintegration, maintains unity in utmost diversity and
> stability in utmost mutability, insists on harmony in the ap-
> pearance of an all-pervading strife and collision. (LD, 151)

It is Supermind which develops the triune principle of
Sachchidananda out of the indivisible unity of the Absolute. It differentiates the three aspects, but does not divide
them. It begins from unity and specifies diversity within.
By this differentiation it is able to emphasize one aspect
over the others—one which nevertheless contains the other
two implicitly—and thus to create a manifold of variety
without ever breaking the primal unity. It remains a one,
not a many; there is as yet no individualization. The
Supermind here is like a many-faceted jewel: strictly one,
containing all principles and all possibilities as its own

8. Haridas Chaudhuri, *Sri Aurobindo: The Prophet of Life Divine*
(2nd ed.; S.A.A., 1960) , p. 27.

faces, each aspect as a function of the others, having no possible being outside the whole.

Holding all reality within it thus, it then freely determines the cosmic relations and the relations of individuals with the universe. (LD, 1160) In it are revealed both the irreducible facts of existence and the interrelations among them.[9] Substance and relation need have no quarrel as to the primacy. But these operations are not an action of knowledge alone, but equally an action of will. The Supermind is a union of self-awareness by immediate self-cognition of reality and of self-limitation by focusing the dynamic potentials which are to be actualized in the cosmos.[10] It is both Light and Force. (LD, 147) It is a "Will to power and works." (LD, 145) Seen from the supramental level, Brahman is "not a rigid Indeterminable, an all-negating Absolute," but also "an Infinite of Power . . . capable of an eternal action and creation." (LD, 372) Creation is a self-manifestation for the Supermind, "an ordered deploying of the infinite possibilities of the Infinite." (LD, 372)

This is why Aurobindo's third name for the Supermind, or Truth-consciousness, is *Real-Idea*. "In Supermind knowledge in the Idea is not divorced from will in the Idea, but one with it—just as it is not different from being or substance." (LD, 154) Real-Idea is "effective self-awareness," a knowledge by identity which projects into manifestation by the very act by which it knows, and thus creates the universe of individuals. Supermind then becomes the original community of all individual selves, each of them "a unique focus and dynamic center of the absolute spirit which does not "arrogate to itself any sepa-

9. *Ibid.*, pp. 28–29.
10. *Ibid.*, pp. 27–28.

rate insular existence."[11] Each of them, while conscious of himself as an individual, is conscious of his union with the All and with each of the other selves on this supreme level.

These three functions of the Supermind: 1) to hold all the differentiation of possibilities within itself as one, 2) to focus the energy of the whole on each of the possibilities differentiated within itself, and 3) to project into actual existence each of the dynamic possibilities and to become the community of such actual individuals—these constitute the three poises of the Supermind. Sri Aurobindo calls them the comprehending, the apprehending, and the projecting poises.

The comprehending consciousness sees any aspect of the differentiation within itself "both as an object of cognition within itself and subjectively as itself." (LD, 283) It is able "to conceive, perceive and sense all things as the Self, its own self, one self of all, one Self-being and Self-becoming, but not divided in its becomings which have no existence apart from its own self-consciousness." (LD, 184) This is the state of "each in all." (LD, 152)

> It is when the reflection of this Supermind falls upon our stilled and purified self that we lose all sense of individuality; for there is no concentration of consciousness there to support an individual development. All is developed in unity and as one; all is held by this Divine Consciousness as forms of its existence, not as in any degree separate existences. Somewhat as the thoughts and images that occur in our mind are not separate existences to us, but forms taken by our consciousness, so are all names and forms to this primary Supermind. It is the pure divine ideation and formation of the Infinite,— only an ideation and formation that is organised not as an unreal play of mental thought, but as a real play of conscious being. (LD, 174)

---

11. *Ibid.*, p. 28.

The apprehending consciousness focuses on each single aspect of its internal differentiation, making it now "an object . . . of cognition within the circumference of its consciousness, not other than itself . . . but a part . . . put away from itself,—that is to say, from the centre of vision." (LD, 283) Instead of the integral action of seeing the aspect as both object and subject simultaneously, there are now, as it were, two sides of the movement, one regarding it as an object distinct from the subject, and then a reverse movement of realizing its union with the subject. (LD, 283) The result is to strengthen the individuality of the diverse aspects, as the apprehending consciousness sees "all existences as soul-forms of the One which have each its own being in the One, its own standpoint in the One, its own relations with all the other existences that people the infinite unity, but all dependent on the One." (LD, 184) This is the state of "all in each." (LD, 152)

> In each name and form [the supramental consciousness] would realise itself as the stable Conscious-Self, the same in all; but also it would realise itself as a concentration of Conscious-Self following and supporting the individual play of movement and upholding its differentiation from other play of movement,—the same everywhere in soul-essence, but varying in soul-form. . . . If our purified mind were to reflect this secondary poise of Supermind, our soul could support and occupy its individual existence and yet even there realise itself as the One that has become all, inhabits all, contains all, enjoying even in its particular modification its unity with God and its fellows. (LD, 175)

The projecting consciousness strengthens the sense of individuality still further, for now the "center of vision" or "supporting concentration" no longer stands back regarding the aspect as an object before it but itself enters into it, "projects" itself into it. (LD, 176) The supramental consciousness can now see each as a whole of its own.

> [It sees] all of these existences in their individuality, in their separate standpoint living as the individual Divine, each with the One and Supreme dwelling in it and each therefore not altogether a form or eidolon, not really an illusory part of a real whole, a mere foaming wave on the surface of an immobile Ocean. . . . but a whole in the whole. (LD, 184)

These are the three poises of the one Supermind, three aspects of one existence. (LD, 184) They are not even really three grades, in the sense of one being higher than the others, but they are the "triune fact of the self-manifestation of Sachchidananda" which the Supermind embraces in "one and the same . . . self-realisation." (LD, 184) We recognize immediately, of course, that they correspond to the three poises of Brahman, the transcendent, the universal, and the individual.

We might also remark here that this analysis of the three poises of the Supermind is another instance of the application of Aurobindo's method of expanded complexity as an instrument of reconciliation. By it he here attempts to draw into a single system the three great schools of Indian philosophy. The comprehending supramental consciousness is knowledge of the Absolute as the unqualifiedly non-dual reality and corresponds to the Advaita philosophical system of Sankara. The apprehending consciousness is knowledge of the Absolute as a whole containing the dependent many beings, and corresponds to the Vishishtadvaita system of Ramanuja. The projecting consciousness is knowledge of the Absolute as a union of distinct individuals and corresponds to the Dvaitadvaita system of Madhava.[12]

---

12. *Ibid.,* pp. 34–35.

Our scheme of the structure of being now shows this arrangement: the utterly transcendent, formless Absolute; the divine maya of Existence, Consciousness with its two aspects of Light and Force, and Bliss; then the Supermind with its three poises; lastly, the undivine maya of Mind, Life, and Matter. (See Diagram I, following this chapter.) The Supermind functions as the mediator, comprehending "all things in itself, as itself the One in its manifold aspects," and apprehending "separately all things in itself, as objects of its will and knowledge." (LD, 314) From this latter activity the Mind is descended, becoming a "movement by which the individual knower regards a form of his own universal being as if other than he." (LD, 283) The first duty of Mind is to render discrete, to "conceive with precise divisions as real," (LD, 149) the various objects of its cognition, "to make . . . this . . . fissure between thought and reality." (LD, 153) And, as we have seen, from this initial fissure proceeds the whole development of the lower world.

Supermind is a mediator between the Absolute One and the relative many. But considering the deep gulf between divine truth-consciousness, which is the nature of Supermind, and the operations of our mind as we know it, it becomes apparent that further mediation is needed between the Supermind itself and the mind. If there are no gradations between the two, it is hard to conceive how the mental consciousness which we now possess can grow into the supramental consciousness to which we aspire. (LD, 325) Mind knows by means of representations and constructions in images and ideas, based on sense experience, liable to many errors and at best only a bright shadow of the reality it seeks to know. Supermind, on the other hand, possesses the truth by nature, and itself produces the forms which mind afterwards attempts to assimilate. It begins from that unity of consciousness and being which knowledge endeavors to recover. It is the perfection of unity, and Mind is, we might say, the perfection of separateness. Is there not some intermediate level between them?

Yes, Aurobindo says, there is a whole range of gradually ascending consciousness above Mind, reaching up to Supermind, the most important of which is the Overmind. In *The Life Divine* Sri Aurobindo describes the characteristics of each of these levels in great detail, both in its knowledge aspect and in its will aspect. To give quickly a sketch of the type of analysis involved, let us trace the advance in the line of knowledge, simplifying a good deal the many modifications which Aurobindo recognizes. *Higher Mind,* while still *conceptual* knowledge, is not a self-critical ratiocination, as is the conceptual knowledge of Mind; it expresses itself in idea constellations, seen integrally, without logical bonds between the separate ideas. (LD, 1118–19) The *Illumined Mind* does not work primarily by thought at all, but by *vision,* thought being regarded as a manifestation or embodiment of a reality perceived by vision, a transcription which inevitably loses a great deal of what it tries to convey. (LD, 1124–25)

However, what is received by Illumined Mind is still only a representative image of the reality. The knowledge which is received by the seer as a vision is itself obtained by *Intuition:* a meeting of the consciousness of the subject with the consciousness in the object, a contactual union. "It is the result of a penetrating and revealing *touch* which carries with it *sight* and *conception* as . . . its natural consequence." (LD, 1126; emphasis added.) Finally, on the level of the *Overmind,* one's cognitive center of gravity is displaced; he may find the universe within himself, or himself within the universe; in either case there is *union and continuity* of what previously seemed to be separate beings. (LD, 1130–31) (See Diagram II, following this chapter.)

Mind sees the whole world—that is to say, all of whatever world it does see—from the pinhole viewpoint of its own individuality, radically separate from all other individuals. It sees everything in terms of its own interest: other beings are relative to it, either as enhancing it or as threatening it. Supermind sees all being as its own self, a great unity having innumerable faces, the bases for development along as many different lines of becoming, and simply rejoices in all this magnificent diversity in unity. Overmind, as intermediate between them, sees the *universe,* basically one but composed of many aspects, the many potentials for separateness all working themselves out, each in its own terms.

> The Overmind follows out diversities and divergent possibilities on their own lines of divergence: it can allow contradictions and discords, but it makes them elements of a cosmic whole . . . obliges them to support each other's existence so that there may be divergent roads of being and consciousness and experience that lead away from the One and from each other but still maintain themselves on the Oneness and can lead back again each on its own path to the Oneness. (LD, 1154)

What is simply a complex unity to Supermind can be dismembered by Overmind and each aspect appreciated separately.

> In overmental and mental cognition it is possible to make discrete and even to separate this original unity [Sachchidananda] into three self-existent aspects; for we can experience a pure causeless eternal Bliss so intense that we are that alone; existence, consciousness seem to be swallowed up in it, no longer ostensibly in presence; a similar experience of pure

and absolute consciousness and similar exclusive identity with it is possible, and there can be too a like identifying experience of pure and absolute existence. (LD, 373)

It is the beginning of the great cleavage of consciousness. In the symbolism of the Veda, the "ten hundred" rays of the sun which "stood together" so that "there was That One"[13] now begin to radiate out, separating as they go, each line of light to find its own development and fulfillment.

If we regard the Powers of the Reality as so many Godheads, we can say that the Overmind releases a million Godheads into action, each empowered to create its own world, each world capable of relation, communication and interplay with the others. (LD, 335) [14]

In this simultaneous development of independent potentialities there is as yet no conflict, even though there is contrariety, for no line of development claims a privileged status.

Each Idea admits all other ideas and their right to be; each Force concedes a place to all other forces and their truth and consequences; no delight of separate fulfilled existence or separate experience denies or condemns the delight of other existence or other experience. (LD, 338)

Nevertheless, this overmental manifold prepares the way for the Mind. It is concerned not with Absolutes, as is the Supermind, but with dynamic potentials. (LD, 339) And once independent development of distinct potentials is admitted, the possibility of each becoming a world unto itself follows. Its action will be determined not by the original oneness but by the principle of independent self-de-

---

13. RV V.62.1
14. Godheads: *Devas,* faculties of knowledge and action.

velopment. And when such centering has in fact taken place, we then have mental existence in the realm of Ignorance. (See Diagram III.)

It is important to stress at this point that Mind is not another *being* than Supermind. Mind itself *is* Supermind, though limited and diminished, and partly blinded, so that it operates on a quite different level. (LD, 320) Indeed, Matter itself is "only a form of Spirit." (LD, 281) Therefore the Supermind pervades all the forms of the lower world "as an indwelling Presence." (LD, 160)

> It is present, even though concealed, in every form and force of the universe; it is that which determines sovereignly and spontaneously form, force, and functioning. . . . It is seated within everything as the Lord in the heart of all existences. (LD, 160–61)

It is "the real creative agency of the universal Existence." (LD, 207)

On the other hand, neither is it separate from the infinite being of Sachchidananda. It is God, as Lord and Creator.

> It is . . . Sachchidananda creating us and the world by the power of His divine Knowledge-Will, spiritual, supramental, truth-conscious, infinite. That is the real Being, Lord and Creator, who, as the Cosmic Self veiled in Mind and Life and Matter, has descended into that which we call the Inconscient. (LD, 668)

It is the ultimate unifying principle of the universe, the bond which makes possible the uninterrupted continuity of the single creative process.

> The Supermind is at once the creative medium of God's descent into cosmic being and the illuminating medium of man's ascent into His unfathomable mystery.[15]

15. Chaudhuri, *Prophet,* p. 27.

The Supermind is not alien to us; it does not belong to another being, separated from us, or to a state of existence to which we cannot aspire. (LD, 144) As "it is evidently the link and means by which the inferior develops out of the superior," it "should equally be the link and means by which it may develop back again towards its source." (LD, 148)

> Since Mind too is created out of it, [and is] a development by limitation out of this . . . mediatory act of the supreme Consciousness; it must therefore be capable of resolving itself back into it through a reverse development by expansion. (LD, 145)

> We may by a progressive expanding or a sudden luminous self-transcendence mount up to these summits in unforgettable moments or dwell on them during hours or days of greatest super-human experience. When we descend again, there are doors of communication which we can keep always open or reopen even though this last and highest summit of the created and creative being is in the end the supreme ideal for our evolving human consciousness when it seeks not self-annulment but self-perfection. (LD, 144–45)

FIFTH CONCLUSION: THE SUPERMIND HAS A DESCENDING
AND AN ASCENDING MOVEMENT

The foregoing analysis has given us the seven principles which Aurobindo calls "the seven-fold chord of Being." (LD, 313) It is composed of notes of different pitch, some higher and some lower, but sounding together in a rich harmony. He means to say by this figure that although the notes are several, the music is one, that all the levels of being are required to achieve the beauty of the whole.

The picture thus far, we have noted, is static. Now we must see Aurobindo's world as it actually is, in motion. Brahman, in its universal and individual poises, is dynamic. Through the mediation of the Supermind, which is substantially identical with both the upper world of Sachchidananda and the lower world of Matter, Life, and Mind, it has a descending and an ascending current. The descending movement we have already seen to some extent. It is the process of creation in the ontological order, in which priority is not temporal: the superior principle gives rise to the inferior in which it limits and diminishes itself, becoming hidden and contained in the inferior. Aurobindo calls this an "evolution downward" from Spirit to Matter. It means, he says, that all that eventually appears in the world of Mind, Life, and Matter was potentially present in Sachchidananda and has only been made explicit. It was *involved* in the upper world. Similarly, in chronological evolution, Life rises out of Matter and Mind out of Life; Mind in turn strives to transcend itself in order to become Supermind. Each successive ascent reveals that the higher level must have been *involved* in the lower.

> In a sense, the whole of creation may be said to be a movement between two involutions, Spirit in which all is involved and out of which all evolves downward to the other pole of Matter, Matter in which also all is involved and out of which all evolves upwards to the other pole of Spirit. (LD, 152)

The seven notes of the chord of Being become now the rungs on the ladder of descent and ascent, of involution and evolution. (LD, 790)

Both movements are the play of the Supermind, what the Indian tradition calls *Līlā*.

> If we look at World-Existence . . . in its relation to the self-delight of eternally existent being, we may regard . . . it as Lila, the play, . . . the poet's joy, . . . creating and re-creating Himself in Himself for the sheer bliss of that self-creation,

. . . Himself the play, Himself the player, Himself the play-ground. (LD, 122)

The various grades of being are not hermetically sealed off from one another, but "the manifestation of the Spirit is a complex weft and in the design and pattern of one principle all the others enter as elements of the spiritual whole." (LD, 308)

> [It is the one] real Being, Lord and Creator, who, as the Cosmic Self veiled in Mind and Life and Matter, has descended into that which we call the Inconscient and constitutes and directs its subconscient existence by his supramental will and knowledge, has ascended out of the Inconscient and dwells in the inner being constituting and directing its subliminal existence by the same will and knowledge, has cast up out of the subliminal our surface existence and dwells secretly in it overseeing with the same supreme light and mastery its stumbling and groping movements. (LD, 668)

Self-expression by fixed types of being would be one possibility for a created world. They would be "typal and not evolutionary"; they would "exist each in its own perfection." (LD, 812) But another possibility is self-expression by self-finding, a process of self-veiling and self-recovery. And this is our world. (LD, 812) Aurobindo's conception of evolution in time is a historical conception. It involves biological transformism, human social, intellectual, and personal development, political expansion and unification, and concrete spiritual achievements by the spiritual leaders of mankind and their disciples.

> It cannot truly be said that there has been no such thing as human progress since man's appearance or even in his recent ascertainable history; for however great the ancients, however supreme some of their achievements and creations, however impressive their powers of spirituality, of intellect or of character, there has been in later developments an increasing

subtlety, complexity, manifold development of knowledge and
possibility in man's achievements, in his politics, society, life,
science, metaphysics, knowledge of all kinds, art, literature;
even in his spiritual endeavour, less surprisingly lofty and
less massive in power of spirituality than that of the ancients,
there has been this increasing subtlety, plasticity, sounding of
depths, extension of seeking. (LD, 1002)

However, Aurobindo does not simply substitute a
mutable world for an immutable one; he sees an integral
union of the two. A merely mobile Nature would give us
only the cyclic rhythm of becoming which is so common a
feature of various ancient theories of the world. It would
not found a true hierarchical evolution which moves toward an ultimate goal. It would not account for "the persistent aspiration of our partial Consciousness . . . to exceed
itself and arrive at . . . the integral conscious knowledge
of all Being." (LD, 621) Even Lila, the game, "carries
within itself an object to be accomplished and without the
fulfilment of this object would have no completeness of
significance." (LD, 995) It is Aurobindo's intention to
hold both visions of the world together in a living union,
the eternal, immutable, and perfect on the one hand, and
the moving, progressive, and achieving on the other. Both
are expressions of the Divine.

Worlds of a higher consciousness are not the only possible
scene and habitation of the perfected soul . . . the material
world, this earth, this human life are a part of the Spirit's
self-expression and have their divine possibility; *that possibility is evolutionary* and it contains the possibilities of all
the other worlds in it. . . . Earth-life is not a lapse into the
mire of something undivine, vain and miserable, offered by
some Power to itself and then cast away from it: it is the
scene of the *evolutionary unfolding* of the being which moves
towards the revelation of a supreme spiritual light and power
and joy and oneness, but includes in it also the manifold
diversity of the self-achieving spirit. There is an all-seeing

purpose in the terrestrial creation; *a divine plan is working itself out.* (LD, 810–11; emphasis added.)

Aurobindo goes so far as to say that the integral life of the world, the fulfilment of God's creative will, is not possible without evolution. (LD, 45)

It is this evolution which has enabled man to appear in Matter and it is this evolution which will enable him progressively to manifest God in the body. (LD, 70) Nor can we find in any unchanging typal world the final or total sense of the Spirit's self-expression in the cosmos. (LD, 810–11)

In particular, our own human condition becomes intelligible only in terms of evolution.

Our mortality is only justified in the light of our immortality; our earth can know and be all itself only by opening to the heavens; the individual can see himself aright and use his world divinely only when he has . . . lived in the being and power of the Divine and Eternal. An integration of this kind would not be possible if a spiritual evolution were not the sense of our . . . terrestrial existence. (LD, 810–11)

It is, therefore, a spiritual evolution which is required, not only the common conception of a material or biological evolution. Aurobindo remarks that although Western science has done a great deal to expose the facts of material evolution, it has neglected the evolution of consciousness.

The science of the West has laid more stress on the growth of form and species than on the growth of consciousness: even, consciousness has been regarded as an incident and not the whole secret of the meaning of evolution.[16]

For Aurobindo the evolution of consciousness is the

16. *Messages of Sri Aurobindo and the Mother,* Second Series (S.A.A., 1952), p. 22.

mainspring of the whole process, expressing itself in the evolution of material forms, and operating by the method of assumption, a taking up of all that has evolved into the next higher grade, so that no quality which manifests the Divine is dismissed in favor of another. It is "an evolutionary self-building of Spirit on a basis of Matter" and shows this triple character:

> An evolution of forms of Matter more and more subtly and intricately organised so as to admit the action of a growing, a more and more complex and subtle and capable organisation of consciousness, is the indispensable physical foundation. An upward evolutionary progress of the consciousness itself from grade to higher grade, an ascent, is the evident spiral line or emerging curve that, on this foundation, the evolution must describe. A taking up of what has already been evolved into each higher grade as it is reached and a transformation more or less complete so as to admit of a total changed working of the whole being and nature, an integration, must be also part of the process, if the evolution is to be effective. (LD, 838; cf. LD, 996)

The operation of these principles can be observed in the lower world of Matter, Life, and Mind. Just as species become dominant at successive periods, so first Matter, then Life, then Mind becomes dominant in its turn. (LD, 792–93) As Matter was the last word of the descent, so is it the first word of the ascent. All other powers are "involved" in it, and it is the foundation of the whole evolution. (LD, 308) Life, Mind, even Supermind are present in the atom, but latent. (LD, 848) On this level the Divine Energy is completely wrapped in the Inconscient. (LD, 815) It appears as a "blind universal force executing a plan . . . without seeming to know what it is doing," and the first result is appropriate: it is a "creation not of beings but of objects." (LD, 1099) Each object has its own properties and the relations between them are mechanical, without any spontaneous participation by the individuals. (LD, 1099)

When the organization of Matter is sufficiently complex, Life emerges. It in turn dominates Matter and complexifies it still further. (LD, 1138) Whereas Matter may be described as profoundly asleep, incapable of waking, Life, when it first appears (let us say on the level of the plant), has so far advanced toward the light of full consciousness as to be called dreaming. (LD, 849) "Force of concealed conscious being has been so much intensified . . . as to develop . . . a new principle of action." (LD, 849) Although there is continuity in evolutionary development, there are also jumps from one level to another.

> The action of evolutionary Nature in a type of being and consciousness is first to develop the type to its utmost capacity by just such a subtilisation and increasing complexity till it is ready for her bursting of the shell, the ripened decisive emergence, reversal, turning over of consciousness on itself that constitutes a new stage in the evolution. (LD, 1003)

In the case of Life, the new stage is evident in the living individual's responsiveness to its environment. It has a power mere Matter does not possess: it can transform contacts with other individuals into its own life-values (e.g., nourishment). The complexity of the material evolution has led to (and been impelled by) an advance in the conscious evolution, and the result is the taking up of the qualities of the previous level into the forms of the new. (LD, 849)

This primitive formulation of conscient life now strives through successive forms toward greater self-finding, more complete self-expression. (LD, 815) In the animal it slowly achieves wakefulness in conscious participation in its interactions with the environment; the animal initiates actions which affect others. (LD, 1099) This transition, too, is effected by the "force of being" becoming "so much intensified . . . as to admit . . . a new principle of existence." The animal has a kind of mentality, an awareness of others, a much wider range of contacts with the environment, and the ability to transform these contacts into vital and sense-mind values. In the higher animals the preparations for human feeling, thought, and will are visible in primitive memories, emotions, practical intelligence involving in some cases planning and invention. (LD, 850) But still, for the most part, the animal only follows instinct; the Life-Force is moving him without his being able to observe what is being done. (LD, 1099)

It is in man that consciousness breaks out into the open. "The world, which he epitomises, begins in him to reveal to itself its own nature." (LD, 850) He observes what is done and he chooses deliberately what he will do. (LD, 1099) The interaction with the environment immediately becomes infinitely more complex and subtle. A whole new power, that of contemplation, of the "self-detaching intelligence," appears. (LD, 850) And this Mind, in its turn, becomes dominant on the face of the earth. Matter and Life become instrumentalities of its self-expression and it is able to subdue them to its purposes in a manner completely transcending the sovereignty of Life over Matter. (LD, 793) Man takes up the animal sense of life and of body and transforms it by his intelligent observation and reflexive consciousness. He takes up the mental life of the animal, absorbs its half-consciousness into rational intelligence, transforms primitive instinct and intuitive invention into technological skill, primitive observation, association, and memory into science, and primitive sensation and emotion into art. (LD, 851) "Life is a scale of the universal energy in which the transition from inconscience to consciousness is managed." (LD, 220)

Nevertheless, man does not escape his origin altogether. Not yet, not on the level of Mind. His understanding is still groping, being either empirical and limited to his restricted observation of the universe, or rational and limited to the theoretical constructions of an itemizing and categorizing consciousness. He does not yet have a "luminous seeing which knows things by a direct grasp. . . . This is evidently not the utmost of which consciousness is capable, not its last evolution." (LD, 1099–1100) Furthermore, he carries with him, even at his greatest heights, "the dead weight of subconscience of body, the downward pull of gravitation towards the original Inertia and Nescience, the control of an inconscient material Nature over his conscious evolution." (LD, 984)

The fully conscious man has still to be evolved. His partial consciousness must become an integral consciousness. He must not only master his environment but unify and harmonize it. He must not only perfect his individuality but expand it to cosmic dimensions and achieve a universal delight in existence. This is "the evident intention of his nature; it is the ideal which the creative Energy has imposed on his intelligence." (LD, 815–16)

All of this magnificent display in the lower world is built on the immensity of the Inconscient and seems to have originated from it and to be supported by it. (LD, 793) And in a sense this is true. But the evolution of consciousness cannot be accounted for unless there is already a concealed consciousness in the first things. (LD, 729) It is the business of evolution to manifest what is from the first hidden within it, says Aurobindo. (LD, 786; cf. LD,

281) Evolution and involution are inverse movements:
the last derived in the downward movement of involution
is the first stage in evolution (Matter), and the original
level from which the descending involution began (Spirit)
is the last level to evolve in time. (LD, 1017) (See Diagram IV.) It is precisely to the extent that the Spirit has
descended into the world that it is possible for the world
to ascend into the Spirit.[17] "A complete involution of all
that the Spirit is and its evolutionary self-unfolding are
the double terms of our material existence." (LD, 811–12)
(See Diagram V.)

Arguments for the necessity of involution to account for
evolution begin almost from the first page of *The Life
Divine* and recur at intervals throughout the text. In the
first chapter, Aurobindo notes that we speak of the evolution of life in matter and of mind in life, but "evolution is
a word which merely states the phenomenon without explaining it." (LD, 4) Why *should* Life evolve out of
Matter, or Mind out of Life? Why else than the reason
already given in the Vedanta (the Upanishads), that "Life
is already involved in Matter and Mind in Life because
in essence Matter is a form of veiled Life, Life a form of
veiled Consciousness." (LD, 4)

In a later chapter on "Ascent and Integration," having
established that evolution means increasing complexity of
material form, increasing consciousness and the assumption of lower levels by higher, Aurobindo urges that "an
evolutionary process must be, by the very terms of the
problem to be solved, a development, in some first established basic principle of being or substance, of something
that this basic principle holds involved in itself." (LD,
839)

17. Maitra, *Introduction,* p. 4.

In the chapter on "Life," he asks, if Life is not involved in Matter, "from where else can it emerge?" (LD, 221) If it is a new creation introduced from outside, then it is either a production out of nothing or a result of material interactions which is not accounted for by these interactions themselves. Both of these suppositions he dismisses as arbitrary. A third possibility, that the new form descended from above, is acceptable (and he works a variation of it into his own scheme), but it does not account for the emergence of Life from Matter unless "this Life-plane exists as a formative stage in a descent of Being . . . into the Inconscient with the result of an involution . . . for a later evolution." (LD, 221) For evidence one would not look for signs of life itself in matter, but for terms in which there could be recognized the same type of energy-formations. What appears as birth, growth, and death on the level of Life is aggregation, formation, and disaggregation on the level of inanimate Matter. (LD, 221–22) The operations of intelligence in both Matter and Life, though unconscious or subconscious, indicate that the same Power is present there as in Mind, only in a lower grade. (LD, 222)

Aurobindo's most developed argument for involution occurs in the chapter on "Indeterminates and Cosmic Determinations," and is based on the observation of a modified determinism in Nature. Nature shows too much order to be the product of mere chance and too much variation to be operated exclusively by a mechanical necessity. There must be "a law of unity associated with a co-existent law of multiplicity, both insisting on manifestation." (LD, 358) The law of unity coexisting with the law of multiplicity is precisely the character of the Supermind, or the "supreme Truth-Consciousness." This Truth-Consciousness is "everywhere present in the universe as an ordering self-knowledge by which the One manifests the harmonies of its infinite potential multiplicity." (LD, 157) It controls and cooperatively joins the infinite potentials of the multiple manifestation in terms of their own individual natures, each of which is nevertheless a reflection of the Supermind itself.

Will this conception of the universe suffice to account for the graded advance of complexity and for the emergence of consciousness out of the inconscient? Aurobindo argues that "if there is necessity which compels the emergence, it can be only this, that there is already a consciousness concealed in the Inconscient." (LD, 358) The hypothesis of an extracosmic creative Deity he rejects because it leads to an insoluble problem of evil. (LD, 360) This problem "would disappear only if the creator were, even though exceeding the creation, yet immanent in it, himself in some sort both the player and the play, an Infinite casting infinite possibilities into the set form of an evolutionary cosmic order." (LD, 360–61)

> The knowledge that creates, because what it creates or releases are forms and powers of itself and not things other than itself, possesses in its own being the vision of the truth and law that governs each potentiality, and . . . its relation to other potentialities . . . ; it holds all this prefigured in the general determining harmony which the whole rhythmic Idea of a universe must contain in its . . . self-conception and which must therefore inevitably work out by the interplay of its constituents. . . . Therefore from the beginning the whole development is predetermined in its self-knowledge and at every moment in its self-working: it is what it must be at each moment by its own original inherent Truth; it moves to what it must be at the next, still by its own original inherent Truth; it will be at the end that which was contained and intended in its seed. (LD, 157)

Behind the movements of cosmic energy there is, then, an involved cosmic Consciousness, "building up through the action of this frontal Energy its means of an evolutionary manifestation, a creation out of itself in the boundless finite of the material universe." (LD, 361)

Aurobindo calls each developing level of evolution "inevitable" because of the involved presence of the Supreme Being in it, even down to the Inconscient. (LD, 791) These developments are "inevitable because that which is involved, must evolve"; (LD, 900) and there are two reasons for this. The Supreme is hidden in each level of being (the physical, the vital, the mental) and each successive level is concealed in those inferior to it. Whatever is hidden in its apparent opposite—as Life in the inanimate or the Unconditioned in the conditioned—will press to manifest itself clearly. And, from the other side, the concealing being will struggle to fulfill itself. But, since its true reality is actually the higher level, and ultimately the Supreme, the struggle for self-fulfillment is essentially an effort for self-recovery. An example of this recovery of the true self is shown by the evolution of Mind from Life:

> Life is an action of Conscious-Force of which material forms are the result; Life involved in those forms, appearing in them first as inconscient force, evolves and brings back into manifestation as Mind the consciousness which is the real self of the force and which never ceased to exist in it even when unmanifest. (LD, 281)

Extrapolating to the next step above, we may expect that Mind, being an inferior power of the Supermind, will in turn evolve and bring into manifestation the involved Supermind, thus finding its own true self.

This whole movement can be summarized as a three-step

involution, emergence, release: involution, the "self-absorption of conscious being into the density . . . of substance," emergence "of the self-imprisoned force into . . . thinking being," and release "of the . . . thinking being into the free realization of self as the One and the Infinite at play in the world." As a result of this movement, the conscious being will recover "the boundless existence-consciousness-bliss that even now it is secretly, really, and eternally." And this triple movement, Sri Aurobindo claims, "is the whole key of the world-enigma." (LD, 135; cf. LD, 839)

Because of involution, the three lower planes of Mind, Life, and Matter are actually powers of the superior principles, but in our present world they are manifest in separation from their spiritual sources and exhibit a divided existence rather than the undivided existence characteristic of the upper world. This separation is responsible for the limited being and knowledge which are typical of our world. Mentality in our world concentrates exclusively on its own immediate concerns with regard to the apparently separated beings and ignores the underlying unity. This is a state which Sri Aurobindo calls "cosmic and individual Ignorance." (LD, 791)

This situation poses a difficult problem for Aurobindo. To appreciate its difficulty, let us review his initial metaphysical commitments. He begins from the premise that Brahman is the sole reality; "all this is Brahman." He goes on to say that it is the nature of Brahman itself to be cosmic and individual. Individuality, as a property of the ultimately real and divine, means that the supreme consciousness actually identifies itself with each possible differentiation of itself: "he [Brahman] delimits himself in that and sets off his other forms against it in his consciousness as containing his other selves which are identical with him in being but different in relation." (LD, 196) But the self-knowledge of Brahman prevents his consciousness from fixing itself in the apparent separation; the divine consciousness is not deceived, it does not forfeit its unity. Diversification of being in individuals is for that consciousness "a definition of things subordinated to its awareness of infinity." (LD, 197) How, then, does the world of our daily experience come to be such a limited, distorted, and confused scene? Why does our usual consciousness experience itself as helplessly limited rather than as freely limiting itself? A new factor of explanation is needed, a faculty for "self-ignoring" which places a veil between our mind and the divine consciousness. This new factor is Avidya.

Avidya is ignorance, literally, not-seeing. It is usually associated in the Indian tradition with Maya and is a state which the yogin must overcome. In all this Sri Aurobindo concurs, but he manages to save a positive role for Avidya, even so. It is the means by which the upper world becomes involved in the lower world. If there were no Avidya, if everything were already seen, there would be no evolution in the lower world. Ignorance is the condition of creation.

What is the nature of this Ignorance, according to Aurobindo, and how does it serve its purpose in the world? The nature of the Ignorance can be put rather briefly: it is a concentration of the All-Conscient on the individual poise, for a particular and limited purpose, to the rigid exclusion of the universal and transcendental poises. (LD, 478) Aurobindo describes it as being "much like that power in our human mentality by which we absorb ourselves in a particular object or in a particular work and

seem to use . . . only such ideas as are necessary for it,—
the rest . . . are put back for the moment." (LD, 478)
And yet, though hidden and unacknowledged, the whole
consciousness is nevertheless present. Ignorance thus is a
power of Knowledge to hold back something of itself. It is
analogous to pain, which is the effect of "holding back" on
the part of the universal Ananda, resulting in a weakness
of the individual with regard to his ability to assimilate
a force that meets him. Just as pain is not a fundamental
opposite of Ananda but a particular working of it in a
limited way, so Ignorance is not a fundamental contrary of
Knowledge but a particular limited and dependent action
of it. (LD, 590–91)

One way of analyzing this activity is to say that it is a
splitting of the original Chit, which is Consciousness-
Force, into Consciousness on the one hand and Force on the
other. The Consciousness aspect, which represents the unitary side, or the universal and transcendent poises, is
neglected, or "involved," and the Force aspect, represent-
ing the manifold side, or an exclusive concentration on
individual material forms, is promoted. When this happens, then the hidden Consciousness "has to struggle back
to itself by a fragmentary evolution which necessitates
error and makes falsehood inevitable." (LD, 343)

As a particularizing mental activity, Ignorance separates
its objects of knowledge, viewing them as divided beings.
Since it ignores the universal and transcendent aspects of
reality, it achieves only a partial knowledge. But because
it nevertheless regards this partial knowledge as if it were
knowledge whole and complete, it is guilty of error. This
is where maya in the sense of deception comes in. (LD,
581–82) "Form and matter asserting themselves as a self-
existent reality are an illusion of Ignorance." (LD, 44)

Each item in its cognizance stands on its separate self. If it relates to others, it is not on the basis of the true underlying unity, but in terms of an artificially constructed whole, composed of the prior and independent units. (LD, 342) It particularizes "first and foremost and always," and leaves unity "as a vague concept to be approached only afterwards, when particularization is complete, and through the sum of particulars. This exclusiveness is the very soul of Ignorance." (LD, 578)

The first effect of the Ignorance is to limit us to a consciousness of surface existence. (LD, 668) "Time presents itself to us as a flow of dynamic movement, Space as an objective field of contents for the experience of this imperfect . . . awareness." (LD, 659) We live almost exclusively in the present, saving only a portion of our experience by means of memory (LD, 659), but for the most part believing the past and future to be inaccessible. We regard the world as separate from ourselves, as the "other," the non-self.

The concentration and limitation of consciousness and action give us also our empirical notion of man:

> What we mean ordinarily by the man is not his inner self, but only a sum of apparent continuous movement of consciousness and energy in past, present and future to which we give this name. It is this that in appearance does all the works of the man, thinks all his thoughts, feels all his emotions. This energy is a movement of Consciousness-Force concentrated on a temporal stream of inward and outward workings. . . . Behind this stream of energy there is a whole sea of consciousness which is aware of the stream, but of which the stream is unaware; for this sum of surface energy is a selection. . . . That sea is the subliminal self . . . the stream is the natural, the superficial man. (LD, 694)

Even that most intimate part of ourselves, the superconscient self, when first experienced, is regarded as something separate and made into an extra-cosmic Deity. (LD, 670) Although a higher consciousness sees that the world lives in us, under the veil of Ignorance we imagine that it is we who live quite independently. (LD, 672)

Worst of all, we are bound by the sense of the ego, "the most formidable of the knots which keep us tied to the Ignorance." (LD, 671)

> For we identify ourselves mentally, vitally, physically with this superficial ego-consciousness which is our first insistent self-experience; this does impose on us, not a fundamentally real, but a practical division with all the untoward consequences of that separateness from the Reality. (LD, 477)

This ego-sense sets up an artificial symbol of self, a usurper of the throne of the real self. Being a structure of the separative Ignorance, this false ego is always egocentric; even its moods of generosity are referred to itself as the doer. (LD, 660)

> We are infinitely important to the All, but to us the All is negligible; we alone are important to ourselves. This is the sign of the original ignorance which is the root of the ego, that it can only think with itself as centre as if it were the All, and of that which is not itself accepts only so much as it is mentally disposed to acknowledge or as it is forced to recognise by the shocks of its environment. (LD, 87)

And yet, even this seemingly hateful ego has its usefulness in Nature's great plan. The individual must regard himself as the center of his experience in order to achieve any consistency in the confusion of contacts and interrelations presented to him. This centralizing ego organizes his responses to the multifarious environment and builds up a pattern of habits for him. "It is this ego-sense that gives a first basis of coherence to what otherwise might be a . . .

mass of floating impressions." (LD, 659) We have to have it for time-experience and time-activity. If we are to live in time, we cannot have all knowledge at once flooding into us. It is a matter of practical convenience, as well as a necessity for the beginning of ordered knowledge, that we perceive individual persons and objects as separate and distinct realities and relate them to one fixed center in the perceiver.

> This primary egoistic development with all its sins and violences and crudities is by no means to be regarded, in its proper place, as an evil or an error of Nature; it is necessary for man's first work, the finding of his own individuality and its perfect disengagement from the lower subconscient in which the individual is overpowered by the mass consciousness of the world and entirely subject to the mechanical workings of Nature. Man the individual has to affirm, to distinguish his personality against Nature, to be powerfully himself, to evolve all his human capacities of force and knowledge and enjoyment so that he may turn them upon her and upon the world with more and more mastery and force; his self-discriminating egoism is given him as a means for this primary purpose. (LD, 824–25)

Egoism is thus a temporary organization of consciousness which endures only until the true self emerges. (LD, 660) The operation of the Ignorance which produces the superficial ego, Aurobindo regards as an action of "the deeper eternal Self in us throwing itself out as the adventurer in Time . . . limiting itself to the succession of moments so that it may have all the . . . delight of the adventure, keeping back its self-knowledge . . . so that it may win again what it seems to have lost." (LD, 605–6)

> It is the play of a secret all-being, all-delight, all-knowledge, but it observes the rules of its own self-oblivion, self-opposition, self-limitation until it is ready to surpass it. This is the Inconscience and Ignorance that we see at work in the ma-

terial universe. It is not a denial, it is one term, one formula
of the infinite and eternal Existence. (LD, 379)

Self-opposition is part of the game. The return from
the plunge into Ignorance by a struggling and groping
consciousness, seeing Consciousness itself under the dual
guise of truth and falsehood, knowledge and error, seeing
its Existence in terms of life and death, and its Delight in
the contrast of pleasure and pain—all this is part of the necessary process of self-discovery. In a world in which evolution is the mode of existence, the pairs of opposites are
bound to appear. (LD, 344)

Ignorance is, then, a necessity in the kind of world we
actually have. If the Infinite Being is to "trace the cycle
of self-oblivion and self-discovery for the joy of it" (LD,
703), then it has to produce individual consciousnesses
absorbed in bodily life, in egoistic separation, in limited
temporal relations with a selected environment.

But why create in Ignorance? Why not create out of
fullness of consciousness? This the Infinite Spirit also does.
This is the creation of the upper hemisphere, what we
might call the "obvious" kind of creation. But for the Infinite to be present and manifest even in the finite? What
a wonder that would be!

It is to find himself in the apparent opposites of his being
and his nature that Sachchidananda descends into the material Nescience and puts on its phenomenal ignorance as a superficial mask. . . . Not to return as speedily as may be to
heavens where perfect light and joy are eternal or to the
supracosmic bliss is the object of this cosmic cycle, nor merely
to repeat a purposeless round in a long unsatisfactory groove
of ignorance . . . but to realise the Ananda of the Self in
other conditions than the supracosmic, . . . to create out of
Matter a temple of Divinity. (LD, 703–4)

Perhaps it is too much of a wonder. Is such a thing really possible? Aurobindo poses the question: "How is even an apparent division effectively operated and kept in continuance in the Indivisible?" (LD, 674) It cannot be ignorant of itself, and since all differentiations are modifications within itself, it cannot be ignorant of them either. We cannot answer by saying that Mind is the seat of ignorance and a product of Maya, the non-Brahman, for we have already committed ourselves to the position that the whole world is integrally one. Any Maya there is must be a power of Brahman, but Brahman cannot be subject to it in any intrinsic or fundamental sense. For a similar reason, we cannot answer the difficulty by asserting that our sense of selfhood alone is subject to ignorance, but that of Brahman is not, and that our consciousness and the consciousness of Brahman are eternally separate. Such an explanation would contradict the very facts of spiritual experience, Aurobindo affirms. We have to continue to hold that we are one in essential being with Brahman but different in "soul-form and in active nature." (LD, 675)

In desperation we might be tempted to refer the whole problem to an unknown origin in a great Unknowable above and beyond our existence and our experience, and let it go at that. But for such an "Unknowable" to escape us completely and forever, it would have to be either an absolute Non-being (out of which nothing, not even Ignorance, can come), or a vast chaos of unrealized potentiality. In that case, there would be no real order in the universe, no real reason for anything, and one opinion would be as valid as another. (LD, 677) Explanation, then, cannot excuse itself by referring the solution of its problem to an "Unknowable." It must, on the contrary, adduce

Something "which being known all is known," in the words of the Upanishads.

The same Upanishadic tradition teaches, as Aurobindo has been arguing up to this point, that that Something is the infinite and absolute Sachchidananda, and therefore the solution must be found somehow in the activity of Sachchidananda itself. But we have already shown that it cannot be in the integral Sachchidananda. It must therefore be in a partial activity of Sachchidananda. (LD, 675)

It is interesting to note at this point that Aurobindo makes it clear that the creation in Ignorance is an *action* of the Supreme, not an intrinsic characteristic of its own nature. "There is no essential reason either in the nature of Being itself or in the original character and fundamental relations of its seven principles for this intrusion of Ignorance." (LD, 573) "Ignorance is not an essential fact but a creation." (LD, 678) It is a creation which is "an action of Nature which is part of the conscious and free movement of the Spirit." (LD, 675) The creation of our world of ordinary observation, then, is a free action on the part of the Supreme Being, in Aurobindo's system.

In order to explain how Ignorance arises from a partial activity of Brahman, Aurobindo recalls the fact that Chit has two aspects, one of Consciousness and one of Force. We had already pointed out above that Ignorance arises when the Force aspect begins to operate in separation from the Consciousness aspect. The Force aspect itself also has two phases, an active and a passive phase. We may get an idea of what is meant by observing that in our own consciousness only a small portion of our total consciousness is involved in any voluntary activity. The rest is what we call "involuntary," "subconscious," or "superconscious." (LD, 679) The whole of our personality stands behind the action, and we are right to speak of ourself as the agent of this action, but the whole of the personality does not express itself in the action, but only a small fragment of it. The rest remains, as it were, a vast reservoir of power, capable of projection in future actions.

Passive consciousness and active consciousness are, obviously, not two different things; they are the same energy, in the one case in a state of reserve, and in the other in a state of expression.[18] "We find that we have the power to arrive at what seems to us an absolute passivity or immobility of our consciousness in which we cease from all mental and physical activity." (LD, 680) The individual soul can move from "the poise of Brahman-consciousness in the world, where it is a fulcrum for the universal action, to or towards the poise of Brahman-consciousness beyond the world, where it is a power for the withholding of energy from the universal action." (LD, 682) This is the dual power that is needed for creation; "the action proceeds on its circuit from the reservation and returns to it . . . the energies that were derived, to be thrown out in a fresh circuit." (LD, 683)

Now the truth is that both of these phases of Force coexist in Brahman; they are simultaneous, not alternate. (LD, 684) But we, in our mental life, experience an alternation between the two phases: on the ordinary level, in the contrast between waking and sleeping, or on the level of yogic experience in the contrast between the perception of the manifold world and the disappearance of this world in the Silent Void (as in Aurobindo's first realization). When our consciousness is in one phase, we are ignorant of the other.

Some philosophers, basing themselves on this experi-

---

18. Cf. Maitra, *Introduction,* p. 55.

ence, have held that when the human soul is engaged in active life, it forgets its passive nature, which is supposed to be its true nature; when it enters into the passive trance of the samadhi and forgets its active nature, it has then attained remembrance of its true nature. (LD, 684) But Aurobindo refutes this position by pointing out that the whole experience of alternating states of consciousness is an experience of only *part* of our being, and we make the mistake of identifying it with the whole. (LD, 684) "We can discover by a deeper psychological experience that the larger being in us is perfectly aware of all that happens even in what is to our partial and superficial being a state of unconsciousness." (LD, 684–85)

We can now put our finger on the source of the Ignorance. When the two phases of Force are not experienced in conjunction with the universal Consciousness but the oscillation between phases of consciousness is accepted as the whole of reality and the logical consequences drawn, then we have Ignorance. (LD, 685)

Ignorance is not a state of being or a property of being, but an action.

> This action cannot be that of the whole being or of the whole force of being,—for the character of that completeness is whole consciousness and not partial consciousness,—it must be a superficial or partial movement absorbed in a superficial or partial action of the consciousness and the energy, concentrated in its formation, oblivious of all else that is not included in the formation or not there overtly operative. (LD, 692)

Concentration in itself is not the cause of Ignorance, not even exclusive concentration on a single object (which necessarily involves a holding back of the rest of knowledge), provided total knowledge is really present in the background of consciousness.

> But if the consciousness erects by the concentration a wall of exclusion limiting itself to a single field, domain or habitation in the movement so that it is aware only of that or aware of all the rest as outside itself, then we have a principle of self-limiting knowledge which can result in a separative knowledge and culminate in a positive and effective ignorance. (LD, 694)

Ignorance is thus shown to have its origin not in something which is not Brahman, nor yet in the absolute and integral Brahman as such.

> It belongs only to a partial action of the being with which we identify ourselves, just as in the body we identify ourselves with that partial and superficial consciousness which alternates between sleep and waking: it is indeed this identification putting aside all the rest of the Reality behind us that is the constituting cause of the Ignorance. (LD, 687)

And here appears a conclusion which is very important to Sri Aurobindo:

> If Ignorance is not an element or power proper to the absolute nature of the Brahman or to Its integrality, there can be no original and primal Ignorance. Maya, if it be an original power of the consciousness of the Eternal, *cannot* itself *be an ignorance* or in any way akin to the nature of ignorance, but must be a transcendent and universal power of self-knowledge and all-knowledge. (LD, 687, emphasis added.)

The Maya-as-illusion theory receives another blow.

After all this, there might be one last doubt: is it not still a mystery how Infinite Consciousness could, even in a partial activity of his consciousness, produce ignorance? But Aurobindo's method of expanded complexity swallows up this apparent contrariety too.

The mystery is a fiction of the dividing intellect which, because it finds or creates a logical opposition between two concepts, thinks there is a real opposition of the two facts observed and therefore an impossibility of co-existence and unity between them. (LD, 707)

Ignorance is a power of Knowledge; all conscious self-limitation is power, not weakness, not a disability. (LD, 707)

The power by self-absorption to become unaware of the world which yet at the same time continues in being, is one extreme of this capacity of consciousness; the power by absorption in the cosmic workings to become ignorant of the self which all the time is carrying on those workings, is the reverse extreme. But neither really limits the integral self-aware existence of Sachchidananda which is superior to these apparent oppositions; even in their opposition they help to express and manifest the Ineffable. (LD, 708)

Looking over the whole picture of evolution now, we can see that it develops through three stages. The first is the stage of involution, even to the depths of the Inconscient, followed by evolution in unconsciousness; this is largely the history of the past. The second is the stage of evolution in the Ignorance, with some possibilities of developing knowledge—"an uncertain spiral in which the human intelligence is used by the secret evolutionary Force of being and participates in its action without being fully taken into confidence." (LD, 844) This is our present condition, a transitional state. Finally, in the future we may confidently expect an evolution in the Knowledge, a "liberation of the spirit into its true consciousness" (LD, 839), a consummation of its self-knowledge and self-power. (Cf. LD, 812)

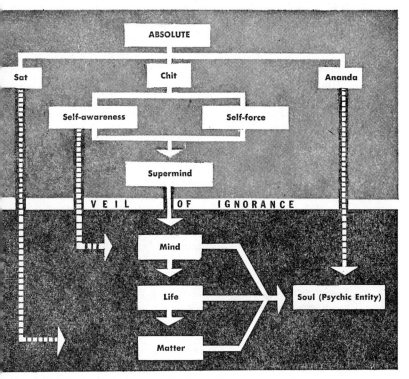

DIAGRAM I

The origin, the continent, the initial and the ultimate reality of all that is in the cosmos is the triune principle of transcendent and infinite Existence, Consciousness and Bliss which is the nature of divine being.

Consciousness has two aspects, illuminating and effective . . . self-awareness and . . . self-force, by which Being possesses itself whether . . . static . . . or . . . dynamic; for in its creative action it knows by omnipotent self-consciousness all that is latent within it and produces and governs the universe of its potentialities by an omniscient self-energy. (cont.)

This creative action of the All-existent has its nodus in the fourth, the intermediate principle of Supermind or Real-Idea, in which a divine Knowledge . . . and a substantial Will . . . develop . . . the movement and form . . . of things in right accordance with their self-existent Truth.

Mind, Life and Matter are a triple aspect of these higher principles working . . . in subjection to the principle of Ignorance. . . . These three are only subordinate powers of the divine quaternary:

Mind is a subordinate power of Supermind which takes its stand in . . . division;

Life is . . . a subordinate power of the energy aspect of Sachchidananda, . . . Force working out form and the play of conscious energy from the standpoint of division created by Mind;

Matter is the form of substance of being which the existence of Sachchidananda assumes when it subjects itself to this phenomenal action of its own consciousness and force.

In addition, there is a fourth principle which comes into manifestation at the nodus of mind, life and body, that which we call the soul; but this has a double appearance, in front the desire-soul which strives for the possession and delight of things, and behind . . . the true psychic entity which is the real repository of the experiences of the spirit. . . . This fourth human principle is a projection and an action of the third divine principle of infinite Bliss. (LD, 313–15)

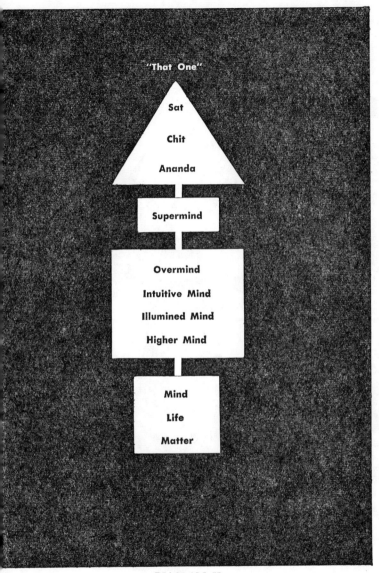

DIAGRAM II

(Cf. LD, 1118–30.)

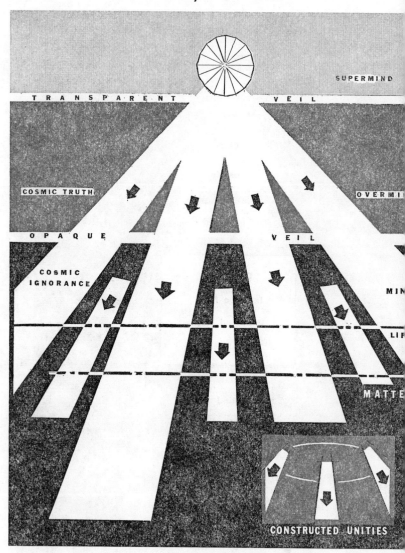

DIAGRAM III

DIAGRAM III

The integrality of the Supermind keeps always . . . the truth of its individual self-determinations clearly knit together; it maintains in them an inseparable unity and between them a close interpenetration and a free and full consciousness of each other; but in Overmind this integrality is no longer there. (LD, 333–34)

For Supermind transmits to Overmind all its realities, but leaves it to formulate them in a movement and according to an awareness of things which is still a vision of Truth and yet at the same time a first parent of the Ignorance. (LD, 333)

A line divides Supermind and Overmind which permits a free transmission, allows the lower Power to derive from the higher Power all it holds or sees, but automatically compels a transitional change. (LD, 333)

Overmind Energy proceeds through an illimitable capacity of separation and combination of the powers and aspects of the integral and indivisible all-comprehending Unity. It takes each Aspect or Power and gives to it an independent action in which it acquires a full separate importance. (LD, 334)

The One Consciousness is separated into many independent forms of consciousness . . . ; each follows out of its own line of truth. (LD, 335)

Overmind in its descent reaches a line which divides the cosmic Truth from the cosmic Ignorance; it is the line at which it becomes possible for Consciousness-Force, emphasising the separateness of each independent movement created by Overmind . . . to divide Mind by an exclusive concentration from the overmental source. (LD, 341)

There has already been a similar separation of Overmind from its supramental source, but with a transparency in the veil which allows a conscious transmission and maintains a certain luminous kinship; but here the veil is opaque and the transmission of the Overmind motives to the Mind is occult. (LD, 342)

Mind separated acts as if it were an independent principle, and each mental being . . . stands similarly on its separate self; if it communicates with or combines or contacts others, it is not with the . . . universality of the Overmind movement, on a basis of underlying oneness, but as independent units joining to form a separate constructed whole. It is by this movement that we pass from the cosmic Truth into the cosmic Ignorance. (LD, 342)

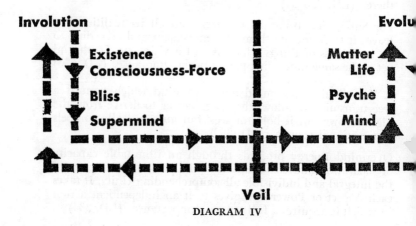

DIAGRAM IV

We may, therefore . . . pose eight principles . . . and then we perceive that our existence is a sort of refraction of the divine existence, in inverted order of ascent and descent.

The Divine descends from pure existence through the play of Consciousness-Force and Bliss and the creative medium of Supermind into cosmic being; we ascend from Matter through a developing life, soul and mind and the illuminating medium of Supermind towards the divine being. The knot of the two, the higher and the lower hemisphere, is where mind and supermind meet with a veil between them. The rending of the veil is the condition of the divine life in humanity. (LD, 316)

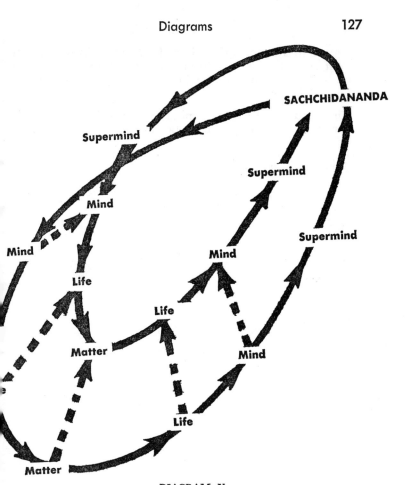

DIAGRAM V

Evolution, [Aurobindo] thought, would not end in Mukti (Liberation) but in Bhukti (enjoyment of the play of God) when there would be accession of spiritual power with the triple capacity to sublimate, to transform, and to render strong.

His diagram of evolution did not lead directly from the

Saguna [relative, manifest] into the Nirguna [Absolute]. It went from the Nirguna down (involution) to Saguna, then up to Nirguna and then again down to Saguna to be taken up to Nirguna.

This circular but eternally spiral movement is the geometric pattern of the dynamic involution-evolution that goes on.

—K. K. Diwakar, *Mahayogi Sri Aurobindo* (Bombay: Bharatiya Vidya Bhavan, 1962), p. 224.

4

Transformation

SRI AUROBINDO'S THEORY OF EVOLUTION HAS SEVERAL RE-
markable features. It is an evolution of consciousness as
well as of matter. It operates by assuming the properties
of the lower levels into the higher levels as they successively appear, or, alternatively stated, the higher levels
descend into and transform the lower levels. Evolution,
or the manifestation of the various properties and principles of being, is an inevitable consequence of a prior
involution of those same properties and principles. Now,
using these special features of his view of evolution, Aurobindo's thought can be seen to approach its climax in a
final conclusion, that evolution has a definite goal, and that
that goal is a divine life on earth.

SIXTH CONCLUSION: EVOLUTION HAS A GOAL

Here two unique features appear: 1) in man the process
of evolution reaches a point of reflexion, or resonance, in
which the product of the process begins to participate in
the agency of the process, and can by his free acts either

prevent or make possible (but not actually effect) the next forward step; and 2) evolution is an individual process as well as a cosmic one and characterizes the development which the person experiences in his own consciousness and spiritual life. It is because of these two features that Aurobindo insists that the practice of yoga, in particular the Integral Yoga, is so necessary and important. He believes that the world and we ourselves can be radically transformed and divinized, but that we must labor in order to realize this high aspiration.

The highest state of evolution we have seen thus far is humanity in the condition of ignorance, struggling for knowledge and control of the environment. Bound down as we are and frustrated by our limited sight and power, we nevertheless experience strong aspirations toward a fuller and freer life. Even before the technological conquest of Nature had reached stages which we now regard as primitive, man was trying to attain a higher spirituality, a level of consciousness beyond sensation and reason. The urge toward increased consciousness is the one outstanding characteristic of his life.

> Man's urge towards spirituality is the inner driving of the spirit within him towards emergence, the insistence of the Consciousness-Force of the being towards the next step of its manifestation. (LD, 1008)

If it is true, as Aurobindo has attempted to show, that evolution is primarily a spiritual evolution, then "man as he is cannot be the last term of that evolution: he is too imperfect an expression of the spirit." (LD, 1009) He must either exceed himself by opening his mind to the higher realms, or he must give place to another creature who will be able to welcome those higher states of consciousness into himself. (LD, 1009)

It is the nature of man to seek to know Matter, Life, and Mind in order to master them. This is the secret urgency of Sachchidananda in him, pressing on to full existence, full consciousness, full delight. This is the problem evolution poses itself, which grows to a paradox in man, in whom evolution is not only self-conscious but apparently self-defeating. Here we have a level of being, the mental man, that has a nature which cannot possibly be fulfilled, for it is the quality of this nature to desire what that nature cannot in itself be. The very core of man, therefore, is the necessity to exceed himself. Until this problem is solved, the human race cannot rest.

> The line of evolutionary creation in which [man] has appeared cannot stop where he now is, but must go either beyond its present term in him or else beyond him if he himself has not the force to go forward. Mental idea trying to become fact of life must pass on till it becomes the whole Truth of existence. (LD, 249–50)

We must bring to bear all our forces, intellectual knowledge, will, practical action, power of enjoyment, all the hidden capacities of our complex consciousness, and focus them on the one object.

> That object is to become, to be conscious, to increase continually in our realised being and awareness of self and things, in our actualised force and joy of being, and to express that becoming dynamically in such an action on the world and ourselves that we and it shall grow more and always yet more towards the highest possible reach, largest possible breadths of universality and infinity. (LD, 818)

Our sense of participation in Nature's workings must increase. We must develop a more intimate intuition which can be in "luminous identity with the movements of Nature" (LD, 1100), so that our being can be brought into harmony with the universe. That would be a "real participation" by the individual in the "working of the universal Consciousness-Force." The person would "become the master of his own executive energy and at the same time a conscious partner . . . of the Cosmic Spirit . . . : the universal Energy would work through him, but he also would work through her . . . the double working [being] a single action." (LD, 1100) As this power of conscious participation grew, the vision of the direction Nature was taking would become clearer together with an understanding of her methods, and alongside the increased knowledge would grow increased freedom. (LD, 1101)

Our present notion of free will, Aurobindo says, is tainted with excessive egoism, and imagines freedom to be the capacity to act with complete independence, in grand isolation, without any determination other than its own choice. But we have no nature with those characteristics. Our nature is part of the cosmos and subject to the supreme Transcendence. The only freedom to be attained is that which is gained by becoming the instrumentality of the Highest Being. Then indeed one would not be subject to any determinism, because one would be united to the source of all determination. Man's will becomes free when it is surrendered to God's Will. (LD, 1102–3)

At present we are subject to the dualities of life and death, joy and sorrow, pleasure and pain, truth and error, good and evil, because we are still caught in the egoistic consciousness of the Ignorance, with its artificially constructed oppositions and unities. But if the human soul can be opened to God, then it will be seen that this egoistic life was only a prelude to a superior human life, even as animal life, with no reflective consciousness at all, was only a prelude to the appearance of man. Such an opening to the Divine would mean the "transformation of the limited ego into a conscious centre of divine unity and freedom." This would be "the divine result toward which the cycles of our evolution move." (LD, 71)

Nature customarily gives hints of the development that is to come. Even in those forms of life which seem to be sunk in unconsciousness, the preparations for sensation can be discovered, and in those capable of sensation the subliminal stirring of mind is evident. (LD, 1014) So it is with our own position in mental life: we can see for ourselves the signs of a superior consciousness to come; we already know the conditions which must be fulfilled if we are to reach it and the characteristics it will display when it emerges. We have argued that if there are planes above, then they must be involved below; and if they are involved below, then they must evolve in the concrete.

> Spirituality emerging in mind is the sign of a power which itself has founded and constituted life, mind, and body and is now emerging as a spiritual being in a living and thinking body. (LD, 1016)

How far the emergence will go, and whether the emergent spirituality will become dominant in its turn, as had mind, life, and matter before it, is the question. Aurobindo feels that the evolution of Supermind and of the supreme Sachchidananda *somewhere* in the universe is assured. (LD, 791–92) The only question is whether man will be the instrument and whether our earth will be the scene of this divine achievement. (LD, 322)

Is such a fantastic goal the only goal which is acceptable? Would not some lower aim be more within our reach and still sufficient to give significance to the movement of evolution? No, says Aurobindo:

If there be any goal to the evolution which finds here its

present crown and head in the human being, other than an aimless circling and an individual escape from the circling, if the infinite potentiality of this creature, who alone here stands between Spirit and Matter with the power to mediate between them, has any meaning other than an ultimate awakening from the delusion of life by despair and disgust of the cosmic effort and its complete rejection, then even such a luminous and puissant transfiguration and emergence of the Divine in the creature must be that high-uplifted goal and that supreme significance. (LD, 316–17)

Aurobindo's basic principle is that Sachchidananda is the beginning, the middle, and the end. Discord cannot be a fundamental principle of His being, but by its existence it implies progress toward a perfect solution. Aurobindo therefore can be satisfied only with a total victory, "a real victory of Life over Matter through the free and perfect use of body by Life,'" "a real victory of Mind over Life and Matter through a free and perfect use of life-force and form by Mind," and "a real victory of Spirit over the triplicity [of Matter, Life, and Mind] through a free and perfect occupation of mind, life and body by conscious spirit." (LD, 279)

> For an evolving life like ours this inevitable culmination must necessarily mean the finding of the self that was contained in the seed of its own birth and, with that self-finding, the complete working out of the potentialities deposited in the movement of Conscious-Force from which this life took its rise. (LD, 250)

The control of mind and life by the higher consciousness has already been achieved to some degree by some men. But the full transformation is still to come, in which divine consciousness will realize "not only in soul but in substance its kingdom of heaven upon earth." (LD, 192)

This earthly life need not be necessarily and for ever a wheel of half-joyous half-anguished effort; attainment may also be intended and the glory and joy of God made manifest upon earth. (LD, 192)

The glorification of God is the vocation of man. "To fulfill God in life is man's manhood. . . . Man's importance in the world is that he gives it that development of consciousness in which its transfiguration by a perfect self-discovery becomes possible. . . . He starts from the animal vitality and its activities but a divine existence is his objective." (LD, 45)

The starting point in animal vitality is governed by the principles of physical evolution.

> There is in the scale of terrestrial existence a development of forms, of bodies, a progressively complex and competent organisation of matter, of life in matter, of consciousness in living matter; in this scale, the better organised the form, the more it is capable of housing a better organised, a more complex and capable, a more developed or evolved life and consciousness. (LD, 996)

Up to this point the evolution has been effected not by the intention of the living being itself but by the automatic operation of Nature, that is to say, by the secret, involved consciousness which was present from the very beginning.

With the appearance of the human being this pattern changes. In mental man there is a self-conscious will to evolve: he has seen that there can be a higher consciousness than he presently possesses, and he desires it. The universality, intensity, and persistence of this desire in mankind may be counted as evidence that this is Nature's will for future development. If so, we will now see a reversal of her usual program. In the evolution below man it was only after the physical vehicle had become sufficiently complex that the next higher level of consciousness could enter into it. But beginning from man, this process will be inverted: the increase in consciousness will transform the physical vehicle! (LD, 1005–6)

> The physical foundation of Matter remains, but Matter can no longer be the foundation of the consciousness; consciousness itself will be no longer in its origin a welling up from the Inconscient or a concealed flow from an occult inner subliminal force under the pressure of contacts from the universe. The foundation of the developing existence will be the new spiritual status above or the unveiled soul status within us. . . . The whole concentration of the being will be shifted from below upwards and from without inward; our higher and inner being now unknown to us will become ourselves, and the outer of surface being which we now take for ourselves will be only an open front or an annexe through which the true being meets the universe. (LD, 863–64)

Thus our humanity moves to fulfill its highest destiny, that of consciously cooperating with the creative force of evolution and of becoming the intermediary between the Inconscient and the supramental planes.[1]

> It is the point in the development of light and power out of the Inconscience at which liberation becomes possible: a greater role than this we cannot attribute to it, but this is great enough, for it makes our humanity all-important for the supreme purpose of evolutionary Nature. (LD, 931)

This liberation is effected through love. Sri Aurobindo says of love that it is "the desire to give oneself to others and to receive others in exchange; it is a commerce between being and being." (LD, 244) It is the working out of the principle of Desire in the world.

---

1. Haridas Chaudhuri, *Sri Aurobindo: The Prophet of Life Divine* (2nd ed.; S.A.A., 1960), p. 18.

[Desire] has to progress from the type of a mutually devouring hunger to the type of a mutual giving, of an increasingly joyous sacrifice of interchange;—the individual gives himself to other individuals and receives them back in exchange; the lower gives itself to the higher and the higher to the lower so that they may be fulfilled in each other; the human gives itself to the Divine and the Divine to the human; the All in the individual gives itself to the All in the universe and receives its realised universality as a divine recompense. Thus the law of Hunger must give place progressively to the law of Love, the law of Division to the law of Unity. (LD, 233)

Even if love begins its progress through evolution as a kind of "extended selfishness," still it leads man to discover through the experiences of self-sacrifice and mutual help that the separated individual he ignorantly took himself to be can be only "a minor term of being" which "exists by the universal."[2] This is the threshold. Once he discovers this, the shell of egoism in Ignorance is broken, and the way is clear for evolution in the higher planes.

He has reached the point at which Mind can begin to open to the truth that there is something beyond itself; from that moment his evolution, however obscure and slow, towards that superior something, towards Spirit, towards supermind, towards supermanhood is inevitably predetermined. (LD, 239)

Man's evolution toward Spirit at this point may be "predetermined," but it is not achieved. The condition is the opening of self to the power above. And this is attained by yoga. Yoga becomes significant precisely at the point at which we pass from natural evolution to conscious evolution.[3] As Maitra says in his *Introduction,* "What philos-

---

2. LD, 239. The level of the universal, we should recall, is the level on which the uniqueness of individuals is preserved and held in a perfect union of community.

3. Satprem, *Sri Aurobindo, or The Adventure of Consciousness* (New York: India Library Society, 1964), p. 97.

ophy establishes theoretically as a fundamental necessity, we can only realize practically through yoga."[4] But even the condition of receptivity on the part of man is not sufficient, for it is not the active principle in this transformation. The transfiguration is accomplished only by the grace of God.

> The supramental change is a thing decreed and inevitable in the evolution of the earth-consciousness; for its upward ascent is not ended and mind is not its last summit. But that the change may arrive, take form and endure, there is needed the call from below with a will to recognize and not deny the Light when it comes, and there is needed the sanction of the Supreme from above. . . . [The actual rending of the veil] can only be done by the Supreme Being; no human effort has the power to do this. Human effort, however, if properly directed, can prepare human beings to receive the Supermind when it descends.[5]

Sri Aurobindo's Yoga is called Integral because its work concerns the integrating of all aspects of life. Its final goal is to see the Supermind freely expressing itself in the matter of the human body, thus binding together in closest unity the highest and the lowest. Just as its goal does not involve escape from the earth, so neither does its way to the goal. It is a life in the midst of the world, mingling all features of human activity. It unites and reconciles the traditional yogas of knowledge, love, and work. It works as much by sending higher powers down into the lower levels as by endeavoring to raise the consciousness to higher planes. It considers that its ideal is the transfiguration and elevation not of the individual yogin alone but of the entire human race.

---

4. S. K. Maitra, *An Introduction to the Philosophy of Sri Aurobindo* (Calcutta: Culture, 1941), p. 10.
5. Aurobindo, *The Mother* (8th ed.; S.A.A., 1956), pp. 83–84.

Aurobindo does not expect that this elevation will take place in the whole human race at once (LD, 1004), but does urge that there be a "general admission of the ideal, a widespread endeavor" in its behalf. (LD, 863)

In yoga, as in everything else, the actual achievement is always the work of the individual. Even the gradually rising general level of cosmic consciousness is made possible only by the individuals who constitute communities. (LD, 825) It is very important to retain individual strength, independence, and plasticity, as against any type of "mass consciousness" if evolution is to continue to progress. (LD, 827) Only through the individual can the recovery of the infinite self be achieved.

> The immense importance of the individual being, which increases as he rises in the scale, is the most remarkable and significant fact of a universe which started without consciousness and without individuality in an undifferentiated Nescience. This importance can only be justified if the Self as individual is no less real than the Self as cosmic Being or Spirit and both are powers of the Eternal. (LD, 900–901)

The role of the individual is crucial in the yoga which brings the world to self-realization because finding the Individual Self, or Soul, is the first step in the transformation leading to the divine life. Conversely, it is the individual's failure to find and live by his real soul that is the source of the malady of the world. (LD, 264)

By "soul," or "psychic entity," Aurobindo means a psychic principle which is "not the life or the mind, much less the body, but which holds in itself the opening and flowering of the essence of all these to their own peculiar delight of self." (LD, 262) The surface "desire-soul" by which almost all of us live, not having found the true soul, is that which operates our vital appetites, our emotions, aesthetic responses, ambitions, curiosity, and so on. (LD, 263) But there is behind it the subliminal psychic entity which is "a pure power of light, love, joy, and refined essence of being. . . . It is when some reflection of this larger and purer psychic entity comes to the surface that we say of a man, he has a soul, and when it is absent in his outward psychic life that we say of him, he has no soul." (LD, 263)

Soul is the manifestation of the Bliss aspect of the Absolute Being. (LD, 262) (Compare Diagrams I and IV.) To seek for delight is the fundamental impulse of life; this motive integrates all the actions of the living being. (LD, 261) At different stages of evolution the impulse toward delight passes into different phases of itself. There is first an inconscient drive, entirely possessed by the universal movement in which it arises. Later comes particular desire, eager to possess but limited in capacity to love, seeking both to possess and to give. Finally, the perfection of these partial tendencies is found in the full emergence of a Love which is "the unification of the state of the possessor and possessed in the divine unity of souls which is the foundation of the supramental existence." (LD, 261) The psychic entity is the principle in the individual which integrates all its other principles and their activities and which manifests the divine Ananda in its individual poise. Just as Sat is manifest in Matter, Chit in Life, and Supermind in Mind, so Ananda is manifest in Soul. (LD, 262)

This subliminal soul is called by the Upanishads the *Chaitya Purusha*, the individual person. (LD, 269) It is ordinarily hidden in man and must be brought to the surface by yoga. The more readily apparent "desire-soul" represents Ananda in the world by responding to its contacts with the environment in terms of pleasure, pain, and indifference. These responses are determined not by the essence of the things experienced but by the subjectivity of the receiving consciousness, and they can be altered by altering the subjective condition. (LD, 265) The desire-soul is the companion of the egoism which binds man to the Ignorance. It is when man breaks the ring of egoism that he is freely on his way toward the supramental life. Bringing the Chaitya Purusha, or true self, to the surface is the way to break this bondage. It replaces the egoistic standards of pleasure and pain by "an equal, an all-embracing personal-impersonal delight." (LD, 267)

As with love, the critical threshold is crossed when the norm of value shifts from the egoistical to the universal. As examples Aurobindo suggests our ability to take delight in all the forms of Nature impartially, without liking some and finding others repellent, or the capacity of the artist or poet to find a universal beauty above what, from a self-seeking or utilitarian point of view, might be ugly or attractive. It is a detached, contemplative attitude as contrasted with a self-centered one. There are such instances as these in which we do manage to live by our inner soul. It is only in those experiences in which we are still too strongly attached to our habitual ego-responses, our physical and emotional pleasures and pains, that the application of the higher principle becomes difficult or impossible for us. We then complain of the contemplative attitude as being too "impersonal." We find detachment repellent when it attacks those desires and standards of judgment most intimate to the desire-soul. (LD, 268) But if we would be completely free, we must permit the Chaitya Purusha to govern us completely.

If the secret psychic Person can come forward into the front and, replacing the desire-soul, govern overtly and entirely and not only partially and from behind the veil this outer nature of mind, life and body, then these can be cast into soul images of what is true, right and beautiful and in the end the whole nature can be turned towards the real aim of life, the supreme victory, the ascent into spiritual existence. (LD, 270–71)

THE TRIPLE TRANSFORMATION AND THE LIFE DIVINE

The *psychic* change just described is the first stage in what Sri Aurobindo calls the "Triple Transformation," by which evolution attains the supramental level. When the transformation is complete, the Supermind will have become the dominant principle in creation and a permanent new order of being will have been established. But at the very outset, in order for the soul to emerge and take over the reins of government of the whole being, there must first be a direct contact in the surface being with the spiritual Reality, that is to say, the soul must consciously touch God. Only such an overpowering contact can integrate all the aspects of our being and energize it to the complete conversion that is required. (LD, 1073)

There are various ways of reaching out for this contact; they are the different yogas. One way is through the thinking mind, leading to the realization of the Supreme Truth and Value above all personal attachments to particular beings. Another way is through the heart, "when the mind goes beyond impersonality to the awareness of a supreme Personal Being" and attains "love of God and men and all creatures." (LD, 1075) A third way is to practice consecration of the pragmatic will and all its actions; practiced perfectly, it enables one to feel "the force or presence acting within . . . governing all the actions, and the personal will is entirely surrendered or identified with this greater Truth-Will." (LD, 1076)

Combining all three of these approaches, as Sri Aurobindo does in his Integral Yoga, a psychic condition is
attained in the surface being in which "there is a larger
and more complex openness to the psychic light within us
and to . . . the Reality now felt above and enveloping and
penetrating us." (LD, 1076) Finally, for the psychic
change to be complete, "the consciousness has to shift its
center . . . from the surface to the inner being; . . . one
must cease to be the surface personality and become the
inner Person, the [Chaitya] Purusha." (LD, 1077) The
soul then becomes the ruler and guide of the whole nature,
and "the whole conscious being is made perfectly apt for
spiritual experience of every kind." (LD, 1081) As the
spiritual experiences flow into the center of the being, the
soul begins to ascend out of Ignorance into Knowledge.
(LD, 1081)

The *psychic* transformation is followed or accompanied
by the second step, the *spiritual* transformation; after the
movement inward to the center, there must be an opening
upward to a higher existence. (LD, 1084)

> If the rift in the lid of mind is made, what happens is an
> opening of vision to something above us or a rising up to-
> wards it or a descent of its powers into our being. (LD,
> 1085) . . . The descent of a higher Light, Knowledge, Power,
> Force, Bliss, Purity into the whole being, even into the lowest
> recesses of the life and body, even into the darkness of our
> subconscience. (LD, 1061) . . . No limit can be fixed to this
> revolution; for it is in its nature an invasion by the In-
> finite. (LD, 1087)

But even this exalted state is not yet the end for Sri
Aurobindo. If the soul were to stop here in its transformation, it might be content to become merely passive to the
world-self. It might rest in the divine Silence from which
it was born, or merge itself with the universal conscious-

ness, or elect to live forever in the presence of the Divine Beloved. "All of these," says Sri Aurobindo, "are great and splendid achievements of our spiritual self-finding, but they are not necessarily the last end and entire consummation; more is possible." (LD, 273) They all still involve some sense of opposition: the silence *or* the action of Brahman, Brahman with qualities *or* without, the Divine Person *or* the Impersonal Existence.

> [The soul] can regard the Person as the sole Reality or the Impersonal as alone true; it can regard the Lover as only a means of expression of eternal Love or love as only the self-expression of the Lover; it can see beings as only personal powers of an impersonal Existence or impersonal existence as only a state of the one Being, the Infinite Person. (LD, 273)

All of these are limited and partial views. There is a higher consciousness, "the supramental Truth-Consciousness," in which the oppositions are transcended in an integral realization of eternal being. (LD, 273) Only this supramental conscious-energy can establish the harmony of spiritual status and world dynamism (LD, 274) which will avoid the greatest disadvantage of partial spiritual achievements, the danger that they will distract the soul from "its ultimate mission here, to lead the nature also towards its divine realisation." (LD, 272)

A person undergoing the transformation, who lives in the presence of these high spiritual experiences, frequently has the sense of being split in two, says Aurobindo. He is aware of an inner self which enjoys the realization of the Divine and of an outer being which is still governed by the values of the Ignorance.

> Only the descent of the Supermind with its perfect unity of Truth-Knowledge and Truth-Will can establish in the outer as in the inner existence the harmony of the Spirit; for it

alone can turn the values of the Ignorance entirely into the values of the Knowledge. (LD, 275)

The third transformation, then, is the *supramental* transformation, "the ascent into the supermind and the transforming descent of the supramental Consciousness into our entire being and nature." (LD, 1062) At this point the passage from Ignorance to Knowledge is completed. An altogether different condition of life prevails. Sri Aurobindo speaks of it as a transition from Nature to Supernature, a transition which the lower Nature is itself essentially incapable of effecting.

> It is . . . impossible for any effort of the mere Mind to achieve; our unaided personal aspiration and endeavour cannot reach it: our effort belongs to the inferior power of Nature; a power of the Ignorance cannot achieve by its own strength or characteristic or available methods what is beyond its own domain of nature. (LD, 1096)

The most that we can do is to prepare ourselves by yoga to receive this grace of the Lord. There is first a stage of seeking and effort, united to an intention to give one's heart and soul and mind to the Highest, then a stage of total conscious reliance on God to aid one's own endeavor, and finally a complete abandonment of oneself in one's entire nature to the action of the Supreme Being. (LD, 1106) This implies the sacrifice by each aspect of the person of its most cherished established ways: the mind must give up its favorite molds of idea formation, all opinions, all habits of observation and judgment; the vital aspect must give up its desires, emotions, habits of sensation, reflex actions; and the physical aspect must give up its instinctive attachment to the laws of the body with its settled grooves of operation. (LD, 1106–7) All of these must be made available for transformation by the descending Supermind.

When the ascent to the Supermind—or its descent into us—begins, it follows certain grades, as all evolutionary processes do. (LD, 1112) It passes through those levels of consciousness which are intermediate between Mind and Supermind: Higher Mind, Illumined Mind, Intuitive Mind, and Overmind. All of these levels Aurobindo calls "gnostic in their principle and power." (LD, 1116) He means that the orientation on these levels of consciousness is no longer based on the sense of exclusive concentration on separated individuals which characterized the Ignorance. These levels are not objects of knowledge, not even ways of knowing or faculties of knowing. "They are domains of being, grades of the substance and energy of the spiritual being, fields of existence." (LD, 1116)

The being which has passed through these levels and is living in terms of Knowledge rather than of Ignorance, Sri Aurobindo calls the "Gnostic Being." It is the name of the new supramental being which now becomes dominant in the world, just as had the living being and the mental being before it. (LD, 1145)

> As there has been established on earth a mental Consciousness and Power which shapes a race of mental beings and takes up into itself all of earthly nature that is ready for the change, so now there will be established on earth a gnostic Consciousness and Power which will shape a race of gnostic spiritual beings and take up into itself all of earth-nature that is ready for this new transformation. (LD, 1151)

The Gnostic, or supramental, Being, having established a new level of life, will assume all of those below itself, elevating them to its own status. It will descend into the world of evolutionary becoming and develop the powers of the divine gnosis in the earthly nature. (LD, 1150) Our former ignorant becoming will be transformed into a "luminous becoming of knowledge and a realised power of being." (LD, 1168) This new power will be essentially a control of spirit over mind, life, and matter. As perfectly possessed instrumentalities of the higher power, the principles of the lower hemisphere will be perfectly transparent and flexible expressions of the spirit. One's own body and life will obey and the environment will come under complete control. (LD, 1238) The infinite Reality, which had been concealed in the lower world from the beginning and was figured in various distorted projections throughout the evolution in Ignorance, now begins to be fully and truly revealed. (LD, 1150)

Whereas the mental being could know an object only as a not-self, an "other," the Gnostic Being will know each being individually, and all of them together, by identity. He will be able to know any object as part of himself because he will no longer regard himself as an ego-bound person but as a universal person. (LD, 1170)

> [The gnostic consciousness] will proceed towards all knowledge, not setting truth against truth to see which will stand and survive, but completing truth by truth in the light of the one Truth of which all are the aspects. (LD, 1170)

All the poises of the Spirit will be real to the Gnostic Being and will be realized in his inner life. He will know himself fused into oneness with the transcendent Spirit; the whole universe will appear to him as the Conscious Being and he will experience all his actions in Nature as those of the World-Mother acting through him; he will feel the divine in every center of his individual consciousness and every cell of his body. (LD, 1156)

> The gnostic individual would be in the world and of the world, but would also exceed it in his consciousness and live

in his self of transcendence above it; he would be universal but free in the universe, individual but not limited by a separative individuality. (LD, 1157)

Furthermore, the gnostic level of life will eliminate the barriers erected in the Ignorance between one self and another on all levels—the level of soul, of mind, of life. (LD, 1236) There will be a direct knowledge of their oneness with one another, knowledge of one another's being, thought, action—direct communication. (LD, 1237) Full and perfect gnostic life must not only take form in the life of the individual but it must be a collective life of many Gnostic Beings as well. (LD, 1211) It will develop a common uniting consciousness, a "spontaneous and innate, not a constructed, unity and harmony." (LD, 1236) This unity, far from overpowering the distinctness of the individuals composing it, precisely enhances their uniqueness.

> The law of the supermind is unity fulfilled in diversity, and therefore there would be an infinite diversity in the manifestation of the gnostic consciousness although that consciousness would still be one in its basis. (LD, 1155) . . . In the supramental race itself, in the variation of its degrees, the individuals would not be cast according to a single type of individuality; each would be different from the other, a unique formation of the Being, although one with all the rest in foundation of self and sense of oneness and in the principle of his being. (LD, 1156)

Only when there is such unity in multiplicity is the delight of harmony possible. (LD, 1237)

Love, for the Gnostic Being, will be a "union of self with self . . . a joy of identity and the consequences of a diverse identity." (LD, 1171)

It is this joy of an intimate self-revealing diversity of the One, the multitudinous union of the One and a happy interaction in the identity, that will be for him the full revealed sense of life. (LD, 1171)

The supramental being will find his joy in bringing joy to others, for their joy will be part of his own joy of existence. He will have no need to practice self-effacement, since the movement of self-donation is integral to his self-fulfillment. (LD, 1161) All oppositions will be overcome in him.

He will not be moved to live for himself, for his ego, or for humanity or for others or for the community or for the State; for he will be aware of something greater than these half-truths, of the Divine Reality, and it is for that he will live, for its will in himself and in all, in a spirit of large universality, in the light of the will of the Transcendence. (LD, 1265–66)

The divine life will be an integral life. There will no longer be any need to practice asceticism because the vision of the world from the viewpoint of the ego will have been overcome and the desire-soul replaced by the true Individual. (LD, 1268) There will be a free acceptance of the whole of material Nature instead of a rejection. There will be "a certain reverence, even, for Matter and a sacramental attitude in all dealings with it . . . an offering of Brahman to Brahman by Brahman," as the Gita says.[6] The Gnostic Being, when using matter, will consider that he is using Spirit in this manifest form of itself. (LD, 1174) His supramental consciousness will "liberate and restore the obscured and spoiled intuitive instincts in the body and enlighten and supplement them with a more conscious action." (LD, 1175) The ability of his consciousness to

6. LD, 1174; cf. Bhagavad-Gita IV.24.

accept contacts with his environment without experiencing pain will increase until "the gnostic evolution at a certain stage must bring about a completeness of this power of self-protection which will fulfill the claim of the body for immunity and serenity of its being and for deliverance from suffering and build in it a power for the total delight of existence." (LD, 1177)

The one form and meaning of the gnostic life will be the will of the Divine Being, the self-expression of His Spirit, whether in simplicity or in complexity. (LD, 1268) Those who attain the gnostic level will be united with the Creator and will share in His action. Instead of being created by the world, as we are in the realm of Ignorance, they will share in creating themselves and the world. (LD, 1213)

This is the culmination of the whole long double evolution, that of the outward being and that of the inward being.

> If there is an evolution in material Nature and if it is an evolution of being with consciousness and life as its two key-terms and powers, this fullness of being, fullness of consciousness, fullness of life must be the goal of development towards which we are tending. . . . The spirit . . . will return to itself . . . not through a frustration of life but through a spiritual completeness of itself in life. (LD, 1271)

Evolution is intelligible, says Aurobindo, only if its goal is an integral and divine life. Escape into the purely spiritual can occur at any point; evolution is not needed to effect that.

> If the sole intention were the revelation of the essential spiritual Reality and a cessation of our being into its pure existence, this insistence on the mental evolution would have no purpose: for at every point of the nature there can be a

breaking out of the spirit and an absorption of our being into it. . . . But if her intention is a comprehensive change of the being, this double evolution is intelligible and justifies itself; for it is for that purpose indispensable. (LD, 1022)

That a comprehensive change of being is Nature's intention—God's will—has been Sri Aurobindo's contention throughout. A merely inward transformation cannot complete the divine manifestation. The outward nature, both individual and universal, must share the transformation, fulfilling the divine glory.

[The goal is] a fulfilment exceeding the individual transformation, a new earth and heaven, a city of God, a divine descent upon earth, a reign of the spiritually perfect, a kingdom of God not only within us but outside, in a collective human life. (LD, 1009)

As the evolution began with Sachchidananda, the absolute and infinite Being-Consciousness-Delight, so, having passed through the ascending levels in the Ignorance and the supramental transformation in the Knowledge, it comes to its goal by totally and integrally *embodying* the divine Sachchidananda, that God may be All in all, transcendent, universal, and individual.

5

Maya and the Mayavada

WE COME NOW TO THE PARTICULAR TOPIC ON WHICH WE WISH to focus: Aurobindo's arguments for the reality and value of the world. This point has been chosen for two reasons: first, it constitutes the heart of Aurobindo's message; and second, it brings up for discussion precisely the area in which Indian philosophy has often been misunderstood in the West. Indeed, Aurobindo charges that there has been a good deal of misunderstanding of the authentic Vedic tradition in India itself, both because of the excessive prestige of the school of Sankara, and because in recent centuries Indian scholars have frequently been content to follow European leadership in the study of their own traditions and thus have repeated rather than corrected the errors. This has given rise to a narrow stereotyped view of Indian philosophy, identifying it with a simplistic interpretation of one of its many schools.

According to the stereotype, Indian philosophy is characterized by the position that the world is an illusion (maya) and the solitary Self (Atman-Brahman) is alone real. Action in an illusory world is, of course, of no significance, except possibly as an exercise to purify the mind in preparation for its union with the Absolute. Whether one renounces all action or whether one practices pious actions, the intention is the same: to escape the world. Therefore nothing is done to develop the world in its own terms and there is no progress in society.

This is, briefly, the mentality Aurobindo is challenging. It is false to take it as characterizing the whole of Indian philosophy, and we will see some demonstration of this in the sections on the term *maya* and on the scriptures. Far more extensive documentation could be made by reference to the whole spectrum of Indian philosophical doctrines, most of which do not take an illusionist or escapist position. But we are concentrating on the structure and orientation of Aurobindo's thought, and much of what he has to say is geared to demolishing the illusionist-escapist mentality. While not characteristic of the whole corpus of Indian philosophy, it was prevalent in the India of his younger days, and Aurobindo set out to counter its deleterious influence on his countrymen. In *The Life Divine* he denies it (LD, 38, 379), he warns against it (LD, 28), he ridicules it (LD, 47, 527), he argues against it (LD, 433–571), he even tries to explain its false attractiveness in terms of the partial truth that is in it. (LD, 805, 493) He exposes the temptations by which minds are drawn to it and shows that for all the impressive and convincing spiritual experience which is offered in evidence for it, it is not the highest experience.

This "illusionist" school of thought is often called *mayavada*, meaning maya-doctrine, or maya-ism. For this reason it will be helpful to survey quickly the history of the word *maya* up to the time of Sankara to see how it acquired the connotation of "illusion." Next, it is only fair

to distinguish between what we may call "extreme mayavada" and the system of Sankara. The illusionist doctrine
is usually linked with his name, but Sankara himself does
not have such a bald and simplistic view. His evaluation
of the world is more ambivalent, but the social effect is the
same: there is no encouragement for action in the world.[1]
Aurobindo, therefore, tends much of the time to class him
and mayavada in general together.[2]

Aurobindo argues against mayavada from both reason
and scripture, and we will summarize his arguments under
these heads in this chapter. However, the arguments which
move him more deeply are the arguments from the effect
of the mayavada mentality on the values of a society. The
following chapter will be devoted to this topic. And finally,
he presents his positive program in contrast to mayavada,
his holistic, or integral, non-dualism in which the world
and each being, society, and activity in it is thoroughly real,
intrinsically valuable, and *progressing* toward greater
value. This will be the burden of the seventh chapter.

HISTORY OF THE WORD *Maya*

Contrary to the popular conception, *maya* does not mean
purely and simply "illusion" or "deception."[3] It is related

1. Cf., e.g., Sankara's *Commentary on the Vedanta-Sutras*, I.1.4, in which
he praises certain scriptural passages for diverting the minds of men
from the objects of natural activity. Translation by George Thibaut
(New York: Dover, 1962), I:35–36.
2. Cf., e.g., this remark from a letter (23 August 1935) published in
Sri Aurobindo on Himself and on the Mother (S.A.A., 1953), p. 239:
"If you deny that these things are material and solid (which, of course,
metaphysically you can), then you land yourself plump into Shankara's
Illusionism, and there I will leave you." Also found in A. B. Purani,
The Life of Sri Aurobindo (S.A.A., 2nd ed., 1960), p. 283. However,
when Aurobindo does treat Sankara explicitly and at somewhat greater
length (as in LD, 540ff.), he admits that Sankara's philosophy is not an
absolute but a modified illusionism, granting a qualified reality to Maya.
3. Ruth Reyna, *The Concept of Maya from the Vedas to the 20th
Century* (Bombay: Asia Publishing House, 1962), pp. ix–x.

etymologically to the Greek *metron* and its literal meaning
is "measure." The broadest sense of the word on which all
scriptural texts and commentators seem to agree is that
which pertains to the relation between the phenomenal
world and the transcendent Absolute.[4] Maya "measures,"
or delimits, the infinite, producing finite forms.

Maya appears as early as the Rig Veda in connection
with the concept of a fundamental Unity on which is based
the phenomenal multiplicity of the world. Indra, the pin-
nacle of the divine hierarchy, is described as "assuming
many forms" (*mayabhih*) [5]: "Indra assumes form after
form, working mayas about his body"[6]; "through mayas
Indra goeth in many forms."[7] The connotation of the word
here may be said to be one of creative power ("making"),
perhaps in the sense of the supernatural ("magic").[8]

In the Upanishadic period, the recognition that the
world depends on a single source (Brahman) for its being
and intelligibility, and the realization that this same ultimate reality (as Atman) is at the center of the individual
conscious subject, raised the question of why this universal
and subjective essence of things was not immediately given
in the objects of sense experience. Why is reality *back of*
appearances? An answer was attempted: these appearances
are *maya:* they both reveal and conceal the Reality.[9] As
revealing the Reality, maya still means the power of the
Supreme Being. But as concealing the Reality, it now
begins to mean the absence of knowledge (avidya); and it

---

4. *Ibid.*, p. 4.
5. Rig Veda X.54.2.
6. *Ibid.*, III.53.8.
7. *Ibid.*, VI.47.18.
8. Cf. also Rig Veda III.38.7; IX.83.3; I.159.4: V.85.5. This sense of the
power of a personal God is retained in some passages of the Upanishads,
as in Svetasvatara IV.10, and in the Bhagavad Gita, for instance IV.5-7;
XVIII.61.
9. Cf. Katha Upanishad II.1.10; Svetasvatara Up. IV.10; Mundaka
Up. I.1.3.

is this, together with the emphasis on the non-duality of the Supreme Being, which seems to have prompted later thinkers to speak of maya as "illusion" and the world characterized by it as (relatively) "unreal."[10]

During this same period, the psychological study of man's consciousness and knowledge became intense. It seems to have been motivated not so much by contemplative wonder as by an effort to obtain deliverance from moral and physical evil.[11] In the course of their efforts to isolate the experience of suffering and neutralize it, the rishis, whose discoveries are recorded in the Vedic scriptures, found that there are several distinct levels of consciousness possible to the human being: ordinary waking consciousness, dream consciousness, the consciousness of the Witness-Self when the mind is withdrawn from the senses, and the total loss of individual self-consciousness when the mind is merged into the Absolute Being which it contemplates.[12] They further observed that these states are not experienced simultaneously: when the mind is in one state, the worlds correlative to the others are either unknown or regarded as unreal. If, therefore, consciousness could be stabilized in a state which was not cognizant of anything which could cause suffering, freedom from pain would be achieved.

If we bear this background in mind in the survey of maya theories and arguments which follow, we will see that this observation of the discrete and mutually exclusive states of consciousness is at the foundation of all these

10. Cf. Prasna Up. I.16.

11. M. Hiriyanna, *Outlines of Indian Philosophy* (London: Allen & Unwin, 1964), p. 18. This is true even of a sophisticated thinker such as Sankara, who says in the prologue to his *Commentary on the Vedanta-Sutras*, "With a view to freeing one's self from that wrong notion which is the cause of all evil . . . the study of the Vedanta-texts is begun." Thibaut, I:9.

12. Also dreamless sleep and intermediate states.

spiritualities and predisposes them to the type of discipline they advocate and the type of liberation to which they aspire. We may say here, by way of anticipation, that what Aurobindo has done is precisely to deny the necessity of this observation and to hold that the unqualified consciousness and the qualified consciousness can be simultaneously experienced. This is one of the derivatives of his doctrine of the three poises of Brahman.

From a psychological context these observations quickly moved into a philosophical context. Reflection on the nature of consciousness and its relation to reality led to an attempt to include all of the states of consciousness within a single theory. But, since it was assumed that they were mutually exclusive, the question reduced to: which level or type of consciousness represented the real truth and which were illusions? Aurobindo distinguishes four types of answer to this question:[13] 1) the cosmic and terrestrial, in which waking consciousness of this material world is real and the other states are unreal; 2) the supraterrestrial, in which this world is only temporarily real and is to be replaced by another world, usually entered into after death; 3) supracosmicism, in which the mystical consciousness alone is real and all others are unreal; and 4) the integral (his own), in which all states of consciousness are real in their respective yet harmonious ways. The various doctrines of maya were developed especially in the "supracosmic" line, because, although this position theoretically denies the reality of all states of consciousness except that of union with the Absolute, it is obliged by the facts of daily life to account for the appearance of this world. "Maya" becomes the way of accounting for an unreal world which appears to be real.

---

13. LD, Part II, chapter 17.

The dialectic of the real and the unreal is masterfully developed by the Buddhist logician and metaphysician, Nagarjuna (second century A.D.) . The Buddhist endeavor to overcome the misery of life had taken the form of analyzing the suffering consciousness into component parts and declaring it a mere aggregate of passing moments of empirical experience with no residue of ego or self. Abandoning the belief in selfhood constituted the enlightenment which gave release from sorrow.

Moving against this background, Nagarjuna began by admitting this view of the world as a process and web of relations. But he charges that the relations themselves are paradoxical and unintelligible (for example, motion and causation) .[14] The things constituted of these relations are therefore not real—neither the external world of sense experience nor the internal world of self-conscious experience.[15] But this does not mean that things do not exist.[16] It means only that empirical things have to be deprived of a fixed essence or selfhood[17] and recognized as a phenomenal stream, a continuous production of appearances.[18] They are thus distinguished from Absolute Reality, the eternal foundation, the infinite, which cannot be spoken of in any of the categories taken from empirical life.[19] This ambiguous condition of being neither real nor totally unreal Nagarjuna called śūnya. The argument was later taken up by Śrīharsa, the foremost dialectician of the school of Sankara, who replaced the term sunya by maya.[20]

---

14. S. Radhakrishnan, *Indian Philosophy* (London: Allen & Unwin, 1923) , I:648; cf. Reyna, p. 11.
15. Radhakrishnan, I:653, 655.
16. P. T. Raju, *Idealistic Thought of India* (London: Allen & Unwin, 1953) , p. 246.
17. Radhakrishnan, I:660.
18. *Ibid.*, I:662.
19. *Ibid.*, I:656, 663.
20. Raju, p. 243.

Gaudapada (sixth century A.D.), the first systematic exponent of the Advaita Vedanta, pushed the idea of the unreality of phenomenal relations to its logical limit, and denied any realistic status at all to the objects of consciousness.[21] They are unreal, both as independent external beings and as distinct items of subjective experience, whether perceived in the dreaming or in the waking state. This is the extreme interpretation of the doctrine of nonduality. There is only one reality: the Atman, or non-dual Self. It and Brahman are identical.[22]

However, after enunciating this most severe and uncompromising doctrine, Gaudapada turns back to the realm of duality and admits that the fact of the appearance of the manifold world as not-self cannot be gainsaid.[23] From an absolute point of view, there can be no phenomenal world at all. But from the point of view of our present experience, it is there and requires an explanation. After having enumerated various possible explanations, including the one that the world is of the nature of dream or illusion, Gaudapada chooses to say that creation is "the inherent nature of the shining one."[24]

Radhakrishnan, in his *Indian Philosophy*, believes that this indicates a realistic conception of the world (on another level or from another point of view than that from which its reality was denied) and quotes other passages in evidence. For instance: "The Atman images himself through the power of his maya."[25] Here maya means, as in the Veda, divine power. Maya is also used by Gaudapada to mean the very nature of the divine; it is "inseparable

---

21. Reyna, p. 13.
22. Radhakrishnan, II:456–57.
23. *Ibid.*, II:459.
24. *Karika* i.7 (Radhakrishnan, II:460).
25. *Ibid.*, ii.12; (*Ibid.*).

from the ever-luminous who is hidden by it."[26] Paradox-
ically, it also means for him the cosmic principle which
veils reality from the mind of man.[27]

THE MAYAVADA OF SANKARA

Sankara (ninth century A.D.), spiritual descendent of
Gaudapada and master spokesman for the school of Advaita Vedanta, modified Gaudapada's position and introduced some important distinctions. While Gaudapada had
classed waking and dream experiences together, thereby
leaving himself open to the charge of subjectivism, Sankara carefully distinguishes them and points out that
waking experiences are linked to existing, though relatively unreal, objects.[28] He also distinguishes the object of
knowledge from the act of knowledge and in this context
admits the existence of an external world.

> That the outward thing exists apart from consciousness, has
> necessarily to be accepted on the ground of the nature of
> consciousness itself. Nobody when perceiving a post or a wall
> is conscious of his perception only, but all men are conscious
> of posts and walls and the like as objects of their perceptions.
> That such is the consciousness of all men, appears also from
> the fact that even those who contest the existence of external
> things bear witness to their existence when they say that what
> is an internal object of cognition appears like something ex-
> ternal. For they practically accept the general consciousness,
> which testifies to the existence of an external world, and
> being at the same time anxious to refute it they speak of the
> external things as "like something external." If they did not
> themselves at the bottom acknowledge the existence of the
> external world, how could they use the expression "like some-
> thing external"?[29]

26. *Ibid.*, ii.19; (*Ibid.*).
27. *Ibid.*, i.16. (*Ibid.*).
28. *Commentary*, III.2.4; (Thibaut, II:138).
29. *Ibid.*, II.2.28; (Thibaut, I:421).

Nevertheless, Sankara holds that these objects, independent of our individual subjective acts of knowledge,
are themselves phases of, or contents of, the Absolute
Spirit.

> In the same way as those parts of ethereal space which are
> limited by jars and waterpots are not really different from the
> universal ethereal space . . . so this manifold world with its
> objects of enjoyment, enjoyers and so on has no existence
> apart from Brahman.[30]

The objects do not exist in and for themselves, and therefore they are not fully *real.*

> The effect is this manifold world . . . ; the cause is the highest
> Brahman. Of the effect it is understood that in reality it is
> non-different from the cause, i.e. has no existence apart from
> the cause.[31]

To be *real* for Sankara means to be eternal, immutable,
and complete,[32] free from self-contradiction and not in
need of being referred to another for an account of its
being.[33] Only the Atman has this type of self-existence.
Genuine *selfhood* alone has the property of *reality.* Atman
alone is Brahman; the experience of Atman, the ground
of anyone's selfhood, is the proof of the existence of Brahman, the Ultimate Reality.

> Of that soul which is to be comprehended from the Upani-
> shads only, which is non-transmigratory, Brahman, different
> in nature from the four classes of substances . . . it is impos-
> sible to say that it is not or is not apprehended . . . that the
> Self is cannot be denied. . . . Different from the agent that is
> the object of self-consciousness, [it] merely witnesses it; [it]
> is permanent in all [transitory] beings; uniform; one; eter-

30. *Ibid.,* II.1.14; (Thibaut, I:321) .
31. *Ibid.,* II.1.14; (Thibaut, I:320) .
32. *Ibid.,* I.1.4; (Thibaut, I:33, 34) .
33. *Ibid.,* II.1.14; (Thibaut, I:326) .

nally unchanging; the Self of everything. . . . And as it is the
Self of all, it can neither be striven after nor avoided.[34]

Sankara sets forth his proof of the "unreality" of the
phenomenal world in his commentary on II.1.14 of the
Vedanta-Sutras. The argument is based on scripture and is
to the effect that the cause (Brahman) alone is real, while
the effect (the manifold world) is "unreal," i.e. not possessing independent existence. Scripture (Katha Upan.
VI.8.7) declares "Thou [individual embodied soul] art
That [Brahman]." Sankara comments:

> This doctrine of the individual soul having its Self in Brah-
> man, if once accepted as the doctrine of the Veda, does away
> with the independent existence of the individual soul. . . .
> And if the doctrine of the independent existence of the in-
> dividual soul has to be set aside, then the opinion of the
> entire phenomenal world—which is based on the individual
> soul—having an independent existence is likewise to be set
> aside.[35]

Sankara appears at this point to be saying two contradictory things, and he himself brings forward this objection:

> The fundamental tenet which we maintain . . . is that the
> creation, sustentation, and reabsorption of the world proceed
> from an omniscient, omnipotent Lord, not from a non-in-
> telligent [material nature]. . . . But how, the question may
> be asked, can you make this last assertion while all the while
> you maintain the absolute unity and non-duality of the
> Self?[36]

The answer is that the Lord is Lord over the creation (a
relation) only insofar as his own Self is considered as limited by the adjuncts of name and form. In reality there are

---

34. *Ibid.*, I.1.4; (Thibaut, I:36–37).
35. *Ibid.*, II.1.14; (Thibaut, I:322).
36. *Ibid.*; (Thibaut, I:328).

no multitude and no relations, not even the qualities of omniscience and omnipotence, for they too are relative qualities, implying something to be known, something to be done.[37] But within the world of Ignorance, so far as the phenomenal world is concerned, all these relations are valid.[38]

> The entire complex of phenomenal existence is considered as true as long as the knowledge of Brahman being the Self of all has not arisen. . . . Hence, as long as true knowledge does not present itself, there is no reason why the ordinary course of secular and religious activity should not hold on undisturbed.[39] . . . When, however, final authority having intimated the unity of the Self, the entire course of the world which was founded on the previous distinction is sublated, then there is no longer any opportunity for assuming a Brahman comprising in itself various elements.[40]

Sankara's view involves two visions: a vision of reality, in which one "realizes," or identifies with, the unitary Brahman, unmanifest and devoid of qualities, and a vision of appearances, in which one beholds the multiple Brahman, manifesting various qualities. The duality is owing to the two states of human consciousness, the condition of ignorance (avidya), in which the soul of man is in bondage to the appearances of the world, and the condition of knowledge (vidya), in which the soul of man is liberated.

The two visions, however, never interpenetrate. In actual life, one is in either one state or the other. Sankara, therefore, feels no obligation to explain the connection between the two states or the two worlds seen in them. When the soul is liberated, the problem of such a connec-

---

37. *Ibid.;* (Thibaut, I:329).
38. *Ibid.;* (Thibaut, I:330).
39. *Ibid.,* II.1.14; (Thibaut, I:324).
40. *Ibid.;* (Thibaut, I:326).

tion disappears, and while the soul is yet in bondage, the Absolute is unavailable.

> As long as a person has not reached the true knowledge of the unity of the Self, so long it does not enter his mind that the world of effects with its means and objects of right knowledge and its results of actions is untrue.[41] . . . For him who has reached the state of truth and reality the whole apparent world does not exist.[42]

Furthermore, in a system already committed to the tenet that there is only one reality, Brahman, there can be no question of "relation" between the two worlds, for that would presuppose distinct terms. The world is not different from Brahman; it is merely the "qualified" Brahman, that which is not the essential truth of the infinite unconditioned Brahman.[43] Brahman cannot be limited to being the sum of what the world is, nor can it be subject to the mutations of the world. But on the other hand, the world cannot be separate from and independent of Brahman, for then Brahman would not be the "one without a second." The best that we can say is that the world is to Brahman as appearance is to reality, but that this is not a logically comprehensible relation.

The term *maya* is used to summarize this situation. It refers to the phenomenal character of the world, neither real nor unreal. It points to the failure of logical categories to account for the relation between the world and Brahman.

> [Maya] is neither existent nor non-existent nor partaking of both characters; neither same nor different nor both; neither

41. *Ibid.;* (Thibaut, I:324).
42. *Ibid.;* (Thibaut, I:330).
43. *Ibid.;* II.1.20 (Thibaut, I:342–43).

composed of parts nor an indivisible whole nor both. She is most wonderful and cannot be described in words.[44]

Maya implies the dependence of the world on Brahman (from the world's view point), but does not imply that Brahman finds its self-manifestation in the world, as if Brahman needed the world for manifestation.

> The germs of the entire expanse of the phenomenal world [are] called in [Revelation] and [traditional commentaries] . . . maya . . . sakti, or . . . prakriti of the omniscient Lord. Different from them is the omniscient Lord himself.[45]

Although some later advaitins did adopt a subjectivist interpretation of the world and could even point to some strong statements of Sankara's in support of their thesis, it would not be correct to say that Sankara himself was a subjectivist. On the contrary, he repudiated the Buddhist subjectivist (Sunyavada) doctrines.[46] Maya, in his view, is not an individual error of judgment. It is a public world: a phenomenon, not a phantasm.[47]

The phenomenal world cannot be a metaphysical zero, because it is obviously a positive content of our experience. Nor is it unreal in the sense of being a formal contradiction, for "round squares" and "barren mothers" cannot function as objects of even imaginary experience. Nor is the world unreal as if it were the product of our imagination, for we experience it as thrust upon us, as given before we begin to act. Nor is the world a projection of our cognitive processes, because we can distinguish between

---

44. *Vivekachudamani*, 109. Translation by Swami Madhavananda (Calcutta: Advaita Ashrama, 6th ed., 1957), p. 40.
45. *Commentary*, II.1.14; (Thibaut, I:328–29).
46. Cf. Radhakrishnan, II:582; Hiriyanna, p. 340.
47. Cf. Radhakrishnan, II:587–89.

such errors and the facts of the given world. All of these points are carefully made by Sankara himself. He is not, therefore, teaching subjective idealism.

The object perceived is objective and real, independent of the observer's perception of it. But this whole situation of perceiver-perceived-perception is relative to the standpoint of Avidya and disappears from the standpoint of Vidya. It is not that the perceiver is real and the perceived unreal. The *perceiver-perceived structure itself* is unreal from the standpoint of Vidya. This being the case, the Mayavadin can very well reply to his critics that there is no problem of how the perceiver-perceived structure is related to Brahman, and he is under no obligation to account for it. This structure is simply *not there* for Brahman.[48]

In the famous image of the rope which appears in the dusk to be a snake, Sankara's point is not that the origin of the appearance of "snake" is the human mind, but rather that regardless of how the rope is perceived—as "snake" or as "rope"—the real rope itself undergoes no change. Furthermore, although the subject has made an erroneous interpretation of his visual data in this case, there is a real foundation for his perception.

Sankara's doctrine on the world follows this analogy. Translated into Western scholastic terminology, he is saying that while the world has a real relation to Brahman, Brahman has no real relation to the world but only a relation of reason.[49] The world appears to us as multiple

48. Cf. Haridas Chaudhuri, "Has Sri Aurobindo Refuted Mayavada?" in *Indian Philosophical Congress* (Silver Jubilee Commemorative Volume), 1950, pp. 106–7.

49. Thomas Aquinas has a passage on the relationship of God and creature that closely parallels Sankara's doctrine. Cf. *Summa Theologica*, ed. Anton C. Pegis (New York: Random House, 1945) I, q.45, a.3, ad 1, p. 437.

through an error of judgment (avidya). What we see as a world of separate entities, divided from each other and alienated from the Infinite Being, is really that Infinite Being itself without separation, a single unity. The world of the pairs of opposites, the experience of which is the "knowledge of good and evil," passes away when the consciousness of nonseparation from Brahman is awakened.

> That this entire apparent world, in which good and evil actions are done . . . is a mere illusion, owing to the non-discrimination of [the Self's] limiting adjuncts . . . and does in reality not exist at all, we have explained more than once. . . . As soon as . . . the consciousness of non-difference arises in us, the transmigratory state of the individual soul and the creative quality of Brahman vanish at once, the whole phenomenon of plurality, which springs from wrong knowledge, being sublated by perfect knowledge.[50]

The Self's "limiting adjuncts" refers to the perceiver-perceived structure discussed above. That structure is judged to be ultimately unreal because of its "plurality," interpreted as "difference," or essential independence, destructive of Brahman's unity.

AUROBINDO'S LOGICAL ARGUMENTS AGAINST MAYAVADA

Aurobindo's extensive arguments against the logical tenability of mayavada are to be found in *The Life Divine*, volume 2, Part I, chapters 3 through 6.

The first chapter takes up the difficulty that is felt by the logical reason in admitting that the individual is in any way eternal or that there is persistence of individuality after liberation has been attained. Applying his usual method, Sri Aurobindo says that such a difficulty of reason

---

50. *Commentary*, II.1.23; (Thibaut, I:345).

(or of spiritual experience) can be overcome only by a larger and more enlightened reason (or spiritual experience). (LD, 434)

The application of wider reason shows that the mind is accustomed to operating in terms of distinctions, and therefore, even when it conceives the final unity, it is secretly still considering it as one arm of a distinction: when a man realizes himself as united with the Transcendent, he is no longer aware of himself as an individual. Such a distinction betrays the fact that this conception has not transcended the mental state. It is still a characteristically mental operation: affirmation of one position by denial of something else from which it can be distinguished. It is an argument which assumes that because the only way we can mentally conceive the infinite and absolute is by contrasting it with the finite and relative, therefore the only way in which one can *exist* in the infinite and absolute is by *ceasing to exist* in the finite and relative. (LD, 435)

We have been used to identifying the individual person with the separative ego rather than with the real Person, with what Aurobindo calls the "psychic entity." Now, it is true that in any spiritual experience which brings one into realization of his union with God and with other beings, he naturally finds that this separative ego disappears like "mist in the sun," or like "a dewdrop in the sea," or like any of the other metaphors which have carried this notion into popular parlance. The reason for this is, Sri Aurobindo holds, that the ego is, on the mental and psychic level, the same type of *constructed* being as the body is on the physical level, and therefore can be thought of as disintegrating or "merging back" into the general store of energy on its level, just as the corrupting body restores its type of energy again to the whole.

This . . . ego . . . is . . . only a practical constitution of our
consciousness devised to centralise the activities of Nature in
us. (LD, 436)

However, this does not mean that true personhood is
lost upon union with God. The application of wider spiritual experience reveals that behind the superficial ego there
is the true Person, our real self.[51] This Purusha (Person)
is not determined by the limited characteristics of the ego;
on the contrary, it is through *his* action in conjunction
with the available world-material, that the ego itself is
formed. (LD, 436–37) But the characteristic action of the
Purusha is to embrace the whole world in his own consciousness, in his knowledge, love, and sense of identification.

By that very fact the individual ceases to be the self-limiting
ego; . . . our false consciousness of existing only by self-
limitation, by rigid distinction of ourselves from the rest of
being . . . is transcended; our identification of ourselves with
. . . a particular mind and body is abolished. (LD, 437) . . .
There is a true individual who is not the ego and still has
an eternal relation with all other individuals which is not
egoistic or self-separative, but of which the essential character
is practical mutuality founded in essential unity. (LD, 442)

He remains an individual. It is he, the individual person, who, as an active center of consciousness, is performing this act of embracing and identifying with the whole
reality. (LD, 438)

The soul still makes the world-becoming the material for
individual experience, but instead of regarding it as something outside and larger than itself on which it has to draw,
by which it is affected, with which it has to make accommoda-
tions, it is aware of it subjectively as within itself. (LD, 438)

---

51. Compare the universal advice of mystics and religious teachers
that one must "lose his self" in order to "find himself."

He does not cease to exist as himself nor does he merge into a world-soul. (LD, 437)

> We cannot understand him if we look only at his present individuality, but we cannot understand him either if we look only at his commonalty, his general term of manhood, or go back by exclusion from both to an essentiality of his being in which his distinguishing manhood and his particularising individuality seem to disappear. (LD, 453)

Because the disvalue of exclusivity has been overcome, there is no further advantage to be gained by merging the individual consciousness in the Absolute One. On the contrary, it is a larger and more divine life to be one with the Transcendent and at the same time act freely in terms of differentiation. Differentiation is the means of greater unity, for it enables us to enjoy union not only with God but with all other individual persons.

> Differentiation has its divine purpose: it is a means of greater unity, not as in the egoistic life a means of divisions; for we enjoy by it our unity with our other selves and with God in all, which we exclude by our rejection of his multiple being. (LD, 440)

Aurobindo does not *deny* that one can merge his consciousness entirely in the One, but he regards this as a lower stage of spiritual experience and not the necessary and final truth.

> Certainly we may prefer the absorption in a pure exclusive unity or a departure into a supracosmic transcendence, but there is in the spiritual truth of the Divine Existence no compelling reason why we should not participate in this large possession and bliss of His universal being which is the fulfilment of our individuality. (LD, 440)

The trick that our logic plays on us, Aurobindo says, is

to make us think that if we have got beyond limitations, then we are bound to stay beyond limitations.

> We readily go on, led by the mind's habit of oppositions, of thinking by distinctions and pairs of contraries, to speak of it as not only not bound by the limitations of the relative, but as if it were bound by its freedom from limitations, inexorably empty of all power for relations and in its nature incapable of them. (LD, 446)

It is this "false step of our logic" (LD, 447) which leads to the hypothesis that the world which we perceive before our illumination and which disappears in the experience of illumination, must be an illusion, since we feel that both experiences cannot be simultaneously admitted to be true. But the logical law of contradiction, so valid in our material experience, is not valid when we are dealing with the Absolute Reality. (LD, 450–51) The making of distinctions is a necessary first approach in understanding which our dividing mind has to take, but we err when we erect these distinctions—either scientific, metaphysical, or spiritual—into absolute truths. Absolute truths are precisely what they are not; being distinctions, they are necessarily *relative* truths. Because the *idea-content* of one of the terms distinguished is "absoluteness," we are deceived into thinking that the distinction itself is absolute. It is a kind of ontological argument for the sole existence of the Absolute.

The world-negating philosophies arise, Aurobindo argues, from a purely mental logic plus a spiritual experience which stops short at the realization of the Transcendent Absolute. (LD, 493) The mind, withdrawing from itself and its structures, *feels* that the world is unreal, but this is because its only knowledge of the world, up to this point in the evolution of the individual consciousness,

has been in the realm of Ignorance. The mental formulations under which we see the world in Ignorance are indeed constructions and "fictions" projected upon the reality, and the sudden discovery of this shocking truth throws
the consciousness into a conviction that there is no reality
at all to its experience of the world. The mind's "little
knowledge," obtained in glimpsing the transcendent and
eternal, has led it into the dangerous error of blanket rejection of what it had previously known in Ignorance.
Even Sankara's mayavada, when reduced to terms of spiritual experience, Aurobindo claims, comes to no more
than an exaggerated expression of this relative unreality.[52]
A "greater knowledge" would bring one back again to the
real world, seen now from the point of view of the Creator of the world. When one stands in the supreme consciousness and knows the world in truth, says Aurobindo,
a theory of illusion becomes superfluous. (LD, 541–42)

According to the classical theory of Illusionism, there is
only the one Reality, the absolute transcendent Brahman,
and we falsely see Brahman in the figure of the cosmic, as
a man might see a rope in the figure of a snake. The universe is not a genuine creation, for only the Absolute
Brahman is a reality. Maya, then, is a principle of "super-
imposition" by which the multiple cosmos is seen where
only the unitary Brahman exists. But we do see it for a
time, and we are able to operate and cooperate with others
in terms of this illusory cosmos. So it cannot be entirely
unreal. (LD, 525)

But if it is true that it is perceived, who is it who perceives it? If Brahman is the only reality, then Brahman
must be the percipient of maya. If Brahman is the percip-

52. Aurobindo, *Essays on the Gita* (New York: The Sri Aurobindo
Library, 1950), p. 279, n.3.

ient of maya, then maya is a power of Brahman-consciousness, and in that case there must be a dual status of consciousness in Brahman, one conscious of the reality, one conscious of maya. (LD, 526) Even if we try to suppose only one status of consciousness, in Brahman, the maya-consciousness, we are forced into duality in order to maintain the illusory character of what maya produces, together with the reality of Brahman itself. (LD, 527)

But this dual consciousness cannot be a knowledge-ignorance dualism, in which Brahman would be subject to maya. It must be a self-awareness joined to a deliberate will to produce a universe of illusion. But is not such a deliberate will to produce a universe an indication of a need to create? Brahman is alone, eternal, perfect, and complete. How can it have a need or a will to produce? Even if it should have such a will, though without need, from what motive would it produce illusion rather than real manifestations of its own reality? (LD, 529–30) The hypothesis of Brahman as the percipient of maya thus leads to the conclusion that maya is more likely a real manifestation of the real Brahman.

To this the Mayavadin would reply that from the standpoint of Brahman the whole question of maya does not arise. There is neither maya nor works of maya; maya is tucchā—nonexistent. Brahman therefore could not possibly be a percipient of maya. When Aurobindo argues that if maya's products are perceived they can be perceived only by Brahman, since Brahman is the only being in existence, he has not taken into consideration the subtlety of the Mayavadin dialectic, according to which the whole perceived/percipient structure is maya.

Let us suppose, then, that Brahman as Brahman is not the percipient of maya, but that Brahman as the individual percipient has entered into maya and can withdraw from it. In order to make the withdrawal—salvation—significant for the individual, he has to have a certain independence of Brahman as Brahman. But that would destroy the non-duality of Brahman. On the other hand, if he is not granted this independence, then Brahman playing at being an individual cannot engage in significant action.

> Salvation cannot be of importance if bondage is unreal and bondage cannot be real unless Maya and her world are real. . . . Brahman, always free, cannot suffer by bondage or profit by salvation, and a reflection, a figment of individuality is not a thing that can need salvation. (LD, 532)

But suppose that this individual reflection of Brahman is conscious and can suffer bondage and enjoy liberation. Whose consciousness, then, is it? There can be only one consciousness if maya is not a real power of Brahman but only an illusion. The conclusion is that in order for salvation to be meaningful, there must be more than one status of consciousness in Brahman, one free from illusion, and one subject to illusion. (LD, 533)

Finally, let us suppose that although maya is not a power of Brahman and both the individual percipient and the perceived universe are ultimately unreal, the maya super-imposition on Brahman has a certain reality which endures as long as the individual is subject to the illusion. But just who is the individual percipient who has a temporarily valid experience of the world, followed by the experience of liberation? If he is ultimately unreal, he cannot suffer from a real bondage or enjoy a real liberation. Only a real self can do these things. But that real self would have to be really subject to maya. That self would have to be either the consciousness of Brahman or the

being of Brahman projected into maya and again withdrawn.

> It is only if a being or a consciousness of the Reality under-
> goes the consequences of the Illusion that the cycles of the
> Illusion can put on any reality or have any importance. . . .
> There can be no solution of our existence in the universe if
> that existence and the universe itself have no reality. (LD,
> 533–34)

Aurobindo concludes from his analysis that the attempts
to explain the nature of maya have failed: they do not show
the inevitability of the hypothesis of illusion. And, he
contends, the burden of proof is on the Illusionists; for
the hypothesis to be accepted, it must be shown to be inevitable. (LD, 538)

Clearly, then, some degree of reality must be granted
the universe. But what reality can a universal illusion
have? Sankara saw the problem and gave it a name:
anirvacanīya, a suprarational mystery.[53]

Sankara, Aurobindo says, distinguishes two orders of
reality, transcendental and pragmatic, absolute and phenomenal, pure Brahman and Brahman in maya. This
makes the individual and the universe real. The individual
self is really Brahman who, within maya, seems to be subject to maya and is released finally into his true being.
Within maya our experience of the universe is valid; the
universe and its experiences are real. (LD, 540)

But in what sense? Aurobindo analyzes the situation
into three possibilities: 1) a true reality which would make
Sankara's theory of illusionism unnecessary; 2) a reality
overlaid with unreality which would shift the problem to
explaining the ignorance which produces the error—something Sankara does not do; 3) an unreal reality, one which

---

53. *Vivekachudamani*, 109; (Madhavananda, p. 40.)

passes away entirely when the subject attains transcendental consciousness, thus revealing that the reality apparently conceded to the world was actually an illusion all the while —the position Sankara actually adopts.

Aurobindo's first argument against this point of view is that it is difficult to see why, if the universe and the individual are real at all, they should be in any sense unreal. They may not be the whole reality, and they need not be real in precisely the way we mentally conceive them, but they need not be unreal. (LD, 541) The classical answer to this objection is that the universe must be unreal because it is temporal rather than eternal; it is only a form, like an earthen pot which is broken and whose material is returned to the earth. But, says Aurobindo, the pot was made of *real* earth and was therefore real while it lasted. Furthermore, although the form can appear and disappear, its manifestation remains an eternal possibility. The power of manifestation must be inherent in Brahman and therefore must participate in Brahman's reality, which argues against its being evanescent. (LD, 542) In general, Aurobindo contends, the denial of reality to the temporal is a purely mental conclusion based on the distinction between the concepts of time and eternity. (LD, 543) Mentally, these are contrary, but in an integral vision, Sri Aurobindo claims, they can be seen as different poises of the same reality.

Similarly, pragmatic truth need not be unreal simply because it is contrasted with transcendental truth. If it were, there could be no dynamic power in the Absolute, and hence no cosmic reality at all, even temporally. If there is a dynamic power in the Absolute, there is no reason to suppose that it is limited to producing illusions. A real power would be supposed—in the absence of evidence to the contrary—to produce realities. (LD, 543)

Both the argument for unreality based on temporality and that based on the pragmatic character of the universe are forms of the argument that only the immutable is real. But again, this is not inevitable. Why should not the Reality be simultaneously static and dynamic? After all, the energy that makes the temporal forms must itself be energy of the eternal being. (LD, 545)

It is argued in Mayavada that the activities of life and thought are finite and temporal because they involve determination, hence limitation and bondage. When the consciousness enters into transcendent reality, these constructions disappear. But, Aurobindo counters, this argument applies only to *mental* thought and action, based on separative egoism. There can be action on higher levels which is not limiting or binding but is nevertheless genuine action. (LD, 546) The deep self is found to be manifesting itself in this action, freely choosing certain limitations for this purpose, without incurring bondage. Thus Brahman engages in becoming as a movement of its own being and appears in time as a manifestation of its own eternity. (LD, 547) There need not be any conflict here.

In Sankara's system, however, there is a conflict between the intuition which feels itself united with the transcendent (Vidya) and the rational intelligence which knows the world as a collection of separate objects (Avidya). (LD, 548) The rational intelligence is bound to the phenomenal world and cannot enter into the transcendent realm. Within the Avidya structure one may speak of relative being and non-being, fact and illusion. Or from the standpoint of Vidya, one may speak of being and non-being. But when an attempt is made to consider the

Avidya realm and the Vidya realm together, this is impossible. There are no categories which can be applied to both in the same sense.

If being is understood in terms of Vidya, as it must be, the Avidya realm is non-being. But, on the other hand, since the distinction of being and non-being has meaning and validity also within Avidya's own confines, neither can Avidya be said to be unreal. Finally, Avidya cannot be said to be both real and unreal, because that would violate the law of noncontradiction. The world of Avidya is therefore "indescribable" (anirvicaniya) from a point of view which pretends to be outside both Vidya and Avidya. From a standpoint within Avidya itself, it is being. From the standpoint of Vidya, it is non-being, or better, the question simply does not arise. As long as the individual's consciousness is subject to Avidya, so long does he operate in terms of its relative reality and unreality, of the facts and illusions of experience within its domain. But when his consciousness passes into Vidya, then all consciousness of multiplicity, differentiation, relative being, and individuality itself disappears.

Aurobindo, in criticizing this position, says that it offers a practical way out—an escape—but that it is not a solution of the philosophical problem. (LD, 549, 555, 465) He ridicules the absurd position into which he considers the Mayavadin to have forced himself:

Who then profits by this escape? Not the supreme Self, for it is supposed to be always and inalienably free, still, silent, pure. Not the world, for that remains constantly in the bondage and is not freed by the escape of any individual soul from the universal Illusion. It is the individual soul itself which effects its supreme good by escaping. . . . But for the Illusionist the individual soul is an illusion and non-existent except in the inexplicable mystery of Maya. There we arrive at the escape of an illusory non-existent soul from an illusory non-existent bondage in an illusory non-existent world as the supreme good which that non-existent soul has to pursue! For this is the last word of the Knowledge, "There is none bound, none freed, none seeking to be free." Vidya turns out to be as much a part of the Phenomenal [World] as Avidya; Maya meets us even in our escape and laughs at the triumphant logic which seemed to cut the knot of her mystery. (LD, 47)

The contradiction is still there: the world was said to be real, but ultimately turns out to be unreal from the viewpoint of the Transcendent.

According to Haridas Chaudhuri, in his contribution to the symposium on the question "Has Sri Aurobindo Refuted Mayavada?",[54] this is the weakest point in the Mayavada presentation. A strictly logical refutation of Mayavada, he concedes, cannot be made, because over the centuries the Mayavadins have learned to answer every objection with another dialectical twist. The best argument against their position, he feels, is the one pointed to in the above passage of Sri Aurobindo's (though not worked out explicitly by him), namely, one which shows that while the Mayavadin aims to establish absolute monism, he is always forced to fall back on a duality in order to account for all experience. It may not be an ontological dualism— he has invented a dialectic for avoiding that—but it is a duality of *standpoints*, that of Vidya and that of Avidya.

Even if Avidya itself, being ignorance, is ultimately unreal, Chaudhuri contends, the *standpoint* of Avidya is terribly real. And this last duality the Mayavadin has left unreconciled. The consciousness is either in one condition or the other. But how such various states of consciousness can exist in one world is not explained by Mayavada.

---

54. See above, n. 48.

Chaudhuri drives the Mayavadin into his own dialectical corner when, having made all the admissions of illusion which the Mayavadin urges, he still argues that the needed account has not been given.

> Taking for granted that we have only a false perception of a false world, there is no getting away from the fact that there is the *appearance* of a true perception of a real world. Taking for granted that the world and our perception of it are equally false, the fact of a false world falsely appearing to false perception must itself be admitted to be an eternal truth. It is an eternal fact, or an eternally true proposition which has got to be explained.[55]

Such an argument shows that the way out of the dilemma is to transcend the whole level of consciousness on which the Mayavada structure stands. In terms of comparing the empirical consciousness of ordinary life with the transcendent consciousness of the state of samadhi, it is true enough and spiritually valuable. But it is not adequate for a comprehensive philosophy of all our experience grasped at once.

Here we see again the importance of the evolutionary factor. If the state of Ignorance, which causes our consciousness to be a mixture of the true and the false, were a permanent condition of the world, then it would indeed be the case that the only way out is the way of escape proposed by the Illusionists. But if the world *evolves* and ignorance is only a temporary state tending toward knowledge, then we are able to find our spiritual destiny within an unqualifiedly real world. (LD, 569)

In summary, Aurobindo says that Sankara went one step further than the Buddha, who had discovered the principle of construction of the world and the way of re-

---

55. "Has Sri Aurobindo Refuted Mayavada?", p. 119.

lease from all constructions. Sankara advanced to dealing explicitly with the suprarational Truth above the constructions—something the Buddha had refused to do.

> Shankara, standing between the world and the eternal Reality, saw that the mystery of the world must be ultimately suprarational, not conceivable or expressible by our reason, *anirvicaniya;* but he maintained the world as seen by the reason and sense as valid and had therefore to posit an unreal reality, because he did not take one step still farther. (LD, 551)

This final step Aurobindo himself supplies in the Purnadvaita, and it is the vision of the world itself from the suprarational consciousness in which it can be seen in its full reality and truth, not in its appearance. For the world cannot be a mystery to the supreme consciousness, an illusion which is not an illusion, or a reality which is unreal. "The mystery of the universe must have a divine sense to the Divine." (LD, 551)

Ultimately the argument is between two types of mystical experience—the transcendental samadhi for Sankara and the supramental realization for Aurobindo. How does one judge between them? The highest experience, says Aurobindo, is the one which is most inclusive. Aurobindo claims that Sankara in his spiritual development skipped the supramental level: he attained the full *height* of the Reality but not its full *extent* and *comprehensiveness.* The experience of the Supermind, on the other hand, allows one to see the reality of both Brahman and the world. Therefore, Aurobindo urges, it is the more inclusive and must be considered to come closer to the truth. (LD, 30)

WORLD-NEGATION IS NOT TAUGHT BY THE SCRIPTURES

Aurobindo insists that his integral position, recognizing

the reality of both the transcendent and the cosmic, is attested by the Hindu Scriptures.

World-negation, he says, is certainly not taught by the Bhagavad Gita, in which each further penetration into the secret of wisdom ends with the admonition to engage in action. Mayavada, which arose about the same time as the composition of the Gita, teaches that maya ceases for the individual when by knowledge he returns to his true and eternal state of identity with the inactive, immutable Brahman. Therefore the renunciation of action is the way to liberation. This is one way of solving the problem of life: escape into something outside the world, void of all qualities and all action.[56] It is the way Arjuna, in the Gita, at first reacts to the prospect of engaging in the terrible action that confronts him in the battle of Kurukshetra. But Krishna, the divine Teacher, will not let him abandon action. He must rather attain to an inner superiority to all claims of the senses, the mind, and the emotions, wherein he will be able to act freely, without being dominated by the forces of life.[57]

The Gita teaches that action is itself the means of liberation, and even after liberation should still be practiced.[58] Inward—not outward—renunciation is the way which leads to calm and self-possessed action in the world, the ideal of the Gita.[59]

Like the Gita, the Upanishads, Aurobindo claims, accept the Becoming of Brahman as real, and with it the validity and righteousness of delight in temporal existence and the effective use of the world's energy. (LD, 797) Of the two great world-negating religions of India, estab-

56. *Essays on the Gita,* p. 78.
57. *Ibid.,* p. 49.
58. *Ibid.,* p. 78.
59. *Ibid.,* p. 51.

lished by two of her greatest thinkers, the Buddha and Sankara, it must be said that with respect to the ancient Vedic and Vedantic tradition, the Buddha's position is heterodox[60] and that of Sankara is only one synthesis and interpretation of the Upanishads among others.

> It is the Upanishads themselves and not Shankara's writings, the text and not the commentary, that are the authoritative Scripture of the Vedantin.[61]

To show how Aurobindo and Sankara differ in their interpretation of the Upanishadic teaching and how Sankara's basic principle of granting only one poise to Brahman is not necessarily a correct interpretation of the Vedantic tradition, we will examine in detail one set of related texts.

Aurobindo frequently refers to the Upanishadic verse, "All this is Brahman," from Mandukya Upanishad 2.[62] Similar verses can be found in Svetasvatara Upanishad III.15: "The Purusha is all this that is, what has been and what is yet to be," and in the Bhagavad Gita VII.19: "All is the Divine Being." Aurobindo interprets these texts as meaning that the world is fully real.

Sankara, however, denies this interpretation in his *Commentary on the Vedanta Sutras,* which are themselves com-

---

60. In the *Essays on the Gita,* Sri Aurobindo, after lamenting the fact that the Gita's view of action had no opportunity to enter deeply into the Indian mind at the time of its composition, because of the overwhelming tide of Buddhist asceticism, appends an interesting footnote in which he says: "At the same time the Gita seems to have largely influenced Mahayanist Buddhism and texts are taken bodily from it into the Buddhist Scriptures. It may therefore have helped largely to turn Buddhism, originally a school of quietistic and illuminated ascetics, into that religion of meditative devotion and compassionate action which has so powerfully influenced Asiatic culture." P. 78.

61. Aurobindo, *The Ideal of the Karmayogin* (S.A.A., 1950), p. 12.

62. Radhakrishnan, *The Principal Upanishads* (London: Allen & Unwin, 1953), p. 695.

mentaries on the Upanishads. Sutra I.3.1, for instance, refers to Mundakya Upanishad II.2.5:

> He in whom the sky, the earth and the interspace are woven as also the mind along with all the vital breaths, know him alone as the one self [ātmānam]. Dismiss other utterances. This is the bridge to immortality.[63]

The sutra itself reads:

> The abode of heaven, earth, and so on is Brahman, on account of the term "own" [sva-śabdāt], referring to ātmānam in the Upanishad.[64]

Sankara, in his commentary on this sutra, takes notice also of verses II.2.10–11 of the same Upanishad:

> His shining illumines all this world.
> Brahman, indeed, is this universe.[65]

Sankara says that these verses might arouse "a suspicion that Brahman is a manifold variegated nature."[66] He counters this interpretation by pointing to the words of the Upanishad which read "know him alone as the one self." In order for the verse to be significant, he says, only the highest Self can be meant, and the highest Self is not manifold.

> The Self is not to be known as manifold, qualified by the universe of effect; you are rather to dissolve by true knowledge the universe of effects, which is the mere product of Nescience, and to know that one Self, which is the general abode, as uniform.[67]

---

63. Radhakrishnan, *Upanishads,* p. 684.
64. Thibaut, I:155–56.
65. Radhakrishnan, *Upanishads,* p. 685, where the verses are identified as numbers 11 and 12.
66. *Commentary,* I.3.1; (Thibaut, I:155).
67. *Ibid.*

He supports this interpretation with a reference to Katha Upanishad II.1.10: "From death to death goes he who sees any difference here."[68] His conclusion is that the statement "All is Brahman," or "Brahman, indeed, is this universe," "aims at dissolving the wrong conception of the reality of the world, and not in any way at intimating that Brahman is multiform in nature."[69]

The *Vedanta Sutras* of Badarayana are an attempt to put together the various teachings found in the Upanishads, and they represent the foundation of the Vedanta school of Hindu philosophy. As such, the work's authority as an authentic Hindu tradition is very high. Therefore, the difference between Sankara and Aurobindo over the interpretation of the points treated in this text is significant for the question of which of them represents a true Vedantic (orthodox) teaching.

Sankara's fundamental position in his interpretation is that Brahman cannot be both qualified and unqualified (as some would argue is required by faithfulness to the Upanishads), since that would be contradictory. Similarly, Brahman cannot be admitted to be really conditioned; therefore, however Brahman may be described, it is always unqualified. The appearance of qualities, the division of the Reality into Brahman with form and Brahman without form, is occasioned, as we have seen, by the different states of consciousness of the human subject: waking, dreaming, deep sleep, and the superconscious state. In deep sleep Brahman is without form; in dream and waking consciousness it is with form; in the superconscious state it is neither.

---

68. Radhakrishnan, *Upanishads,* p. 634.
69. *Commentary* I.3.1; (Thibaut, I:156).

However, the researches of **P. M. Modi**[70] on the *Vedanta Sutras* (also known as the *Brahma-Sutra*) have indicated that Sankara's interpretation is not to be accepted without further question. S. N. Dasgupta, in his Foreword to Modi's *A Critique of the Brahma-Sutra*,[71] says that while Modi has been "sympathetic and fair to Sankara" and has not "read his own philosophical creed into the Brahma-Sutra," he has "proved to our satisfaction that at least in many places Sankara's interpretation is either doubtful or unacceptable. Sankara seems to have been often interested in reading his own philosophy in the Sutras and loyalty to the Sutras does not seem to be his strong point."[72]

Modi's view is that the author of the Sutras denies precisely this contention of Sankara's that Brahman's being with form or without form depends on the state of consciousness of the subject. He holds rather than Brahman is both with form and without form in all the states.[73] Modi submits that the two aspects of Brahman, personal and with form, on the one hand, and impersonal and without form, on the other, are recognized by Badarayana as objective and of an equal status.[74] They are aspects of Kārana Brahman, Brahman as making, doing, performing, or producing.[75]

It is Modi's opinion that Badarayana probably obtained his doctrine of the twofold Brahman from earlier Vedantic

---

70. Professor of Sanskrit, Samaldas College, Bhavnagar; Ph.D. from Kiel, where he learned to apply a full-scale critical apparatus to these ancient texts.
71. Published in Bhavnagar: P. M. Modi, 1943.
72. P. 7. S. N. Dasgupta is the author of the standard *History of Indian Philosophy* in 5 vols. (Cambridge: Cambridge University Press, 1922–1955).
73. Modi, p. 4.
74. *Ibid.*, p. 5.
75. *Ibid.*

writers who had applied to Brahman Yaska's[76] interpretation of Vedic deities as both personal and impersonal.[77] This would make the acceptance of Brahman as having two poises, without form and with form, or transcendent and cosmic, appear to be an authentic strain in Indian philosophy which was offset only by the work of Sankara.

A supporting argument can be found in the discussion of causality where, according to Modi, the author of the Sutras takes the position that the effect of Brahman's action is identical with Brahman and that all changes come from Brahman's own action.[78] This, taken together with the conception of Karana Brahman, would seem to affirm full reality for the world.[79]

From the interpretation of these key texts from the Upanishads themselves and their most revered commentary, we see that Sankara's world-negating position is not to be uncritically assumed as the orthodox view of the Indian philosophical tradition. Aurobindo has considerable support from textual critics in his contention that world-negation is not taught by the Scriptures and that the twofold Brahman is.

If the true interpretation of the Upanishads is questionable, that of the Vedic hymns is almost unknown. Two interpretations have been popular among scholars: the

---

76. An early interpreter of the Vedic hymns. On the twofold Brahman, cf. Prasna Upanishad V.2.

77. Modi, p. 7.

78. *Ibid.*, pp. 5–6.

79. Cf. a somewhat similar dispute which Aurobindo has with Sankara over a passage in the Gita. Sankara reads "Brahman is the jiva itself" (his theory of superimposition), whereas Aurobindo holds that the phrase means "Brahman has become the jiva"—a real creation. The grammarian, Kapali Sastry, through a detailed analysis of the construction of the passage and other uses of the words concerned, shows that Aurobindo's rendering is correct. Cf. T. V. Kapali Sastry, *Sri Aurobindo: Lights on the Teachings* (Madras: Sri Aurobindo Library, 1948), pp. 155ff.

ritualistic, following Sayana, and the naturalistic, the construction of European philologists. It is one of Aurobindo's most important contributions that he offers a new interpretation of the Veda which gives a more profound meaning to the ancient literature.

According to Aurobindo, the Vedic sages were not possessed of the impatience of later spiritual aspirants (such as the Mayavadins) who, eager to rest their minds in the One in a way that they could logically understand, forsook the paradox of the created Many and thus missed union with the "great Unknowable." (LD, 42) Not that this impatience was an unnatural reaction in an age which isolated the religious quest from the rest of natural activity. Once the spiritual ideal of life had been separated from the other motives of man's life (his vital needs, his desires, and his ethical aspirations), life itself was deprived of genuine significance.

But in Vedic times it was not so. A balanced view prevailed which recognized four aims of life: Atharva (material goods), Kama (pleasure), Dharma (righteous conduct), and Moksha (liberation). Periods within a lifetime were provided in which to cultivate each of them. A man would be successively a student, a householder, a recluse, and a renunciate.

The world-view of the Veda is one which recognizes the joys of life.[80] It concerns itself not only with spiritual and moral values but with material well-being, speaking of an optimum life-span of a hundred years of unimpaired efficiency of the senses and limbs, adequate prosperity, knowledge, progress, and happiness.[81]

80. B. G. Gokhale, *Indian Thought through the Ages: A Study of Some Dominant Concepts* (London: Asia Publishing House, 1961), p. 87.

81. A. C. Bose, *Hymns from the Vedas* (New York: Asia Publishing House, 1966), pp. 10–11.

Throughout the Samhitas there is a sense of elation at the beauty and glory of the material world and of buoyant optimism. It may be said that while the Upanishads seek Satya, Truth, in the absolute sense (Vedanta), the Samhitas lay greater emphasis on Rita (that includes Satya on the ethical plane) in its aesthetic, ethical, social and ritualistic senses, as Eternal Order. Thus the Samhitas want both [the spiritual leader] and [the secular ruler] to work energetically and in mutual concord.[82]

The reality of the world was never questioned in Vedic times.[83] The world was not only real but full of promise, wealth, and opportunity.[84] There was "no basis for any conception of the unreality of the world" in the Vedic mentality; the world was not "a purposeless phantom, but . . . the evolution of God."[85] Maya, for the Vedic seers, meant a selective faculty of knowledge which differentiated finite phenomena within the infinitude of the Reality. "It is by maya that the Infinite finitizes, the static being becomes dynamic becoming, and out of the Absolute the world of phenomena emerges."[86]

This sense of the One diversified in the Many is a recurrent theme in the Veda.

One in many births, a single ocean holder of all streams of movement, sees our hearts.[87]

Such am I [the One] and the Gods have found me established in the Many, permeating and taking possession of the Manifold.[88]

82. *Ibid.*, p. 50.
83. M. Hiriyanna, *Outlines of Indian Philosophy* (London: Allen & Unwin, 1964), p. 44.
84. Gokhale, p. 123.
85. S. Radhakrishnan, *Indian Philosophy* (London: Allen & Unwin, 1923), I, 103.
86. S. Chatterjee, "Mind and Supermind in Sri Aurobindo's Integralism," in H. Chaudhuri and Fr. Spiegelberg, eds., *The Integral Philosophy of Sri Aurobindo* (London: Allen & Unwin, 1960), p. 40.
87. Rig Veda, X.5.1.
88. *Ibid.*, X.125.3.

This world exists in Him; He is merciful. This God is One only. All Gods or worlds become one in being in Him.[89]

He is the One and One alone, and in him all Devas become the One alone.[90]

Aurobindo's own researches in the Vedic texts uncovered for him a psychological and mystical interpretation of the verses which not only cast light on the significance of the hymns but illumined his own spiritual experience. He claimed to have found the lost secret of the Veda. The "secret" says that the Divine is already present, planted deep in every being, the same Divine in all. As infinity incarnate in the finite, it expands; this is the spiritual-material evolution of which our world is the (thus-far) product.

The sense of a living synthesis of the spiritual and the material is strong in all the Vedic Samhitas. The hymns pray for intellectual and spiritual power, for moral purity and strength, but also for physical health and material prosperity. The rishis speak freely of Heaven as Father and Earth as Mother and pray unabashedly,

O Godhead, guard for us the Infinite and lavish the finite.[91]

Considering passages such as this, typical of the general tenor of the ancient Vedic hymns, Aurobindo feels justified in charging that Mayavada is not faithful to the Vedic view of life and in claiming that his own integral non-dualism is an orthodox position.

89. *Ibid.*, X.121.21.
90. Atharva Veda, XIII.4.
91. Rig Veda, IV.2.11.

6

The Destruction of Values in Mayavada

WE CAN SEE FROM THE DISCUSSION THUS FAR HOW INTER-
woven are the questions of the reality of the world and
the value of the world. As was remarked earlier, for Indian
philosophy existence and value are always one. We might
almost say in Aurobindo's case that what is at stake in
this issue is not so much the ontological state of the
world as the value of the world, not a doctrine about the
world but an attitude toward the world.

Aurobindo's argument against all of the theories of
world-negation comes down to this: unless bondage is
real, salvation cannot be real. And real bondage means a
real maya and a real world. (LD, 532) In this chapter we
will follow his arguments as he shows why one is tempted
to call the world unreal, what genuine experiences seem
to support this conclusion, and what spiritual advantages
are attached to these experiences. He then goes on to show
why, if one stops with this experience and this philosophical position, a dangerous situation results. One may be
tempted to deny the reality of the world in order to solve

the problem of the evil of the world; but, on the other hand, if one holds the unreality of the world, he will not be prepared to work for the resolution of its evils, and this leads to practical disaster.

India's misery has been owing in large measure to this "revolt of Spirit against Matter," in Aurobindo's view, and while he grants that the sense of the cosmic illusion is not the whole of Indian thought, he still holds that "all have lived in the shadow of the great Refusal, and the final end of life for all is the garb of the ascetic." (LD, 28)

Sri Aurobindo hated every type of evasion of life, which he considered to be escapism and cowardice. Life was meant to be vigorous and adventurous and to achieve its goals, not to be abandoned as a bad job.[1] His own life was full of struggle and he accepted it as his sadhana.[2]

The fact that the forms and values of our present life do not endure forever was no argument in his mind for not accepting them as real and valuable in their own temporal context. Kapali Sastry calls this "a salient feature of this Teaching":

> It recognizes the reality of Manifestation. . . . It is opposed to all those lines of thought that lead to the negation of values or sermonize upon what they conceive to be the chimerical character of values for the supposed reason that they do not endure for ever or in another state of consciousness or elsewhere in another world-existence or non-cosmic existence which is the Absolute. It avoids the untenable position of looking at values obtaining under given conditions as nonexistent or fanciful because they are not the same under different conditions or for all time and everywhere.[3]

1. R. R. Diwaker, *Mahayogi Sri Aurobindo* (Bombay: Bharatiya Vidya Bhavan, 1962), p. 147.
2. Cf. a letter to Dilip, quoted by Diwakar, p. 175.
3. T. V. Kapali Sastry, *Sri Aurobindo: Lights on the Teachings* (Madras: Sri Aurobindo Library, 1948), pp. 106–7.

In an evolving world, one does not expect any particular form of being or any particular value to endure forever. These temporal manifestations of the divine are themselves part of the larger being and greater value of the growing and changing image of the Supreme. But without the knowledge of evolution, one might very well interpret and evaluate his experience in the world differently.

TEMPTATIONS TO DENY THE WORLD

Aurobindo was not unaware of the tremendous spiritual forces tempting man to the denial of the world. Beginning from the first human recognition of the three areas of man's concern, himself, the world, and God, there has been a struggle to attain unity of understanding, some kind of comprehension of how these three fit together. The pull toward unity has in fact been so strong that many times men have espoused systems of thought which achieved this unity by affirming one of the three fundamental areas at the cost of suppressing the others.[4]

Following on the search for unity, there often comes the "intuition of a beyond" (LD, 804), a sense that there is something more than terrestrial experience. Then, enflamed by spiritual ardor, intellectual intolerance, and the discouragement of the vital being over the difficulties and evils of life, "this perception of the supracosmic is easily associated . . . with a sense of the entire vanity and unreality of all else than that remote Supreme." (LD, 805) The physical mind discovers that the senses play it many

---

4. LD, 820. This can be done in various ways: God alone is real, man and the world are illusion; man alone is real, the world is dependent on his perception, God on his imagination; the world is the basic reality, man is a subclass within it and God a subclass of man's activity, his value-system.

tricks, the vital mind finds its appetite for novelty and enjoyment always exceeding its satisfactions, the thinking mind builds and unbuilds one system of certitudes after another until it realizes that all are equally its own constructions, and the soul finally exclaims in its frustration that everything here is relative and useless. Only the Absolute and the Eternal is real. The world is "a vast delirium, an immense cosmic Illusion. . . . The principle of negation prevails over the principle of affirmation. . . . Thence arise the great world-negating religions and philosophies." (LD, 493; cf. LD, 1023)

Aurobindo speaks of this attitude as "impatience of heart and mind, vehement attraction to an ultimate bliss which sought the One to deny the Many and because it had received the breath of the heights scorned and recoiled from the secret of the depths." (LD, 43; cf. LD, 277) This, Aurobindo undertakes to show, was not the attitude of the Vedic rishis, and it is to their "steady eye of . . . wisdom," he advises, that we should return.

But the greatest source of temptation to deny the world has been the obstacle encountered in the human body itself. It seems not only to stand between man and his spiritual aspiration but positively to taunt him with his bondage to the earth.

> Therefore the eager seeker of spiritual fulfilment has hurled his ban against the body and his world-disgust selects the world-principle above all other things as an especial object of loathing. The body is the obscure burden that he cannot bear; its obstinate material grossness is the obsession that drives him for deliverance to the life of the ascetic. To get rid of it he has even gone so far as to deny its existence and the reality of the material universe. Most of the religions have put their curse upon Matter and have made the refusal or the resigned temporary endurance of the physical life the test of religious truth and of spirituality. (LD, 277)

However, "the older creeds . . . the ancient mysteries . . . more patient, more . . . profound," did not react with such violence. Aurobindo urges a renewal of their type of integral reverence for "Earth the Mother and Heaven the Father." (LD, 277)

> The touch of Earth is always reinvigorating to the son of Earth, even when he seeks a supraphysical Knowledge. It may even be said that the supraphysical can only be really mastered in its fullness—to its heights we can always reach—when we keep our feet firmly on the physical. "Earth is His footing," says the Upanishad[5] whenever it images the Self that manifests in the universe. And it is certainly the fact that the wider we extend and the surer we make our knowledge of the physical world, the wider and surer becomes our foundation for the higher knowledge, even for the highest, even for the Brahmavidya. (LD, 13–14)

Admittedly, a spirituality of a real world is more difficult. One's developing spiritual consciousness would have, if the world is ultimately real, to receive and assimilate into itself the influences coming from this world and endeavor to perfect them. But this involves working with material which is unconscious, or very weakly conscious, and not entirely under our control.

> It is . . . always easier to spiritualise the inner self-sufficient parts than to transform the outer action; a perfection of introspective, indwelling or subjective spirituality aloof from the world or self-protected against it is easier than a perfection of the whole nature in a dynamic, kinetic spirituality objectivised in the life, embracing the world, master of its environment, sovereign in its commerce with world-nature. (LD, 1142–43)

Sri Aurobindo experienced in his own sadhana the necessity for purification and strengthening of the lower powers of his being. This work, he said, has to be done

---

5. Mundaka Upanishad II.1.4.

over and over again with inexhaustible patience, because
it forms the foundation for the integral realization of God.
Even these "least brethren" of the Highest—the vital and
material levels of being—have to be served as the Lord
Himself in order that they may attain their proper perfection, which is "to hold consistently and vividly the settled
perception of the One in all things and beings, in all qualities, forces, happenings, in all this world-consciousness and
the play of its workings."[6]

But the laying of this foundation of Unity meets a
vicious rebellion on the part of the lower powers, because
their activities have up to now been founded not on unity
but on division, on the contrast-consciousness which enabled them to build up their initial strength. Their surrender now and assumption into a higher unity comes only
with difficulty, and it is the temptation of many spiritual
paths to abandon these aspects of the life-energy which
give them trouble and to attempt to attain the higher
realms of being without integrating the lower into them.

> It is this to which our nature is most recalcitrant. It persists
> in the division, in the dualities, in the sorrow and unsatisfied
> passion and labour, it finds it difficult to accustom itself to
> the divine largeness, joy and equipoise—especially the vital
> and material parts of our nature; it is they that pull down
> the mind which has accepted and even when it has long lived
> in the joy and peace and oneness. That, I suppose, is why
> the religions and philosophies have had so strong a leaning
> to the condemnation of Life and Matter and aimed at an
> escape instead of a victory. But the victory has to be won; the
> rebellious elements have to be redeemed and transformed,
> not rejected or excised.[7]

6. Letter of Aurobindo to the Mother, June 26, 1916, quoted in A. B.
Purani, *The Life of Sri Aurobindo* (S.A.A., 2nd ed., 1960), p. 190.
7. *Ibid.*

THE VALIDITY AND VALUE OF THE NIRVANA EXPERIENCE

In the face of these strong temptations to bypass the problem of the world, and in view of the very real difficulties encountered in the spiritual life when one attempts to rise above the material, vital, and mental levels of existence to the transcendental states of consciousness, it is not surprising that the aspiration to the Nirvana experience should have become the strongest driving force in the various religious traditions at some point in their history.

When the spiritual aspirant draws back from the mind and its experiences coming from the material, the vital, and its own actions, he discovers his identity with a timeless and immobile self, unattached to any of these experiences, actionless, without ideas, thoughts, memories, imagination, or will. He experiences it as self-absorbed and self-sufficient. (LD, 603–604) If the aspirant should fall into this state suddenly, the contrast between it and the world he had long taken for granted as the only real world is so striking and so complete, that he is moved to believe—and indeed to believe that he *perceives*—that the multiple world is utterly unreal and that this deeper silent Self alone is real. (LD, 538)

When the inner, hitherto secret, Self thus breaks through into consciousness, it has the effect of rendering the subject "cosmically conscious," as it is often said. That is, he experiences himself as a single self inhabiting the entire universe, and he may even lose all sense of individuality, so convincing is his sense of being merged with the world-being. Or he may experience this union as an

openness to the universal energy with absence of any sense
of individual action. (LD, 644)

The reason for this experience, Sri Aurobindo explains,
is that ordinarily there is a thick veil between our inner
self and our ignorant surface self, and again another veil
between this surface self and the objects of our experience.
Mental knowing, under these conditions, necessarily takes
the form of a subject receiving—or meeting—an object on
the "outside." However, when these veils are pierced by the
subliminal inner being's coming into self-consciousness,
the object no longer appears to be "outside" the subject,
and the individual subject himself—always up to now defined by his relation of opposition to the object—seems to
disappear. (LD, 643)

It must be remembered that Aurobindo himself had
experienced this state[8] and knew with what force it over-
whelms the consciousness of the one to whom it comes.

> It comes upon us with a great force of awakening to reality
> when the thought is stilled, when the mind withdraws from
> its constructions, when we pass into a pure selfhood void of
> all sense of individuality, empty of all cosmic contents: if the
> spiritualised mind then looks at individual and cosmos, they
> may well seem to it to be an illusion, a scheme of names and
> figures and movements falsely imposed on the sole reality of
> the Self-Existent. Or even the sense of self becomes in-
> adequate; both knowledge and ignorance disappear into sheer
> Consciousness and consciousness is plunged into a trance of
> pure super-conscient existence. Or even existence ends by
> becoming too limiting a name for that which abides solely
> for ever; there is only a timeless Eternal, a spaceless Infinite,
> the utterness of the Absolute, a nameless peace, an over-
> whelming single objectless Ecstasy. (LD, 557)

And he adds, unequivocally:

There can certainly be no doubt of the validity—complete

_____
8. See above, chapter 1.

within itself—of this experience; there can be no denial of
the overwhelming decisive convincingness . . . with which this
realisation seizes the consciousness of the spiritual seeker.
(LD, 557)

There are many ways of approaching the Supreme Reality. According to the way taken, so will be the nature of
the culminating experience of the seeker. For this reason
we must not hold any one of these ways to be the only way,
or its crowning experience the sole judge of all reality.
(LD, 558) But is this Nirvana (blowing out) of world-
consciousness and individual-consciousness only one among
the other ways, or is it itself the Ultimate of all ways, the
final end to which all paths eventually come? Sri Aurobindo's answer to this will be that beyond the Nirvana
experience is a still higher and more inclusive spiritual
realization which grants a place of validity to both the
Nirvana experience and to the world-consciousness of
which it is the negation. We will consider this claim of
his later; at present we wish to recognize his admission of
the valid place of the Nirvana experience in the spiritual
life.

The Nirvana experience is in fact necessary on the way
to the spiritual goal, in Aurobindo's view, for by it we
realize our freedom from the determinations of Nature.
(LD, 377) Only in this way can the fundamental Self
recover its position as pure consciousness.[9]

Becoming can only know itself wholly when it knows itself
as Being; the soul in the Becoming arrives at self-knowledge
and immortality when it knows the Supreme and Absolute
and possesses the nature of the Infinite and Eternal. To do
that is the supreme aim of our existence. . . . Therefore . . .
Illusionism itself, even if we contest its ultimate conclusions,

9. Cf. Ruth Reyna, *The Concept of Maya from the Vedas to the 20th
Century* (Bombay: Asia Publishing House, 1962), p. 27.

can still be accepted as the way in which the soul in mind, the mental being, has to see things in a spiritual-pragmatic experience when it cuts itself off from the Becoming in order to approach and enter into the Absolute. (LD, 786)

If we were to rest in phenomenal nature and see the world only as phenomenal experience presents it to us, we would never know the truth, even of our becoming, for the truth back of the becoming is the divine force of being, the transcendent and universal Spirit.[10]

In our ordinary consciousness, says Sri Aurobindo, the consciousness with which we set out on the spiritual path, we conceive of ourselves falsely and all the principles of our personal and communal life are rooted in this falsity. The falsehood is one of mistaken identification: we identify with our separate-seeming bodies and personalities. We say "I am this body, I am this life, I am this mind."[11] If the soul sees no further, it will conclude "I am a mind in a living body." If it sees a little further and becomes aware of the persistence of mental personality, it may think of itself as a mental soul occupying a body, once or repeatedly, and passing from earthly life to a mental world beyond where it mentally enjoys or suffers. Or it may penetrate yet deeper and foresee the possibility of a dissolution of the mental being into some wider realm of being which it will call, by contrast with the mental, a Void or an Infinite, and it will say of its own relation to this state, "There 'I' will cease to be."[12]

To believe in the false identification is to believe in an illusion, for the view of the universe and the individual which the mind and senses give us, as long as they are

10. *Essays on the Gita* (New York: The Sri Aurobindo Library, 1950), pp. 237–38.
11. Aurobindo, *Synthesis of Yoga* (S.A.A., 1957), pp. 383–85.
12. *Ibid.*, p. 385.

unenlightened by a higher faculty, is an imperfect construction, an incomplete and distorted figure of the truth.[13] To this extent and in this sense Aurobindo would admit that the world (as we in ignorance perceive it) is an illusion.

The truth, Aurobindo teaches, is that our reality is that of a Self which is a "pure existence of which all these things are becomings."[14] At some point the spiritual seeker must discover that the finite is "nothing but a definition, a face-value of the Infinite's self-representations to its own variations of consciousness; the real value of each finite phenomenon is an infinite in its self-existence, whatever it may be in the action of its phenomenal nature, its temporal self-representation."[15]

Man is not a rigidly separate self-existent individual but humanity in a mind and body of itself, and humanity in turn is not a rigidly separate self-existent species but the universal Godhead expressing itself in the form of humanity.[16]

This is the truth which we have to realize, to make operative in our inner and outer life. And here enters the value of asceticism, leading to the Nirvana experience. It begins with the negative way, saying "I am not the body," "I am not the life," "I am not the mind," and ends with the affirmation "I am That, the pure, the eternal, the self-blissful."[17] If the soul loses sight of its ultimate goal— which is to move consciously in its becomings, knowing itself to be rooted in pure being—the goal to which this ascetical technique was a first step, and becomes fixed in

---

13. *Ibid.*
14. *Ibid.*, p. 386.
15. *Essays on the Gita,* pp. 136–37.
16. *Ibid.*, p. 137.
17. *Synthesis of Yoga,* pp. 386–87.

the consciousness of the transcendent alone, then it is only
caught in another, though more refined, falsehood.

A second spiritual discipline is required to build the
realization of the Absolute's immanence on the foundation
of the realization of the Absolute's transcendence.[18] We
begin with the desire to release ourselves from bondage
to Nature, a desire which has two branches: on the one
hand, a drive to establish the supremacy of spiritual consciousness, even if Nature must be totally rejected, and on
the other hand, an urge to extend the realization of
spirituality throughout all the levels and parts of Nature.
(LD, 1024) Of these two desires, the former must be fulfilled first. Until the realization of transcendence and absolute freedom is firmly fixed in consciousness, the realization of the immanence of the pure Spirit in the variety
of the multiple world cannot have any deep significance.

> It is the foundation of the pure spiritual consciousness that
> is the first object in the evolution of the spiritual man, and
> it is this and the urge of that consciousness towards contact
> with the Reality, the Self or the Divine Being that must be
> the first and foremost or even, till it is perfectly accomplished,
> the sole preoccupation of the spiritual seeker. It is the one
> thing needful that has to be done by each on whatever line is
> possible to him, by each according to the spiritual capacity
> developed in his nature. (LD, 1024)

The establishment and protection of this inner life is
the first and necessary obligation of the man who seeks
reality. To the extent that he finds the world of Ignorance
intractable, he must ruthlessly separate himself from it.
Only from the security and truth-vision of this inner life
can he act effectively on the world, in any case.

This is the transcendence aspect of the spiritual life and it
_____
18. *Ibid.,* p. 388.

is necessary for the freedom of the spirit; for otherwise the identity in Nature with the world would be a binding limitation and not a free identity. (LD, 1164)

Union with the transcendent Absolute, however, implies union with the Absolute's own dynamic nature and action, i.e., with "a necessity of manifestation." (LD, 786) The ascetic rejection of the finite will no longer need to characterize the life of the Gnostic Being, the one who has attained to supramental knowledge.

> The one rule of the gnostic life would be the self-expression of the Spirit, the will of the Divine Being; that will, that self-expression could manifest through extreme simplicity or through extreme complexity and opulence or in their natural balance. (LD, 1268)

Sri Aurobindo could well say with Gandhi that his rule of life was the Gita's dictum, "Renounce and enjoy."[19] Renunciation is the necessary first stage of the spiritual life. If it is perfectly practiced, it then frees one for the second stage, enjoyment in union with the Divine Will.

THE DANGERS OF ESCAPISM

Valid though the experience of Nirvana is, and necessary though the negation of the world is as a first moment in the passage from Ignorance to Knowledge, there remains the great danger of stopping half-way, of resting in this negative moment, of satisfying one's impatience by tying the knot too soon. Sri Aurobindo recognizes that it is the pressing problem of evil that drives many spiritual aspirants to this extreme. They have realized the ever-pure, the perfect, the blissful, the infinite. How account then

---

19. Cf. *Thoughts and Glimpses* (S.A.A., 1964), p. 16; Satprem, p. 242.

for the seeming tolerance on the part of the Perfect One of this world of impurity, falsehood, evil, and suffering? If we have no answer—and an acceptable answer must make sense not only in the mind but also in action—then we have no recourse but to withdraw to the pure inner Presence and deny the external world altogether. As Sri Aurobindo says, it is an escape rather than a solution. (LD, 465)

If man opts for this escape, believing all things to be fixed in their present mode of being, himself also fixed in his human weakness, sin, and suffering, then he forfeits forever his chance to cooperate in the divine action. God, moving in the evolving world, is liberating from the concealing veils of ignorance and falsehood images of His own knowledge and truth; out of evil and ugliness He is developing goodness and beauty; out of weakness, He makes power, out of suffering, delight. But for the escapist the whole world of manifestation is hopeless. Abandoning human ignorance, he abandons likewise human knowledge; he leaves human goodness along with human evil, human joy with human sorrow. They cannot be transformed, he decides; hence they must be destroyed. Every decision bears its fruit; the escapist's harvest is a certain kind of heaven, but it is not human.

> Whether the result will be an individual enjoyment of the absolute divine nature or of the Divine Presence or a Nirvana in the featureless Absolute, is a point on which religions and philosophies differ: but in either case human existence on earth must be taken as condemned to eternal imperfection by the very law of its being. (LD, 484)

It is a possible stance, and at first sight appears to be very pure and holy. But Sri Aurobindo finds it to be destructive of values on all levels: of intellectual values because its doctrine is not the highest truth and does not allow for fruitful development of the intellect on other levels of inquiry; of religious values because it is not devotion to God in His dynamic aspect of self-manifestation; of personal values because the individual person loses all significance from its point of view and cannot fulfill himself under its ascesis; of social values because the society which follows this way will make no effort to reform its evils.

The intellectual life that withdraws from the world to pursue its own aesthetic, ethical, or theoretical speculations may often result in benefits for the world. But its seclusion is justified only by these benefits. The elevation of the lone thinker himself may be some achievement, but it is a poor and limited fulfillment compared with the uplifting of the entire race.

> The progressive mind is seen at its noblest when it strives to elevate the whole race to its own level whether by sowing broadcast the image of its own thought and fulfilment or by changing the material life of the race into fresh forms, religious, intellectual, social or political, intended to represent more nearly that ideal of truth, beauty, justice, righteousness with which the man's own soul is illumined.[20]

By contrast, world-negation by means of intellectual discipline destroys even itself in the end, for in straining toward the infinite and eternal, it is obliged to deny its own mode of being.

> It . . . cuts away from us all that we seem to be in order to get from it to the nameless and impersonal reality of our being. The desires of the heart, the works of the will and the conceptions of the mind are rejected; even in the end knowledge itself is negated and abolished in the Identical and Unknowable.[21]

20. *Synthesis of Yoga,* p. 26.
21. *Essays on the Gita,* p. 300.

Just as this knowledge is imperfect as knowledge, so is it imperfect as a union with God.

> No God-knowledge can be integral, perfect, or universally satisfying which leaves unfulfilled [the] absolute claim [of the will, the heart, and the comprehensive mind], no wisdom utterly wise which in its intolerant asceticism of search negates or in the pride of pure knowledge belittles the spiritual reality behind these ways of the Godhead.[22]

Aurobindo will not admit the common idea that when a man becomes interested in the spiritual life and takes up the path of yoga he is expected to be lost to the rest of the community with its pressing concerns. In his view, God gave man life on earth precisely in order that the higher might be expressed in the lower and the lower transfigured in the higher. To refuse this vocation is neither to serve God nor to fulfill one's own manhood.[23] To reject the world altogether is to miss "the Divine Being's larger joy in cosmic existence . . . the total sense of creation and the entire will of the Creator." (LD, 806)

> If in passing from one domain to another we renounce what has already been given us from eagerness for our new attainment, if in reaching the mental life we cast away or belittle the physical life which is our basis, or if we reject the mental and physical in our attraction to the spiritual, we do not fulfil God integrally nor satisfy the conditions of His self-manifestation. We do not become perfect, but only shift the field of our imperfection. (LD, 45)

The Divine Being is essential unity, it is true, but to admit this does not compel us to call God's workings worthless or unreal, nor to say that the best use we can make of them is to renounce them. (LD, 454–55) Brahman

---

22. *Ibid.*, p. 301.
23. *Synthesis of Yoga*, pp. 6–7.

has not cast all of this energy out of Himself only to be lost in some unreal external Void. (LD, 683)

Commenting on Aurobindo's teaching in this respect, K. D. Sethna says that to spurn the earth is almost as evil as to remain enmeshed in it. It is only the opposite pole of the same error, the same want of balance and the same distorted perspective. Only those who are still attached to worldly goods through ignorance feel the need to cut themselves off from these with such violence. To refuse God's manifestation is, says Sethna, to despise Him for having "taken the form of common clay." The ascetic is assuredly in a better state than the profligate, but for all that, he still bypasses the riddle of the universe.[24]

The spiritual man who has the proper detachment from the world and does not feel obliged to do violence to it or to himself, is able to see that this whole world is in fact God's own living action, and that devotion to God means cooperation in creating the world.[25]

Cooperation with God in creating the world is indeed the vocation of man in Aurobindo's eyes. And it is the individual man who fulfills this vocation. If we lose the individual man, we lose our link with the earth and we fail to achieve our goal of transformation.[26]

The worth of the individual person is the value Aurobindo is most concerned to protect. Whenever he critcizes other views, it is usually because they do not allow sufficient significance to the person, the individual man.[27] It is on this ground that he most passionately battles both the materialist and the illusionist-escapist. The question of the

24. *The Indian Spirit and the World's Future* (S.A.A., 1953), p. 226.
25. *Essays on the Gita*, p. 97.
26. Satprem, *Sri Aurobindo, or The Adventure of Consciousness* (New York: India Library Society, 1964), p. 170.
27. See, e.g., his arguments, against other oriental views, in favor of rebirth of the individual as a persistent reality. (LD, 899ff.)

reality of the material and spiritual worlds is a very concrete question, and it is the effect that its answer has on
the individual person that moves Sri Aurobindo most
strongly.

> The difference, so metaphysical in appearance, is yet of the
> utmost practical import, for it determines the whole outlook
> of man upon life, the goal that he shall assign for his efforts
> and the field in which he shall circumscribe his energies. For
> it raises the question of the reality of cosmic existence and,
> more important still, the question of the value of human
> life. (LD, 24)

Stressing the unreality of the world brings us only conclusions of despair—"the fictitious character of the individual ego, the . . . purposelessness of human existence, the
return into the Non-Being or the relationless Absolute as
the sole rational escape from the meaningless tangle of
phenomenal life." (LD, 25) Aurobindo is not deceived by
the apparent concessions made in the Mayavada system
with a view to validating life and personality during the
time of the sadhana. What it comes down to in the end is
that "whatever rule can help us soonest to get back to self-
knowledge and lead by the most direct road to Nirvana"
is the true law of life. (LD, 796) The fact that the Vedan-
tins call their ideal "self-finding" does not clear it of the
charge of vanity, because it could only be a genuine self-
finding of the individual in the Absolute if both he and
the Absolute were interrelated realities. The final self-
affirmation of the Absolute by the destruction of all individual and cosmic existence is inevitably an ideal which
regards our life as a radical vanity. (LD, 797)

> An uncompromising theory of Illusion solves no problem of
> our existence; it only cuts the problem out for the individual
> by showing him a way of exit: in its extreme form and effect,

our being and its action become null and without sanction, its experience, aspiration, endeavour lose their significance; all, the one incommunicable relationless Truth excepted and the turning to it, become equated with illusion of being, are part of a universal Illusion and themselves illusions. God and ourselves and the universe become myths of Maya. (LD, 555)

The Mayavadin's answer to these reproaches may be that the demand for personal significance and persistence is an error of our consciousness in its present state of ignorance. Or a less rigid Vedantin might urge that for the individual to be a temporary becoming of the eternal Brahman should be a quite sufficient significance. Nevertheless, Aurobindo observes, the whole interest of these philosophies centers precisely on this insignificant or only temporarily significant individual person. It is *his* release from ignorance into salvation that is at stake. The theoretical value accorded the person is far too weak in these philosophies to sustain the weight of motivation which it is asked to bear.

The value put on individual perfection and salvation is too great to be dismissed as a device for a minor operation, the coiling and uncoiling of an insignificant spiral amid the vast circlings of the Eternal's becoming in the universe. (LD, 798)

Sri Aurobindo's own ideal for man includes a "real and always existent Person who maintains and experiences the stream or mass of phenomena" (LD, 890), "a personal individuality not dependent on the material body" (LD, 892) but at home in a wider range of being. It is the individual man, in his view, who is the living laboratory in which the evolving Spirit is seeking to work out the Superman.[28]

28. Cf. Haridas Chaudhuri, *Sri Aurobindo: The Prophet of Life Divine* (2nd ed.; S.A.A., 1960), p. 21.

I have said that the Supreme Being that we want to realize is not an impersonal Infinite but a Divine Personality; and in order to realize Him we have to grow conscious of our own true personality. You must know your own inner being. This Personality is not the inner mental, the inner vital and the inner physical being and its consciousness, as is many times wrongly described, but it is your true Being which is in direct communication with the Highest. Man grows by gradual growth in nature and each has to realize his own Divine Person which is in the Supermind.[29]

It is this pressure from Nature herself, experienced in the individual, which develops the aspiration toward the higher life. (LD, 55) And the individual in turn uses the universal Nature to realize himself. Yet, as he universalizes himself, he still preserves "a mysterious transcendent something of which his sense of personality gives him an obscure and egoistic representation." (LD, 55)

We must recognize that our primary aim in knowledge must be to realise our own supreme Self . . . for that is the pressing need of the individual, to arrive at the highest truth of his own being, to . . . mount to its source. But we do this not in order to disappear into its source, but so that our whole existence and all the members of this inner kingdom may find their right basis, may live in our highest self. . . . And if we do this rightly we shall discover that in finding this supreme Self we have found the one Self in all.[30]

THE DECLINE OF INDIA UNDER THE ASCETICAL IDEAL

We have followed Aurobindo's attack on Illusionism and its concomitant escapism for being destructive of the values of the intellect, of religion, and of the human person. It remains to show how it is destructive of social values.

29. Speech of Sri Aurobindo on August 15, 1924, quoted in Purani, p. 228.
30. *Synthesis of Yoga*, p. 390.

The ascetic life inculcated by the philosophy of world-negation seeks to save individuals by withdrawing them from the social body with its obligations and temptations, its pleasures and pains. The more this aim of saving humanity succeeds, the more individuals are withdrawn from society and the more humanity suffers from want of highly developed individuals to serve and elevate it. The immense resistance of material Nature is not overcome in this way.[31] And yet this is the problem. It is the escapists' own problem, the reason for their desire to escape. Denying the problem does not solve it.

> The discord and apparent evil of the world must in their sphere be admitted, but not accepted as our conquerors. The deepest instinct of humanity seeks always and seeks wisely . . . an ultimate victory and fulfilment, not the disappointed recoil of the soul from its great adventure. (LD, 38–39)

The refusal of the ascetic can lead only to the bankruptcy of life, and India is the historical proof of it, say Sri Aurobindo and the scholars in his train.[32]

> Nothing precipitated the decline of the country so much as the acceptance by it of the anti-pragmatic ideal of monasticism and other-worldliness.[33]

In India, Aurobindo says, for the last thousand years spiritual life and material life have gone their separate ways, with the result that the country has fallen into decadence. Spirituality gained the right to renounce any attempt at progress by fixing its eyes on a higher goal. And at the opposite pole, material society was granted the

31. *Ibid.*, p. 24.
32. LD, 11. Aurobindo adds that Europe is the evidence of the bankruptcy in things of the spirit which results from too exclusive a concern with material progress.
33. Sisirkumar Mitra, *The Vision of India* (New York: Laico, 1949), p. 88.

privilege of drowsing in conservatism and inertia. Each reinforced the other. When the best spirits turned their backs on society, society had little hope for advancement. Life in society being a hopeless bondage to a material world of suffering, escape was the only rational response.[34]

The spiritual disciplines of this period cooperated in the separation and the stalemate. Individual liberation was the only aim, renunciation of the world the only way. The collective body of humanity had no place in the ideal of life. And so the vast majority of the people suffered, for the ordinary man cannot live with such rarefied ideas. These high thoughts only succeeded in making him dissatisfied with his life, which he came to understand was in some way unreal or without genuine value. Why should he exert himself for such a life? How indeed could he find a sufficient motivation to move his life out of the rut in which it circled? A culture-wide unnerving of the life-impulse was the inevitable result. (LD, 805)

The decline began, according to Aurobindo, with Buddhism, which disturbed the balance of the old Aryan world by making Spirit revolt against Matter. This turned the Indian mind astray. (LD, 28) The Buddha had discovered the way of escape from constructions, the constructions of experience in which are rooted the sufferings of mankind. (LD, 551) But he overshot his mark, in Aurobindo's opinion, by emphasizing exclusively the transcendent realization.[35]

---

34. *Synthesis of Yoga*, p. 29. Cf. Chaudhuri, *Prophet*, p. 245.
35. *On Yoga* (S.A.A., 1958) II–I:406. Cf. Chaudhuri, *Prophet*, p. 22. Cf. also Diwakar, who says in support of Buddhism that it threw doubt on the value of life only in its intellectual part. Dynamically it gave new and strong values to life, such as *karuna,* compassion. (Pp. 270–71) Likewise, Mitra says that "by its insistence on freedom Buddhism liberated the social life of India from many of its cramping evils and thereby created conditions favorable to the growth and advancement of culture." (*Vision,* p. 18)

Sankara, also, although he opposed the errors of the degenerate form of Buddhism of his day, continued to stress the evanescence of life and therefore could not reveal to India its true soul. He did not understand that what was necessary was a restoration of the harmony between spirit and life which had characterized the Vedic age.[36]

Between the Buddha and Sankara the Bhagavad Gita was composed, with a teaching quite opposed to both of them. Sri Krishna, according to Aurobindo's interpretation of the Gita, lays great stress on the perfect Yogin's cleaving to life and human activity, regardless of their relation to his personal sadhana, for the good of the world itself.[37] His teaching in this respect echoes many verses from the Upanishads, which themselves hark back to the Vedic hymns, voicing the joy of life, giving rules of conduct, and generally orienting themselves in a social context.[38]

> For the Yoga of the Gita, as for the Vedantic Yoga of works, action is not only a preparation but itself the means of liberation; and it is the justice of this view which the Gita seeks to bring out with such unceasing force and insistence,—an insistence, unfortunately, which could not prevail in India against the tremendous tide of Buddhism, was lost afterwards in the intensity of ascetic illusionism and the fervour of world-shunning saints and devotees and is only now beginning to exercise its real and salutary influence on the Indian mind.[39]

The point is not that renunciation is not to be practiced, but that it is to be practiced inwardly by the rejection of desire and egoism, not by the rejection of action. Sri Aurobindo feels that a deeper penetration into the meaning of renunciation itself as taught by the Gita would

---

36. Mitra, *Vision*, p. 89.
37. Cf. Aurobindo, *The Ideal of the Karmayogin* (S.A.A., 1950), p. 11.
38. *Ibid.*, p. 10.
39. *Essays on the Gita*, p. 78.

have led spiritual aspirants much sooner to a form of
spirituality which elevated the nation instead of depress-
ing it.

> Asia temporarily failed not because she followed after things
> spiritual, as some console themselves by saying,—as if the
> spirit could be at all a thing of weakness or a cause of weak-
> ness,—but because she did not follow after the spirit suffi-
> ciently, did not learn how entirely to make it the master
> of life.[40]

Neither a gulf between Spirit and life, nor a compro-
mise between them is the answer, but a conquest of all by
the Spirit,[41] which will give its full legitimate value to each
part of our composite being and find the key to their unity
in an evolutionary synthesis. (LD, 806) Such a synthesis
was attempted in the ancient Indian culture, and Aurobindo and his followers hope to reestablish and perfect it,
making India once again the world's leader in a spirituality
which will serve man and lead him to an integral goal.
K. D. Sethna expresses it thus:

> If we Indians are to march in the van of the world and fulfil
> a mission which no other people can accomplish, we must
> feel that our genius is a dynamic world-transforming spiritu-
> ality which lives in a concrete contact and communion with
> a Perfect Being, Consciousness, Power and Bliss. . . . If the
> Divine is the centre of things there can be nothing on even
> the remotest periphery without an invisible radius running
> out towards it. We must find the radius and discern in the
> peripheral object the point at which contact is made. . . . The
> labour of discovering . . . a point of contact, however subtle,
> with the spiritual goal of mankind calls for intellectual no
> less than intuitive examination. To that labour we must
> pledge ourselves and put no limits to the field which is to
> be examined.[42]

40. Aurobindo, *The Human Cycle* (New York: The Sri Aurobindo
Library, 1950), p. 268.
    41. *Ibid*.
    42. K. D. Sethna, *The Indian Spirit and the World's Future* (S.A.A.,
1953), pp. 20–22.

7

The Value of the Universe and of the Person

MOST OF THE ARGUMENTS OUTLINED ABOVE HAVE BEEN directed against the supracosmic position. Equally unsatisfactory, to Aurobindo's mind, is the supraterrestrial view,[1] which considers the world as only temporarily real, or as real but not intrinsically valuable. There are those who call this a "transitory world," and a "vale of tears." We are caught in it, the evil actions of the past producing fruits of evil experiences in the present, and in this environment still further evil actions are committed, so that the wheel continues to turn. This is the nature of things; we must not expect perfection in "this world."

> The general conception of existence has been permeated with the . . . theory of the chain of Karma and with the consequent antinomy of bondage and liberation . . . liberation by cessation from birth. . . . All voices are joined in one great consensus that not in this world . . . can there be our kingdom of heaven, but beyond. (LD, 28–29)[2]

---

1. Cf. *The Life Divine*, (S.A.A., 1960), Part II, chapter 16; also chapter 5 above.
2. For a Christian counterpart, substitute "original sin" for "Karma" and "death in the state of grace" for "cessation from birth."

NOT A TEMPORARY TESTING GROUND

What, then, is the purpose of this world, if it is full of evil and cannot be perfected? There are those who contend that it is a temporary testing ground for souls whose real destiny lies in another world. The characteristics of this position are: 1) belief in individual immortality of the human spirit, 2) belief in that spirit's life on earth as only a temporary passage to a heaven beyond, and 3) belief in the development of ethical and spiritual values as the means of passage to the world beyond. (LD, 803)

The typical model of this view in Aurobindo's mind is the Christianity with which he was acquainted. He describes it (without identifying it) in these words:

> There is . . . the idea of certain religions, long persistent but now greatly shaken or discredited, that man is a being primarily created as a material living body upon earth into which a newly born divine soul is breathed or else with which it is associated by the fiat of an almighty Creator. A solitary episode, this life is his one opportunity from which he departs to a world of eternal bliss or to a world of eternal misery either according as the general or preponderant balance of his acts is good or evil or according as he accepts or rejects, knows or ignores a particular creed, mode of worship, divine mediator, or else according to the arbitrary predestining caprice of his Creator. (LD, 801)

It must not be supposed that Sri Aurobindo disagrees with the three characteristics enumerated above. On the contrary, he himself holds them with certain modifications. The "human spirit" which is immortal is for him the psychic entity, not the empirical personality; the development of ethical and spiritual values is certainly the way to perfection—together with the cultivation of mental, vital, and physical values *through* the spiritual; and earthly life *in its present condition* is, of course, a temporary stage on the way to life in its full glory.

But what Aurobindo would insist upon is that it is this very life and this very earth which are capable of and destined to a perfection which will be the adequate manifestation of the glory of God. As against a typical Indian view, he will not admit that the world is so essentially evil that the very will to create or to manifest must be withdrawn in order to obtain salvation.[3] And as against a typical Western view, he will not admit that the "next world" is of prime importance and the regeneration of earthly life of only secondary or instrumental importance.[4] Such a view neglects the truth that the worlds of higher consciousness are not the only possible habitations for a perfected soul, for this life also is part of the Supreme Spirit's self-expression.

> The ascent of man into heaven is not the key, but rather his ascent here into the spirit and the descent also of the spirit into his normal humanity and the transformation of this earthly nature. For this and not some post-mortem salvation is the real new birth for which humanity waits as the crowning movement of its long, obscure and painful course.[5]

Of course, surrounded as we are by the evidence of our peccability, we naturally tend to be profoundly sceptical about the possibility of our attaining any integral perfection in what we call "this world" or "this life."[6] Perfection would demand a radical transformation of our present nature. Perhaps this is why the death of the organic body

---

3. Aurobindo, *The Riddle of This World* (S.A.A., 1951), p. 87.
4. Cf. Aurobindo, *The Human Cycle* (New York: The Sri Aurobindo Library, 1950), p. 295.
5. *Ibid.*, pp. 295–96.
6. Cf. Haridas Chaudhuri, *Sri Aurobindo: The Prophet of Life Divine* (2nd ed.; S.A.A., 1960), p. 19.

is looked upon by many religions as the locus of this transformation, it being the most far-reaching change which
observable man ever undergoes.

Aurobindo agrees that a radical transformation is required, so radical that it involves completely new types of
consciousness and new powers over the material universe.
However, he (and the Hindu tradition generally) does not
locate this transformation at the moment of death of the
body but at the moment of enlightenment or self-realization. This would seem to account for the fact that while
those spiritualities which localize transformation at death
can grant a temporary reality and usefulness to the world,
those which do not so localize it must face without any
mitigation the question of the essential value of the world.

The problem organizes itself in this way for some of
the latter: God is perfect and we believe that if He completely governed the world, it would be perfect also. But
we observe the world to be imperfect. To overcome this
dissonance, let us say that the world and God are two different realities, and if we wish to reach God, we must
leave the world. (LD, 471–73)

Clearly, what is missing from this argument is the
dimension of time, the notion that the world, though
presently imperfect, might be in process of becoming
perfect—and even that this process might be God's mode
of government. This is why the doctrine of evolution is
all-important to Aurobindo's thesis. Without it, he would
have no ground for holding that the world is worthwhile.
And if the world were to lack value, then it could not be
granted reality in a universe where the perfect God is the
origin, essence, and finality of all beings. Put another way,
the goodness of God, plus our experience of evil, require
the world to evolve if it is to have any intelligibility at all.

But, having granted this much, there is then no reason to foreshorten the evolution of the world, to set bounds to the perfection and goodness it may attain. Indeed, to stop it at any point short of divine perfection would only return us to the argument's initial position and the unreality of the world. The world, then, must attain divine perfection, and therefore cannot be viewed as only temporarily real and valuable.

Faith in God present in evolution is what makes possible the spirituality and the philosophical position of Aurobindo. If the forms of the world were fixed, then either resignation to our lot or escape to another world would be the proper answer.

But if in us there is a spiritual being which is

emerging and our present state is only an imperfection or half-emergence . . . if an evolution of being is the law, then what we are seeking for is not only possible but part of the eventual necessity of things. (LD, 1231)

Aurobindo draws the alternatives clearly for us. If there is no evolution or if it cannot attain the goal of divine fulfillment, one of two things must happen: the human spirit will either cut short the whole context of earthly life and seek to escape from the world into the divine, or if not capable of this, it will find itself imprisoned in its own egoism and will simply revolve in the circle of the satisfactions and frustrations available to its limited experience. (LD, 807)

But there is scientifically verifiable evidence for material and biological evolution in this world, and Aurobindo argues that such a progression in this world can only have for its aim some kind of self-fulfillment here. Had withdrawal from the world been the ultimate intention of God, the complex and tedious process of evolution would never have appeared. (LD, 813) And the recognition that this evolution is essentially a *spiritual* evolution is the key to joining our understanding of earthly life to our vision of the life of the spirit. (LD, 807)

There is no reason to conclude that the passage from our present imperfect life to the perfect life to which we aspire can be achieved only by a passage to a heaven beyond. This conclusion would be valid only if the dark power of Ignorance were the whole of the meaning of the world-manifestation and there were no force of self-transcendence at work in Nature. (LD, 1007) But all the actions of Nature testify that there is such a power of self-transcendence. It has already achieved marvelous and apparently impossible things. Why should it not continue?

> [Sri Aurobindo] saw the very secret of evolution to be the manifestation in earth-nature of what superficially looks impossible—the quivering forth of vitality and sensation in seemingly lifeless Matter, the glimmering out of mind and reason in apparently instinctive animality, the all-perfecting revelation of Supermind in ostensibly groping intelligence, stumbling life-force and mortal body. So there never could be for Sri Aurobindo either a surrender to ordinary world-conditions or a flight into peace away from the world.[7]

It is Aurobindo's position, then, that it is not the Creator's intention that we should escape this world, nor is it necessary to escape this world in order to escape misery and evil. It is the intention of Nature to conquer all imperfections, and the pain we experience is but a spur to our endeavor to achieve this victory.

Every weakness and failure is a first sounding of gulfs of

---

7. K. D. Sethna, *The Indian Spirit and the World's Future* (S.A.A., 1953), p. 204.

power and potentiality. . . . All this imperfection is to us
evil, but all evil is in travail of the eternal good, for all is
an imperfection which is the first condition . . . of a greater
perfection in the manifesting of the hidden divinity. . . . If
we have first to face and endure [evil and imperfection], the
ultimate command on us is to reject, to overcome, to transform the life and the nature. (LD, 482)

The divine life, according to Sri Aurobindo, is to be
lived not in a heaven of disembodied spirits but on earth,
in matter, in the human body. "It must be a concrete being
—and not an abstract power—who enjoys immortality."
(LD, 443) The divine life is to assume the lower forms
of activity in the human being just as each other successive
development in consciousness assumed those activities beneath it.

> As the mental life does not abrogate but works for the
> elevation and better utilization of the bodily, so too the
> spiritual should not abrogate but transfigure our intellectual,
> emotional, aesthetic, and vital activities.[8]

This assumptive and assimilative character thus runs all
the way down from the highest spiritual life to the very
matter of the body. When the body passes under the direct
control of the Supermind, rather than of Mind, it will no
longer be subject to weakness, disease, or death.[9] The object of the birth of the soul in the human body, says Sri
Aurobindo, is "to realize the Ananda of the Self in conditions other than the supracosmic . . . even in . . . an
embodied material existence. . . . To . . . embody the All-
Delight in an intense summary of its manifoldness . . .
to create out of Matter a temple of Divinity." (LD, 704)

---

8. Aurobindo, *Synthesis of Yoga* (S.A.A., 1957), p. 20.
9. S. K. Maitra, *An Introduction to the Philosophy of Sri Aurobindo*
(Calcutta: Culture, 1944), p. 8. Cf. Aurobindo. *The Supramental Manifestation* (S.A.A., 1952), pp. 62–64.

THE WORLD IS GOD'S OWN SELF-EXPRESSION

In Aurobindo's view the world has to be judged in terms of its value for God, rather than its value for man. When we regard it in terms of its value (or disvalue) for ourselves, we are tempted to escape it, to "renounce" it, or to use it merely as an instrument by which we may strengthen our souls in the virtues which give us entrance into an extraterrestrial heaven. It is when we regard it in terms of its value for God that we recognize its right to endure and to have its own destiny. As our point of view gradually becomes less self-centered, our attitude toward the world shifts from considering it as that *from* which we are to be saved, to that *through* which we are to be saved, to that *together with* which we are to be saved. Nature too has a right to deliverance. (LD, 482)

In fact, Nature in all its stages of development must have some profound meaning of its own.

> The fact that the Formless has assumed form, that it has manifested itself in name and form, is not merely Maya or a capricious whim. Manifestation of the Spirit through form has some profound purpose.[10]

A world turning on a wheel of Ignorance, with no issue except finally a chance of stepping out of it, is not a world with any real reason for existence. (LD, 960) Rather, the world as such must have a meaning. Sri Aurobindo finds that meaning in the expression of the divine possibilities of the finite.

> The Divine potentialities of the Infinite Self are latent in the finite and it is the revelation of the Divine Nature and infinitude hidden in the finite that is the purpose of the

10. Letter of Aurobindo to Barindra, 1920, quoted in R. R. Diwakar, *Mahayogi Sri Aurobindo* (Bombay: Bharatiya Vidya Bhavan, 1962), p. 194.

Limitless Self discovering himself in limitation of the finite.[11]

The working out of this purpose Sri Aurobindo likens to a great yoga of the whole of Nature.

> All life, when we look behind its appearances, is a vast Yoga of Nature attempting to realise her perfection in an ever increasing expression of her potentialities and to unite herself with her own divine reality.[12]

Aurobindo's view is not precisely that the teleology of Nature is aimed at the emergence of man as its crown. Man appears within the vast teleology of Nature, as "her thinker" and through him she "devises self-conscious means and willed arrangements of activity by which this great purpose may be more swiftly . . . attained."[13] Nature's progress in her yoga, prior to and apart from man, is slow and tentative, a groping in the dark, but through him she is able to proceed with greater speed and clearer direction.[14]

There is no question, then, about whether Nature's evolution and man's yoga (effort to realize union with God) might be working at cross-purposes.

> Integral Nondualism maintains that man's highest ideals are as much an expression of the immanence of the Infinite in Man as the evolutionary urge is an expression of the immanence of the Infinite in Nature. In truth, it is the immanent finality of Nature herself brought to focus in human consciousness that gives birth to the deepest aspirations of man.[15]

11. Kapali Sastry, *Lights on the Fundamentals* (Madras: Sri Aurobindo Library, 1950), p. 78.

12. *Synthesis of Yoga,* p. 4.

13. *Ibid.,* pp. 204–5.

14. Rishabhchand, "The Philosophical Basis of Integral Yoga," in H. Chaudhuri and Fr. Spiegelberg, eds., *The Integral Philosophy of Sri Aurobindo* (London: Allen & Unwin, 1960), p. 219.

15. Chaudhuri, *Prophet,* p. 139.

The whole world, man included, is the expression of God and exists for this purpose. Aurobindo's metaphysical scheme of the world, with its hierarchy of planes of consciousness, each with its own principles and powers, organically and harmoniously related, makes the teleological significance of the immanence of the Creator in the world seem to be evidently integral self-manifestation.[16] And his religious representation of the Supreme Reality as Sachchidananda makes the release of the world-being from His own being natural to God, because of the bliss-nature of Sachchidananda.[17] The self-manifestation applies not only to the spiritual creation but also to the mental, vital, and physical. Otherwise, says Aurobindo, God would not be integrally fulfilled. Brahman is in the world to represent Himself in the values of life. (LD, 45)

Because the world is God's self-manifestation, Aurobindo argues, devotion to God implies acknowledgment and respect for the world. Spurning the earth is as bad as remaining enmeshed in it. It is to despise God. We must accept Becoming as divine, just as we accept Being. (LD, 50)

Aurobindo comments that the Bhagavad Gita recognizes a distinction between being and becoming but does not elevate it to the rank of an opposition, thus endangering the unity of Reality.

> The Godhead is one in his transcendence, one all-supporting Self of things, one in the unity of his cosmic nature. These three are one Godhead; all derives from him, all becomes from his being, all is eternal portion or temporal expression of the Eternal.[18]

Having denied that the world is a fiction of Maya,

16. Rishabhchand, p. 220.
17. Sastry, *Fundamentals*, p. 77.
18. *Essays on the Gita*, p. 310.

Aurobindo holds that the cosmic Truth-consciousness is creative of a true universe. (LD, 519) But these forms are created not outside but within the divine existence, consciousness-force, and bliss, as part of the working of the divine Real-Idea. (LD, 191) The world, the forms, the Becoming thus is and yet is not God. It cannot be other than He for there is nothing independent of the Divine Being.

> The Infinite Being must . . . be capable of an eternal action of creation: but this . . . must be an action in itself, a creation out of its own self eternal and infinite, since there could be nothing else out of which it could create; any basis of creation seeming to be other than itself must be still really in itself and of itself and could not be something foreign to its existence. (LD, 372)

But, of course, the world does not exhaust the Divine. Perhaps it is best said to be a "sign" of God.

> This extended universe is not all that the Spirit is, there is an Eternal greater than it by which alone its existence is possible. Cosmos is not the Divine in all his utter reality, but a single self-expression, a true but minor motion of his being. . . . The divine Reality is something greater than the universal existence, but yet all universal and particular things are that Divine and nothing else,—significative of him, we might say, and not entirely That in any part or sum of their appearance, but still they could not be significative of him if they were something else and not term and stuff of the divine existence. That is the Real; but they are its expressive realities.[19]

Aurobindo speaks freely of "creation." We may wonder just what he means by this term and whether it corresponds to the usual meaning to be found in the Western tradition. If by "creation" is meant "made as a potter might make a vessel" (LD, 425), separated from the Cre-

---

19. *Ibid.*, p. 279.

ator in substance and existence but causally dependent on Him, then Aurobindo would prefer to speak of "manifestation," for the product, he holds, is inherent in the producer.

> Energy seems to create substance, but, in reality, as existence is inherent in Consciousness-Force, so also substance would be inherent in Energy,—the Energy a manifestation of the Force, substance a manifestation of the secret Existence. (LD, 362)

He distinguishes his view from "the normal theistic conception" (LD, 425) in that he holds that "the many are themselves the Divine One in their inmost reality, individual selves of the supreme and universal Self-Existence." But still "the many exist by the One and there is therefore an entire dependence of the manifested being on the Ishvara [Creative Lord]." (LD, 425)

Aurobindo's chief objection to the "normal theistic conception" of creation is the "ex nihilo" factor. This is why he presupposes involution in his evolutionary account of the development of the universe.[20] He considers creation out of nothing to be an "arbitrary conception," something "magically and unaccountably introduced." (LD, 221) Such creation is metaphysically unacceptable, he holds, because it would make Nothing a second reality alongside the Creator.

> It is not possible that they are made out of a Nothing, a Non-existence other than the Absolute; for that will erect a new dualism, a great positive Zero over against the . . . one Reality. (LD, 371)

He feels, too, that if the creature is not of the same substance as the Creator, then its reality is in question; it

---

20. See above, chapter 3.

becomes "phenomenal . . . an arbitrary . . . cosmic construction . . . a sort of imposition." (LD, 379) "Imposition" is Sankara's term for the relation of the observable
Many to the real One; the apparent universe is "imposed,"
or "superimposed," upon the Reality. To admit that the
universe was created out of the Void (Sunya) would be,
for Aurobindo, tantamount to surrendering to Mayavada.
He feels that the only way to protect the reality of the
manifold world is not to permit any "cut and separation
between the uncreated Eternal and created existences." If
the world is of the very substance of Real Being, then it is
inescapably real. (LD, 566–67)

> The creations of the absolutely Real should be real and not
> illusions, and since it is the One Existence, they must be
> self-creations, forms of a manifestation of the Eternal, not
> forms of Nothing erected out of the original Void—whether a
> void being or a void consciousness—by Maya. (LD, 543–44)

"Manifestation," in Aurobindo's usage, is a self-formu-
lation of Consciousness-Force (LD, 336, 385) , an ordered
deployment of the infinite possibilities of the Infinite.
(LD, 372)

> In fact the Infinite does not create, it manifests what is in
> itself, in its own essence of reality; it is itself that essence of
> all reality and all realities are powers of that one Reality.
> The Absolute neither creates nor is created,—in the current
> sense of making or being made; we can speak of creation
> only in the sense of the Being becoming in form and move-
> ment what it already is in substance and status. (LD, 395–96)

Kapali Sastry, in his *Lights on the Fundamentals,* a work
approved by Sri Aurobindo as being in consonance with
his own teaching, describes "manifestation" as a movement
by the Shakti of the Lord which is "thrown out" from

Him,[21] by which He "releases these worlds inseparable from Himself."[22] Aurobindo himself notes that the Sanskrit word for *creation* means a "loosing or putting forth of what is in the being." (LD, 397 n.1) To appreciate the atmosphere of the Indian approach to this question, it may be useful to quote in full one verse from Sastry's work, with his commentary on it.

> The Supreme One, the Lord as the vibrant Word, is and becomes the Powerful, incubates, increases, releases these worlds inseparable from Himself.
>
> The Supreme Sole Being has been already stated to be the fundamental consciousness and this latter, while static in the conserving poise, is by the very nature of its infinitude, endued with an expressional aspect which translates itself into a movement for Self-manifestation, connoted by the word Shabda, the vibrant consciousness. He is Shakta, Powerful, ever fresh with a power to bring out something of himself; He maintains it in himself, by the force of Tapas, in the heat of what may be called the creative incubation, *tapati,* preparing what is to be brought out of himself for the assumption of huge and varied dimensions, of gradations in degree and kind, of difference in stress and quality and feature. By virtue of this poise of His Consciousness which is the agency for manifesting something of the Unmanifest which is beyond all formations, He may be said to increase, *vardhate.* From such an increase, the outflow of something in himself in the form of these worlds results. This is called the release, *visristi,* of the worlds. And these again are not separable from himself since He is said to be the Indivisible One out of whom these worlds are loosened, released and set forth.[23]

One last remark on the subject of creation might be made. Both Aurobindo and Kapali Sastry go out of their way to show that God's creation of the world is undertaken

21. (Madras: Sri Aurobindo Library, 1950), p. 4.
22. *Ibid.,* p. 7.
23. Pp. 7–8.

deliberately and in freedom, not by an indifferent mechanism, or, on the other hand, out of any determinism, necessity, or need to create.[24] But it is interesting for a Westerner to notice that in all the discussions examined here of the teleology of the universe and of the creative activity or self-manifestation of God, the motive of love is not ascribed to the Lord. Self-expression of the Ananda which is His own nature comes the closest to it. (LD, 995ff)

In continuing discussion of the argument for the world's having value in itself, it is pertinent to note Sri Aurobindo's attitude toward history. Indian philosophers traditionally have not dealt with the topic and in fact the main reason why it is so difficult to date events and literary remains in Indian culture is that the sense of history has been lacking among Indian scholars of the past. Aurobindo, however, feels that the integrity of God's purpose in the world appears particularly in history. The history of mankind, especially its history of spiritual development, Sri Aurobindo regards as "a constant development of a divine purpose, not a book that is closed, the lines of which have to be constantly repeated."[25]

History, Aurobindo considers, is governed from above by the Supermind, not from below either by a mechanistic determinism or by a completely free-wheeling indeterminism such as Spengler suggests.[26] The fault of causal determinism is not that it is determinism but that it is determinism by an outside agency. And complete indeterminism, the idea that "the historical process is a pure

24. *Ibid.*, p. 15.
25. *Sri Aurobindo on Himself and on the Mother* (S.A.A., 1953), pp. 194–95.
26. See the detailed discussion by S. K. Maitra, "Sri Aurobindo and Spengler: Comparison between the Integral and the Pluralistic Philosophies of History," Chaudhuri and Spiegelberg, pp. 60ff.

flow which does not know toward what it is flowing and which is absolutely undetermined by any goal or destination,"[27] is the negation of all philosophy.[28]

History is guided, according to Aurobindo, by a greater reason and by its own logic in which relations and connections are seen and executed. To our finite reason, he says, it may look like magic, but to the Infinite it is logic.[29] Aurobindo holds that because the historical process has a definite goal before it, it cannot be stopped before it reaches that goal. Even if there occur crystallizations of cultures from time to time, that is not the end of their life, because new stimulations come to arouse them to fresh activity.[30]

In Sri Aurobindo's view, history is linear, not cyclical. A cyclical view would make evolution a farce, for a genuine goal would never be achieved. In this he not only separates himself from Spengler, according to Maitra, but from the traditional Indian version of history as an endless revolution of the four yugas (ages).

> [Evolution is] progress all through, not progress followed by regress and vice versa. . . . Even in the case of rebirth in the present state of our evolution, Sri Aurobindo does not accept the traditional view of our country, namely, that the fate of the soul after death is determined by the law of Karma. For him the law of Karma is to yield to the higher principle of the evolution of the Spirit, and therefore there is no lapse into a lower state.[31]

27. *Ibid.*, p. 75.
28. A much longer discussion of Aurobindo's views on determinism would be profitable. There are three planes to be considered: causal *determinism* on the lowest levels of Nature, superseded by *freedom* in man, which in turn, having done all it can, finally achieves its goal by the *grace* of God.
29. Maitra, "Aurobindo and Spengler," p. 74; cf. LD, 298.
30. *The Human Cycle*, p. 237.
31. Maitra, "Aurobindo and Spengler," p. 78.

Aurobindo also objects to the traditional cyclic view because it holds that a new epoch emerges only on the total extinction of the previous one. As he sees the evolving world, each new epoch builds on, absorbs, and transforms its predecessors.[32] This historical process of transformation does not rest with the expansion of human consciousness to the dimensions of the universe, nor does it aim at the absorption of all beings into the static perfection of the Absolute. It has as its goal the production of increasingly higher grades of self-manifestation of the Divine: a new order of free advance in divine knowledge.[33]

It is not man only, then, who is to be saved. Outer Nature, too, has a right to deliverance. The travail of the world is not disregarded by the great souls who have begun to glimpse the reality and the power of the supramental state. There is such a unity among all beings that the liberation of the whole is intimately joined to the liberation of any one. (LD, 482)

This is one of the strongest reasons for Sri Aurobindo's vigorous opposition to the Mayavada. Its attitude would keep us from our duty to Nature.[34]

> [The belief in the unreality of the world] can bring about . . . an unnerving of the life-impulse and an increasing littleness of its motives . . . an absorption in an ordinary narrow living . . . a failure of the great progressive human idealism by which we are spurred to a collective self-development. (LD, 805–6)

The immanence of the Spirit itself in this world would have no meaning if the world did not eventually reach perfect transfiguration. Only if the supreme Bliss can be

32. *Ibid.*, p. 78.
33. Chaudhuri, *Prophet,* pp. 255–56.
34. Satprem, *Sri Aurobindo, or The Adventure of Consciousness* (New York: India Library Society, 1964) , p. 40.

brought down into the lowest regions and made to dwell there will "all the long labour of Nature . . . end in a crowning justification and her evolutions reveal their profound significance."[35]

Our work in the world is not to be undertaken for our own sakes, as a set of exercises done with a good intention in order to accumulate merit for our own souls. It is to be done for the sake of the value itself thereby achieved.[36] Nor are we to work for material goods. Sri Aurobindo distinguishes himself, for instance, from the Vedavadins, who make sense-enjoyment the object of action and its fulfilment the highest aim of the soul.[37] We must work in the world, but it is not work practised with desire, "not the claim for the satisfaction of the restless and energetic mind by a constant activity, the claim made by the practical or kinetic man."[38] We are not to live directly for the world but for God and then for the world in God."[39]

> The yoga we practice is not for ourselves alone, but for the Divine; its aim is to work out the will of the Divine in the world.[40]

Action in the world and for the world, then, is a matter of devotion to God.[41] God Himself works for and in the world.[42] Aurobindo, summarizing Krishna's message in the Gita, has him say:

> I am the eternal Worker within you and I ask of you works. I demand of you not a passive consent to a mechanical

---

35. *Synthesis of Yoga,* pp. 18–19.
36. *Ibid.,* p. 26.
37. *Essays on the Gita,* p. 89.
38. *Ibid.,* p. 93.
39. *Ibid.,* p. 29.
40. Aurobindo, *The Yoga and Its Objects* (S.A.A., 1964) , p. 1.
41. *Essays on the Gita,* p. 97.
42. *Ibid.,* p. 488.

movement of Nature from which in your self you are wholly separated, indifferent and aloof, but action complete and divine, done for God in you and others and for the good of the world.[43]

Every part of life is to be taken up by the spiritual: the intellectual, the aesthetic, the ethical, and also the dynamic, the vital, the physical. Each power of nature is to be converted. As the Divine is concealed in all, all can be made into instruments of divine life.[44] These powers of Nature, formerly used in an egoistic spirit and for undivine ends have now to be used in a spirit of surrender to the Divine and for the divine work.[45] Whereas at present the world seems to create us, in the perfection of the spiritual life we shall create ourselves and the world. (LD, 1213)

> The whole principle of the Yoga is to give oneself entirely to the Divine alone and to nobody and nothing else, and to bring down into ourselves by union with the Divine Mother all the transcendent light, power, wideness, peace, purity, truth-consciousness and Ananda of the Supramental Divine.[46]

THE IMPORTANCE OF THE INDIVIDUAL PERSON

The world has its own meaning and its own value, but it is through the individual person that it attains its destiny. It is the spiritually aware man who is able, as we have just read, to lift his consciousness to the Divine Mother and surrender himself as a channel and an instru-

43. *Ibid.,* p. 521.
44. *The Human Cycle,* p. 297.
45. Aurobindo, *A Practical Guide to the Integral Yoga* (S.A.A., 1965), p. 25.
46. *Ibid.,* pp. 25–26.

ment through which the world beneath him may also be transformed. Both the individual and the world are derived from the transcendent Reality which is manifest in them (LD, 368), but the world achieves its finality through man. It is true that man, in his present state, is only an incomplete revelation of the divine nature, but that is part of his significance. He is the embodied Godhead in the course of its evolution, where evolution is understood as the pattern of the divine Lila. (LD, 368) Within the evolution, he is the mediator between Ignorance and Knowledge.

> He alone can work out at its critical turning-point that movement of self-manifestation which appears to us as the involution and evolution of the divine consciousness between the two terms of the Ignorance and the Knowledge, (LD, 458)

The individual poise of the Divine Being has specific values of its own, quite distinct from those of the cosmic poise.

> The immense importance of the individual being, which increases as he rises in the scale, is the most remarkable and significant fact of a universe which started without consciousness and without individuality in an undifferentiated Nescience. This importance can only be justified if the Self as individual is no less real than the Self as cosmic Being or Spirit and both are powers of the Eternal. (LD, 900–1)

It is the individual who, by his power of self-consciousness, is able to realize his union with both of the other poises, the Transcendent and the Universal, and thus to constitute the unity of the whole. (LD, 458)

> He must be the Transcendent itself dealing with a cosmic manifested in his own being. (LD, 550)

The presence of the individual is neither an illusion nor a "subordinate circumstance in a divine play . . . a continuous revolution through unending cycles . . . without any higher hope." (LD, 459) He exists for a specific and a grand purpose.

Since he is not caught in a cycle, man's end is not escape from the cycle. His "liberation," or realization of his true nature and status in Reality, is a preliminary condition for his conscious cooperation in God's drama of evolution.[47] In this drama he has a significant role to play because he possesses the power, through his own individual evolution to the supramental state, of transforming the lower world, speeding and guiding its cosmic evolution.[48] This in turn means that the infinite Bliss and self-conscious Existence, which can never be entirely expressed in phenomena, comes through evolution to know itself—by intuition, by self-vision, by self-experience.

> It becomes itself in the world by knowing itself; it knows itself by becoming itself. . . . This becoming of the infinite Bliss-Existence-Consciousness in mind and life and body,—for independent of them it exists eternally,—is the transfiguration intended and the utility of individual existence. Through the individual it manifests in relation even as of itself it exists in identity. (LD, 52–53)

The individual is the key to the evolutionary movement because it is he who becomes conscious of Reality. (LD, 1248) If there is any goal to evolution, Aurobindo says, it must be the completeness, in the individual and in the community of individuals, of the Divine existence-consciousness-bliss. Absolute completeness cannot be had in the finite, therefore not in any order of cosmic being;

47. Haridas Chaudhuri, *Sri Aurobindo, The Prophet of Life Divine* (2nd ed.; S.A.A., 1960), p. 213.
48. Maitra, *Introduction*, p. 70. Cf. LD, 459.

"the only final goal possible is the emergence of the infinite consciousness in the individual." (LD, 135) The universe seeks to represent the infinite consciousness, the divine immensity and omnipresence, by its spatial extension and variety of form, but it thereby becomes diffuse. In the self-conscious individual it finds a point of concentration by reflection, through which it can reach into another dimension to image the Divine Reality. It is the individual who by self-transcendence enters into the Absolute, carrying the cosmic with him. (LD, 566)

But if the individual person really enters into the Absolute and experiences the infinite consciousness in his own being, then he is no mere by-product of Nature. He is not just the means by which the cosmic being expresses itself and attains divine realization, but he must also be a distinct poise of the Absolute Being itself, another phase of the manifestation of the Transcendent, a branch of independent rank as compared with cosmic being. He is not a temporary formation of the cosmic Spirit (LD, 788–89), nor "a mere accompaniment or auxiliary product of the play of consciousness in the body but . . . a persistent reality, an eternal portion of the Eternal Spirit."[49] Even when extended in universality of consciousness, man possesses a certain transcendence.

> If the individual is a persistent reality . . . if his growth of consciousness is the means by which the Spirit in things discloses its being . . . then, secure behind all the changings of our personality, upholding the stream of its mutations, there must be a true Person, a real spiritual Individual. (LD, 901)

What is this personhood? What does Aurobindo mean by personality? His use of these terms does not quite co-

_____
49. *Ibid.*, p. 71.

incide with their usual connotations in the West. Aurobindo felt that the concepts of individuality and personality which had been developed in Western philosophy
and theology were the result of intellectual speculation,
which he holds to be incapable of reaching the ultimate
truth.[50]

Aurobindo is at pains to distinguish true personhood
from the ego-personality. The individual ego is, in fact, a
pragmatic fiction, "a translation of the secret self into the
terms of surface consciousness, or a subjective substitute
for the true self in our surface experience." (LD, 742)
It is a necessary development in Nature's movement from
Inconscience to evolutionary self-expression, but it is not
the persistent and surviving Person, the one who enters
into transcendental consciousness and the bliss of the Absolute. This ego-personality is only a temporary manifestation and instrument for the real Person. (LD, 973) It is
essentially separative and is the seat of all selfishness and
the focal point of moral evil. Far from being the self in its
abiding reality, it is composed of many changing elements.

What in the West, especially in popular parlance, is
usually called the "personality" is really a complex of
impersonal characteristics. The various marks by which
we recognize and judge "personality" are themselves uni-
versals: certain qualities, certain forms of energy. The variety of combinations of these forces and qualities constitutes the variety of "personalities." The true Person is
the being supporting this collection of impersonal characteristics.

50. C. A. Moore, "Sri Aurobindo on East and West," Chaudhuri and
Spiegelberg, p. 91. Bolle, in *The Persistence of Religion* (Leiden: Brill,
1965), a work on Tantrism and Aurobindo, says that individualism in
the West arose as "a recent revolution against authority" and remarks
that in India it does not appear in this context. P. 105.

What we call the personality of the Person is his expression in nature-status and nature-action—he himself being in his self-existence, originally and ultimately, much more than this, it is the form of himself that he puts forth as his manifested . . . being . . . in nature. (LD, 1181)

The spiritual Person is "not a personality in the sense of a pattern of being marked out by a settled combination of fixed qualities, a determined character." (LD, 1182) In his essential being, he is a "formless, unlimited self" (LD, 1182) ; his manifestation as a formed, limited individual is "his personal expression of what is impersonal, his personal appropriation of it."[51]

The Person puts forward the personality as his role, character, *persona,* in the present act of his long drama of manifested existence. But the Person is larger than his personality. (LD, 1183; cf. 612–13)

Just as the real person is not defined by a set of specific qualities, neither is he a being rigidly separated from all other persons. The common notion of an individual is of a mental-vital-physical being separate from all other beings, incapable of unity with them by its very individuality. We even think of the soul as an individualized being separate from all others, incommunicable by nature, capable only of sympathy but not of real unity with others. Sri Aurobindo is emphatic in denying this idea as untrue to the real individual.

It is therefore necessary to insist that by the true individual we mean nothing of the kind, but a conscious power of the Eternal, always existing by unity, always capable of mutuality . . . a conscious being who is for our valuations of existence a being of the Eternal in his power of individualizing self-experience. (LD, 443)

51. LD, 1181; "personal" and "impersonal" here have the sense of "particular" and "universal."

Besides thinking of our soul and personality as incommunicable and separate from other finite beings, we also tend to think of it as naturally separate from the Infinite Being and independent of Its action. Sri Aurobindo denies this also, calling it an instance in which he will grant the analysis of Sankara!

> The one thing that can be described as an unreal reality is our individual sense of separativeness and the conception of the finite as a self-existent object in the Infinite. . . . [The surface personality] has no independence or separate reality. Individual independence, entire separativeness are not necessary for individual reality, do not constitute it. (LD, 553) . . . The ordinary . . . man . . . finds himself in the world thinking and willing and feeling and acting and he takes himself . . . as a separate self-existent being who has the freedom of his thought and will and feeling and action. He bears the burden of his sin and error and suffering and takes the responsibility and merit of his knowledge and virtue; he claims the right to satisfy his . . . ego and arrogates the power to shape his own destiny and to turn the world to his own uses. . . . What is true of his spirit he attributes to his ego-personality and gives it a false application, a false form and a mass of ignorant consequences.[52]

Thus we mistake both the individual's relation to the universe and his relation to the Transcendent. The solution to this confusion is to be found in Aurobindo's basic premise that the Absolute has three poises: Transcendent, Universal, and Individual.

In his *Philosophy of Integralism,* Haridas Chaudhuri has an excellent summary and commentary on the topic of the individual in its relation to the other two poises.[53] The true individual, he says, is "a concrete universal in the sense that consistently with its possession of some centrality of reference it includes other individuals within

---

52. *Essays on the Gita,* pp. 492–93.
53. Pp. 262–64.

itself as much as it is also itself included within other individuals."[54] Similarly, the person who has realized his true self sees the Transcendent within himself and himself within the Transcendent. It is in this sense that the Individual is intimately related to both the Universal and the Transcendent.

Chaudhuri gives here some very useful corrections of possible misconceptions which are only too easy to form in an effort to grasp Aurobindo's subtle doctrine of the three poises of Brahman. First of all, the Individual is not *part* of Brahman, because the Absolute has no parts but is infinite and indivisibly present in each Individual. Nor is it an *image* of the Absolute, because it is not a reflection of Brahman in an independent substance. But, on the other hand, it is not absolutely nondifferent from Brahman, for it is not a mere illusory product of Ignorance. It cannot be defined in terms of the Universal, the objective world, because it transcends all empirical conditions. It is not even advisable to speak of it as "a conscious power of being of the Eternal," because it is not impersonal.

> The truth about the mode of being of the Individual Self is that it is a concrete Person who enjoys immortality. . . . The Individual Self is in its deepest essence a poise of being of the Absolute, just as cosmic universality and supracosmic transcendence are other poises of being of the same Absolute. As a poise of being of the Absolute, the Individual has an aspect of transcendence as well as an aspect of universality. . . . Each Individual Self is a unique centre of action and medium of self-manifestation of the Absolute.[55]

This is a lofty doctrine of the true essence of the individual person. But the man of the present age, as we experience him, how is he to come into a full realization of

54. *Ibid.*, p. 262.
55. *Ibid.*, pp. 264–65.

this essence of his? Sri Aurobindo answers that he has to get rid of his ego-personality. As long as he identifies himself with that, the divine life is unattainable.

> The ego is a falsification of our true individuality by a limiting self-identification of it with this life, this mind, this body; it is a separation from other souls which shuts us up in our own individual experience and prevents us from living as the universal individual: it is a separation from God, our highest Self, who is the one Self in all existences and the divine Inhabitant within us. (LD, 881)

The ego-life is by nature incompatible with the divine life, for the divine life is boundless and vast, while the ego "exists by its limits and perishes by the loss of its limits." (LD, 882)

By a strange paradox, the first step on the way to realizing oneself as the true Person is the cultivation of an attitude of impersonality.

> Impersonality is a denial of limitation and division, and the cult of impersonality is a natural condition of true being, an indispensable preliminary of true knowledge and therefore a first requisite of true action.[56]

If we are to attain unity with all existence, we clearly cannot remain simply identified with this limited personality of the empirical ego, because it is by nature—and by necessity—self-centered in its outlook and in its action. It is our image of ourselves as identified with this personality that makes the practice of unselfishness, generosity, forgiveness, and the other virtues seem hard and unnatural. Liberated from this narrow image of ourselves, we find compassion and selfless concern for all beings perfectly natural and the life of virtue spontaneous.[57]

56. *Essays on the Gita*, p. 475.
57. *Ibid*.

The practice of this first step of the Integral Yoga involves the familiar renunciation of personal likes and dislikes, attachments and aversions. The correct understanding of the so-called "renunciation of the world" is this rejection of selfish attitudes and action in the world. In Aurobindo's yoga—and here he is following the Gita—such renunciation is only a preparation for the transformation of life into a divine outlook and divine action. Union with the universal Brahman follows and makes possible supreme love and devotion to the Personal God.

The second step of the yoga, therefore, is a passage back from impersonality to a personal orientation again, but this time centered in the Person of the Lord, spoken of in the Gita as the Purushottama, the Supreme Person.

> Here there is the supreme Soul and its supreme nature, here there is the Purushottama who is beyond the personal and impersonal and reconciles them on his eternal heights. The ego personality still disappears in the silence of the Impersonal, but at the same time there remains even with this silence at the back the action of a supreme Self, one greater than the Impersonal. There is no longer the lower blind and limping action of the ego . . . but instead the vast self-determining movement of an infinite spiritual Force. . . . All Nature becomes the power of the one Divine and all action his action through the individual as channel and instrument. In place of the ego there comes forward conscious and manifest the true spiritual individual in the freedom of his real nature, in the power of his supernal status, in the majesty and splendour of his eternal kinship to the Divine.[58]

The individual man attains perfection when he merges his will with the Divine Will.[59] But this does not mean that there is only one pattern for all men. On the contrary, divine perfection implies the perfection of variety in the

58. *Ibid.*, pp. 477–78.
59. *Ibid.*, p. 185.

realm of the Many. The uniqueness of each person is not only preserved but enhanced. Each unrepeatable manifestation of the divine One may now develop freely according to its own special way of expressing the divine nature.[60] Individuality as such perdures. We should not conclude that the perfected spiritual man, the gnostic being, is an inhuman supramental self without a personality. To Aurobindo's mind this would be just as bad as a blank of pure being. (LD, 1180) Rather, in the supramental consciousness, both the impersonality that overcomes egoism and the personality that expresses in a limited concrete way the transcendent soul within are real and worthy of respect. (LD, 1181)

Here we can see another instance of the advantage of Aurobindo's thesis of the three poises of Brahman, as compared with other Indian systems. He has no difficulty in admitting the union of the human spirit with the Absolute and at the same time preserving the individuality of man. Just as bodily life need not be given up when mental life is attained, so individual actions are not inconsistent with cosmic consciousness and transcendent realization. (LD, 46) An integral spiritual consciousness links all the levels of being into an indivisible whole. It does not abolish the individual existence but transforms it by revealing its true nature as nonseparate from the Divine Reality. (LD, 756)

> The soul can in its consciousness identify itself with other souls, can contain them and enter into and be contained by them, can realise its unity with them; and this can take place, not in a featureless and indistinguishable sleep, not in a Nirvana in which all distinctions and individualities of soul and mind and body are lost, but in a perfect waking

---

60. Satprem, pp. 24, 171.

which observes and takes account of all distinctions but exceeds them. (LD, 688–89)

This is the doctrine of the Bhagavad Gita, says Aurobindo, which appears to admit an eternal plurality of souls, sustained by their eternal unity. There is somehow a "vast identity of conscious being . . . behind all this apparent separativism of relative existence"[61] and yet there is no disappearance or "annullation of the individual soul in the Infinite."[62] Both positions are maintained simultaneously. This is the ancient Hindu tradition, Aurobindo claims, as exemplified by the Isa Upanishad when it tells us that Brahman is both mobile and immobile, one and many, knowledge and ignorance, and so on, and that to hold one side of the truth without the other is to remain in darkness.

Sri Aurobindo and his followers emphasize that his doctrine does not admit the thesis that the individual soul is ever lost by merging with the Absolute. Diwakar, for instance, says:

> It is of utmost significance to know and understand thoroughly why Aurobindo was not satisfied only with the gospel of Adwaita Vedanta which preaches absorption of the individual soul in the universal Soul. He stood rather for bringing the power of the Universal Soul down into the earth consciousness, so that mind, life, and matter are transformed and made capable of a Divine life here on earth.[63]

Chaudhuri also points out:

> The true spiritual individuality of a man is not dissolved even after the attainment of full spiritual illumination. . . . The noblest fruition of individuality would lie not simply in returning to the bosom of the Infinite from which he was

---

61. *Essays on the Gita,* p. 390.
62. *Ibid.,* p. 391.
63. P. 249.

separated through Ignorance, but in functioning as a perfect medium of self-manifestation of the Divine in material conditions and under the aspect of temporality.[64]

Sri Aurobindo himself declares:

> The meeting of man and God must always mean a penetration and entry of the Divine into the human and a self-immergence of man in the Divinity. . . . But that immergence is not in the nature of an annihilation. Extinction is not the fulfilment of all this search and passion, suffering and rapture. The game would never have been begun if that were to be its ending.[65]

Annihilation of the individual in the Absolute would result in a pure and blank unity in which there could be no harmony. But in the union Sri Aurobindo sees, of the individual with the Absolute and with other individuals, there would be a perfect harmony in the multiplicity which is at the same time a spontaneous expression of the unity: a "mutuality of consciousness aware of other consciousness by a direct inner contact and interchange." (LD, 1237) Far from being dissolved, the individual consciously dwells in God[66] in both His divine poles, the One and the Many. (LD, 182)

This point needs to be remembered constantly to avoid any misconception when one reads passages by Aurobindo in which he speaks of "merging," of "fusion," of "essential unity." For instance, according to one text, a doctrine "falls short of the whole truth if it denies the essential unity of God and Soul or their capacity for utter oneness or ignores what underlies the supreme experience of the merger of the soul in the Divine Unity through love,

---

64. *Prophet,* pp. 205, 213.
65. *Thoughts and Glimpses* (S.A.A., 1964), p. 11.
66. *Essays on the Gita,* p. 397. The Gita uses the expression *mamamsah, sanatanah,* which Aurobindo renders "eternal individual."

through union of consciousness, through fusion of existence in existence." (LD, 789–90) And again he says,

> When the liberated soul comes into union with the Transcendent, it has this self-experience of itself and cosmos which is translated psychologically into a mutual inclusion and a persistent existence of both in a divine union which is at once a oneness and a fusion and an embrace. (LD, 442)

But the context shows that this implies no loss of personhood, for in the same paragraph he says:

> We find that the individual being also comes in the end to include the world in its consciousness, and since this is not by an abolition of the spiritual individual, but by his coming to his full, large and perfect self-consciousness, we must suppose that the individual always included the cosmos. (LD, 441)

And in another place he says plainly:

> It is not . . . merged in the sense of being extinguished or abolished but is there inherent in it, indistinguishable from the self of awareness and the self-effectuating force of the Bliss of Being. (LD, 1177)

The difficulty, he grants, is with our language. We have only a rational language with which to operate and it is inadequate to convey these spiritual realities. Our language was formed by Mind for the mental purpose of dealing with the finite appearances of the phenomenal world. Its definitions and images refer to conceptions of physical space and circumstance and the experiences of the senses. (LD, 441, 442) What does "dissolve" or "merge" or "fuse" mean? Do not these words automatically bring up physical images? How can we expect them to give accurate renditions of the mode of spiritual existence? These images of a small particle disappearing into a large mass—such as the "dewdrop" slipping into "the shining sea," which has misled so many—express precisely what does *not* take place in the perfection of the spiritual life, according to Sri Aurobindo. That type of unity is the effect of external coercion and can only result in "an effacement of the personality by its extinction in the mass or subjugation to the mass." (LD, 1221) But *inner* growth enables the individual "freely and effectively" to "universalize and transcendentalize his being." (LD, 1221)

The type of union with the Absolute which Sri Aurobindo is trying to describe is far more complex than any simple fusion or confrontation or being a "part" of another. It is, in a way, a reconciliation of what each of these images points to, but based on a more subtle, a more complex, and consequently a more adequate foundation, namely the triply poised Brahman. By means of this conception of the Godhead he is able to grant a place to each of the three traditional Indian ways of thinking of the ultimate state of the soul: the pure oneness of the Advaita, the distinction within unity of the Vishishtadvaita, and the confrontation of the Dvaita. Also, the yogas of knowledge, work, and love are each recognized.

> All relations with the Divine will be his [who enters into the divine life]: the trinity of God-knowledge, divine works and devotion to God will open within him and move towards an utter self-giving and surrender of his whole being and nature. He will live in God and with God, possess God, as it is said, even plunge in him forgetting all separate personality, but not losing it in self-extinction. The love of God and all the sweetness of love will remain his, the bliss of contact as well as the bliss of oneness and the bliss of difference in oneness.[67]

Sri Aurobindo does not claim that this doctrine is orig-

---

67. *The Supramental Manifestation* (S.A.A., 1952), pp. 85–86.

inal with him but refers it to the Bhagavad Gita. One of
the aims of the author of the Gita had evidently been to
provide a reconciliation of the traditional yogas and ways
of conceiving the goal. Aurobindo, in his commentary on
the Gita, shows how refined is the Gita's treatment of this
question, how delicate its analysis and thorough its integration:

> The liberation of the Gita is not a self-oblivious abolition
> of the soul's personal being in the absorption of the One . . . ;
> it is all kinds of union at once. There is an entire unification
> with the supreme Godhead in essence of being and intimacy
> of consciousness and identity of bliss . . . for one object of
> the Yoga is to become Brahman. . . . There is an external
> ecstatic dwelling in the highest existence of the Supreme . . .
> for it is said, "Thou shalt dwell in Me". . . . There is an
> eternal love and adoration in a uniting nearness, there is
> an embrace of the liberated spirit by its divine Lover and
> the enveloping Self of its infinitudes. . . . There is an identity
> of the soul's liberated nature with the divine nature . . . for
> the perfection of the free spirit is to become even as the
> Divine. . . . The orthodox Yoga of knowledge aims at a
> fathomless immergence in the one infinite existence. . . ; it
> looks upon that alone as the entire liberation. The Yoga of
> adoration envisages an eternal habitation or nearness as the
> greater release. . . . The Yoga of works leads to oneness in
> power of being and nature . . . : but the Gita envelops them
> all in its catholic integrality and fuses them all into one
> greatest and richest divine freedom and perfection.[68]

THE INDIVIDUAL AND THE COLLECTIVE

One last topic remains to be touched on briefly—the relation of the individual person to the community. For
Sri Aurobindo the goal of humanity is not merely an
individual affair. It is also a matter of the community,

---

68. *Essays on the Gita,* p. 354.

of the world as a whole. There is a collective salvation to be attained as well as an individual one. Having emphasized the importance of the individual as against the herd, the mass consciousness which is still close to the Inconscient or Subconscient, Aurobindo goes on to show that through the individual this collective consciousness can come to its own awakening.[69]

> While [Nature] organises the separate object and the body and mind of the individual being, it creates also collective powers of consciousness which are large subjective formations of cosmic Nature; but it does not provide for them an organised mind and body, it bases them on the group of individuals, develops for them a group mind, a changing yet continuous group body. It follows that only as the individuals become more and more conscious can the group-being also become more and more conscious; the growth of the individual is the indispensable means for the inner growth as distinguished from the outer force and expansion of the collective being. (LD, 825)

The community exists by the individual, not vice versa (LD, 1247), and a perfected community exists only by the perfection of its individual members. (LD, 1249) The community exists to serve the individual, but it is also right for the individual to sacrifice himself for the sake of the community.[70] Sri Aurobindo's own long efforts to bring down the Supermind into the lives of men on earth is a sacrifice of this kind.[71] He acted not for himself alone but for mankind. If one attains the goal, then it becomes easier for others.[72]

---

69. Aurobindo's theories of collective life are dealt with at length in his works *The Ideal of Human Unity* (New York: Dutton, 1950) and *The Human Cycle*. They will not be developed here for this would involve us in his philosophy of politics.
70. *The Ideal of the Karmayogin*, p. 35.
71. Purani, p. 279.
72. Diwakar, p. 191.

The individual is the instrument of the desired transformation, but an isolated individual transformation is not enough and may not be wholly feasible. The individual's own transformation can be secured in permanency only if it is embedded in a transformed world. (LD, 1145) For the complete and perfect fulfillment of the evolutionary movement, illumination and transformation must take place on every level of the individual, and not only in the individual but in the collective life of illumined individuals. (LD, 1211) A whole new order of beings, a new race, is needed for the change in the world which Aurobindo sees as the goal of evolution. (LD, 1212)

This coming race, according to N. K. Gupta, a disciple of Aurobindo, will practice a kind of "spiritual communism" which will embrace both individualism and collectivism, unifying them in a higher truth. Collectivism, the rule of the "herd," was the primitive form of human society. Individualism appeared as a revolt against the tyranny of the group, but is no more the complete answer than was collectivism.[73] Individual freedom and self-determination are here to stay, but the truth of collectivism too must be acknowledged: that the individual is not to live for himself alone but for his neighbor as well, finding his own fulfillment in the fulfillment of others.[74] In the future harmonization of collectivism and individualism, the individual will be the center, the group the circumference, and the two will form one whole circle.[75] In Aurobindo's words:

We have to recognise once more that the individual exists not in himself alone but in the collectivity and that indi-

73. N. K. Gupta, *The Coming Race* (Madras: Sri Aurobindo Library, 1944), p. 50.
74. *Ibid.*, p. 54.
75. *Ibid.*, p. 55.

vidual perfection and liberation are not the whole sense of
God's intention in the world. The free use of our liberty
includes also the liberation of others and of mankind; the
perfect utility of our perfection is, having realised in ourselves the divine symbol, to reproduce, multiply and ultimately universalise it in others.[76]

The problem of the relative claims of the individual
and the community, which is so difficult for us now, in
what Aurobindo calls our state of ignorance, will not be a
problem in the transformed world. We are now laboring
to build some approach to unity and harmony, but it is an
externally constructed unity—an association of egos under
law by convention, for the balancing of egoistic interests.
(LD, 1230) When there are no egoistic interests to balance against one another, then there is no conflict between
the ideals of individualism and those of collectivism, for
both are terms of the greater Reality. (LD, 1266)

The supramental man will experience the whole world
through his own subjective experience. (LD, 1165) All
beings will be to him as his own selves (LD, 1157) , selves
of himself in the one existence (LD, 1164) . As Satprem
puts it, the ideal would be as if each could taste each other
and the whole.[77] And it must inevitably be this way, for
the Transcendent must express itself in a collectivity of
individuals because it is only one being and its unity must
find a reflection in the multiplicity.[78] The evolution of the
world is linked inextricably to the totality of the world:
nothing can be saved unless all is saved.[79]

It is the claim of the Integral Yoga that it effects this
divine unity among men. It is a unique feature of Sri

76. *Synthesis of Yoga.* p. 30.
77. P. 272.
78. Satprem, pp. 299–300.
79. *Ibid.,* p. 209.

Aurobindo's yoga, as compared with the traditional yogas of India.[80]

> We regard the spirit in man not as solely an individual being travelling to a transcendent unity with the Divine, but as a universal being capable of oneness with the Divine in all souls and all Nature and we give this extended view its entire practical consequence. The human soul's individual liberation and enjoyment of union with the Divine in spiritual being, consciousness and delight must always be the first object of the Yoga; its free enjoyment of the cosmic unity of the Divine becomes a second object; but out of that a third appears, the effectuation of the meaning of the divine unity with all beings by a sympathy and participation in the spiritual purpose of the Divine in humanity. The individual Yoga then turns from its separateness and becomes a part of the collective Yoga of the divine Nature in the human race.[81]

The perfection of this Yoga in what Aurobindo calls the gnostic life breaks down the barriers between soul and soul. Divine living includes not only the individual life of the being but "the life of others made one with the individual in a common uniting consciousness." (LD, 1236) This sense of unity, which is spontaneous, not contrived, comes from each individual's realization of his and the others' real natures as expressive selves of the One Self. (LD, 1236) This unites all while leaving each one free to develop full expression of his own "self-nature (swabhava)."[82] While guided by Mind and under the rule of Ignorance, we tend to think of unity as sameness, but this would not at all be the case in the gnostic life. On the contrary, "the greatest richness of diversity in the self-expression of oneness would be the law of the gnostic life." (LD, 1202)

80. Chaudhuri, *Prophet*, p. 53.
81. *Synthesis of Yoga*, p. 700.
82. Gupta, p. 127.

But if the gnostic being does not live for his separate ego, neither does he live for any collective ego. (LD, 1225) Supramental self-realization gives freedom from both kinds of egoism.[83] The coming race of Supermen will not descend to our common experience of the strife of collective ego with collective ego any more than they will tolerate strife between individual egos. (LD, 1230) The new world calls for many gnostic beings (Supermen) to form a new common life. This Supermanhood is not a privilege of the few or a gift restricted to an elite. It is the next level of development of the whole human race. (LD, 1226) Supermanhood is "an ideal of collective transformation or racial evolution, not an ideal of individual over-growth."[84] If it could be realized, we might find, as Chaudhuri reminds us that Bernard Show prophesied, that the salvation of the world lies in its producing "a democracy of supermen."[85]

83. Mitra, *Vision,* p. 257.
84. Chaudhuri, *Prophet,* p. 148.
85. *Ibid.,* p. 171.

8
Spiritual Evolution of the Real World: Summary and Evaluation

AUROBINDO'S THOUGHT IS CLEARLY SITUATED IN THE CONTEXT of Indian philosophical and spiritual traditions. He deals with the classical problems of the phenomenal world and the transcendent One, the relative merits of the different states of consciousness, and the ultimate goal of human life. He accepts traditional Indian orientations on many points: the non-dual nature of the ultimate Reality, its identification as Sachchidananda in abstract terms and as the divine incarnation of Lord Krishna in personal terms. He develops the Shakti tradition and reconciles the popular yogas. He offers interpretations of the Hindu Scriptures and is eager to show that his doctrine is orthodox by being in conformity with them.

But his thought is not limited to this setting. The basic problems which concern him concern all men. Questions of the meaning of life, of God, of evil, of the world, of action, and of selfhood are not special to one culture. These problems are universal, and they seem also to be perennial. Aurobindo's answers to them, however, while taking advantage of wisdom from the recent and distant past, are characteristically modern. The theory of evolution is the mainspring of his structure, and his zest for progress and his attitude of optimism belong to the present age.

Reconciliation and integration of every kind are among his chief gifts. Eastern spiritual patience and Western material progress, extreme otherworldliness and down to earth practicality, traditionally contrary philosophical systems and spiritual disciplines—all come together in his scheme of life. The two doctrines which enable him to accomplish this integration, in my view, are the doctrine of the three poises of Brahman and the doctrine of spiritual evolution. Each of these deserves a brief summary before the critique of his work as a whole.

ADVANTAGES OF THE DOCTRINE OF THE THREE POISES

The doctrine of the three poises of Brahman is the cornerstone in Sri Aurobindo's edifice of reconciliation. It enables him to hold simultaneously several theses which in other systems are incompatible.

The first and most important reconciliation it makes possible is that between the real world and the non-dual Absolute. By maintaining that Brahman itself *is* the world, or becomes manifest as the world (cosmic poise), Aurobindo indicates that the world is not a second substance, other than Brahman. Thus Brahman remains "one without a second." At the same time, the world becomes real, because Brahman is real and its act of manifestation is real. But by insisting that Brahman also has a transcendent poise, he avoids the error of pantheism which would simply identify God and the world. The world, in Aurobindo's system, has no reality which is not Brahman's reality, yet the reality of Brahman is not exhausted by the reality of the world.

Making the world consubstantial with Brahman is the surest way to protect its reality against the type of eventual dissolution to which it is subject in Mayavada. A creation out of nothing would not suffice for this purpose, Aurobindo feels. "Nothing" is too reminiscent of Sunya, the Void. That which is made out of nothing is essentially nothing, is an illusion. Here, of course, those familiar with the creation doctrine of the West will feel disappointed that Aurobindo so far failed to understand this thesis as to reject it in this naïve way. He nowhere considers the possibility that God could give an act of existence of its own to a creature which previously had no reality whatsoever. However, Aurobindo was not a student of Western metaphysics, nor was he assembling his arguments in terms of a Judaeo-Christian theological context. His context was the Mayavada, and against that background any suggestion of a creation out of nothing would have weakened his case for the reality of the world.

As it is, Aurobindo's position is neither creationist nor emanationist—or else it is a reconciliation of chosen aspects of each view. If we consider theories of the relation of the one to the many with regard to only two notes, necessity of production and consubstantiality, there are four possibilities: 1) production is not necessary and the product is not consubstantial with the cause (Christian creationist position); 2) production is necessary and the product is consubstantial with the cause (Spinozan emanationist position); 3) production is necessary but the product is not consubstantial with the cause (Avicennan emanationist position); and 4) production is not necessary but the product is consubstantial with the cause (Aurobindo's position).

Aurobindo's stance could be called incarnationist. He remarked once that the full implications of the dogma of the divine Incarnation had not been appreciated in the West because this idea had not entered the general consciousness of the people but had been restricted to a single instance. On Aurobindo's view, the whole world as a cosmos, and each individual being in it, is an incarnation of God. (He also believes in the special divine incarnations, the avataras, but he sees these as acts of the divine mercy within the larger framework of general incarnation.) In this way he is able to preserve both the freedom of God's action in producing the manifold world and the absolute reality of the world, since it is of the substance of God Himself.

By introducing a third poise of Brahman, the individual, Aurobindo protects the individual against an indiscriminate fusion with the cosmos as a whole and reconciles the claims of the collective and the individual. God not only becomes incarnate as the universe but as each individual being, or at least each individual *human* being. It is not clear what status Aurobindo grants to lower creatures, nor what his criterion of individuality is. When he speaks of "the individual," it is apparent from the context that he has in mind individual men.

The individual's various motives for action can also be reconciled in this system, because action in the world has intrinsic value of its own, and yet it is a divine value. A debate has recently arisen in the West over what constitutes a sufficient motive for altruistic action in the world. Traditionally, good works have been undertaken because they are pleasing to God and productive of reward in the next life. Now there are increasing numbers of people who claim to find a sufficient motive for such actions in the values intrinsic to the actions themselves. Furthermore, they claim that theirs is a purer and less self-centered motive. Aurobindo's affirmation of the cosmic and individual poises of Brahman would reconcile these two views by making the value of a good work simultaneously intrinsic and divine. One performs an action to improve the world or help another person for the sake of the world or the person himself, but this is identical with doing it for God's sake, because neither the world nor the person has any reality except the divine reality.

The chief advantage of the three-poise formulation, of course, is the one Aurobindo was most concerned for: it assures the reality and the value of the world. But it also allows him certain other positions which he favors. It reduces the sting of the problem of evil, if it does not eliminate it, by putting God Himself in the suffering world, rather than outside, permitting evil to be endured by others. It assures personal immortality and avoids the conception of life as a trial followed by judgment and reward or punishment. It gives man the high dignity of a divine incarnation, a cooperator in the divine action of evolving the world, yet saves his unique individuality and his capacity for personal relations with other men and with God. The three poises make understandable the variety of spiritual states and allow each of them an equal dignity: the individual may be united with the Personal God in love, he may attain cosmic consciousness, or he may merge his consciousness in the transcendent.

Are there any difficulties with the three-poise position? Someone might ask how a man can have true individual selfhood if he is essentially a manifestation of the one Divine Being and does not have his own independent existence. Or one might ask simply how it is possible for the Absolute to have three such different postures. Aurobindo might reply by saying that these are his axiomatic positions, the radical propositions from which he starts and which he does not prove—though in *The Life Divine* he offers various arguments to show their feasibility. And he might further point out that they are no more difficult to assimilate intellectually than the fundamental propositions of Christian theology, according to which the Absolute is a single Being with three hypostases and there is a divine incarnation in which one hypostasis has genuine individual selfhood while remaining the transcendent Deity. Aurobindo has, in fact, referred to these Christian doctrines in relation to his own teaching. His remark about the implications of the Incarnation has been mentioned above, and he explicitly disclaimed any originality in the construction of the three-poise doctrine, on the grounds that the dogma of the Trinity already expressed it.

> The distinction between the Transcendental, the Cosmic, the Individual Divine is not my invention, nor is it native to India or to Asia—it is, on the contrary, a recognised European teaching current in the esoteric tradition of the Catholic Church where it is the authorised explanation of the Trinity—Father, Son and Holy Ghost,—and it is very well-known to European mystic experience.[1]

These are, perhaps, ultimate mysteries of being, as far as we can penetrate them at present, and we may simply have to accept them in their mystery. By observing and reasoning we can conclude that holding other positions seems to lead to greater difficulties than holding these positions, whereas these give fruitful results when applied to our experience.

---

1. *The Riddle of This World* (S.A.A., 1951) , p. 72. The author is not aware of this interpretation as the "authorised explanation of the Trinity" by the Catholic Church.

THE CRUCIAL IMPORTANCE OF EVOLUTION

There has been a long tradition among humanity, both in India and in other cultures, teaching that man's ultimate goal cannot be found in this world. All of the great religions have taught it in one form or another. The doctrine of the unreality of the world is only the most extreme expression of this attitude. The notion that the world is a field for the development, or the trial, of a soul which will then find its home elsewhere belongs to the same general class. Both views measure the worth or the reality of the world in terms of its value or disvalue for man. If the world is seen only as a disvalue, it is declared unreal. If a temporary usefulness for the world can be seen, then it is accorded that much reality, but is assumed to be destroyed once its role is finished.

Aurobindo rejects both of these views, and his arguments reduce to two main lines: 1) the world has meaning and value of its own in relation to God without reference to man; and 2) it is not impossible for man to achieve his goal within this world through a continuous transformation. The first line is supported by the doctrine of the three poises of Brahman. The second is dependent on the doctrine of evolution.

If there were no evolution, then the above attitude of either immediately or eventually escaping this world would be perfectly right, for it is certainly clear that man cannot attain his goal in this world as it presently exists. The question is whether it is necessary to break radically with the present world. In the West, for instance, the religious tradition does not declare the world unreal, but it looks for "the end of the world" and expects "a new heaven and a new earth." There is every indication that this is to be conceived as a radical discontinuity with the present world. Aurobindo feels that our knowledge of evolution, plus our spiritual experience, is sufficient to enable us to entertain the possibility that the "new earth" can be attained without this radical break, by a continuous transformation instead.

Aurobindo does not argue about whether there is evolution. He feels that the scientific evidence for cosmic evolution is so strong that this may be taken for granted. He proceeds to argue that since there is evolution, it must be for some purpose. If God intended man merely to break out of the world, there would be no intelligibility to the long, slow, arduous development of the multiplicity of natural forms, the gradually rising spiritual life of intelligence, love, and freedom, the continual strengthening of the individual, and all the other characteristic features of natural evolution as we observe it.

The intention of the Creator must make use of evolution; it must be intrinsic to His purpose. But only up to a point? Is it merely to evolve man to a certain stage from which he can then make a radical break to an entirely different form of life? This does not amount, in Aurobindo's mind, to a sufficient reason. If, for instance, man has to be possessed of a certain degree of freedom in order to make the crucial leap, why not create him with this freedom in the first place? Why bring him up gradually from lower organic forms and these in turn from the inorganic? Also, if God's interest in man is only in his spiritual perfection, a certain purity of his will, why involve all these complex transformations of organic Nature? If evolution is to be intelligible, Aurobindo concludes, it must be intrinsic to God's purpose, and it must go on until it attains a goal in which all its features are integrally perfected. Stopping short halfway will not accomplish this, and leaving material evolution without a final fulfillment will not accomplish it. Either would make evolution an extraneous factor, not integral to the divine action, and thus reflect on the wisdom of the divine action itself.

It is not clear, Aurobindo contends, that it is *impossible* for man to attain his goal in this world, if this world is sufficiently transformed. It is not inconsistent, for instance, that he be united with the Infinite and still be incarnate in a world of finite forms. It is only our mental logic which would persuade us that these are incompatible. If God Himself can be incarnate in a finite form, clearly the two are not contradictory.

It is important, therefore, to pinpoint the obstacle to salvation in this world. If it is not finitude as such, not limitation, not being with form, that is the barrier to union with the Absolute, what is it? It is the false identification of ourselves with the separative ego, says Aurobindo, the belief that we, and all other beings, are separated entities excluded from direct communication with one another and with God. If we can overcome this divisive sense of ourselves and the centering of our own self-interest, we will be able to transform the world so that we can attain our goal. In any case, Aurobindo would say, in this world or elsewhere, *this* is the spiritual prerequisite to the divine end. It is not getting rid of the world that makes the difference but getting rid of the ego.

The question then becomes, can this be done in this world? Does not, for instance, our present union with the human body make it impossible to perfect this transformation? Aurobindo replies that the evolutionary forces of

Nature already have done things which we would have said were a priori impossible, such as bringing forth life and sensation from inert matter, and intelligence and freedom from instinctive animality. Why should they not support us in the accomplishment of this task? It is clearly in the line of what Nature seems to be moving toward: increasing consciousness, greater richness of diversity within a more interiorized unity, and greater transparency for the divine self-expression. It is the obvious next step. Why should we not trust the power of God in the evolving world to accomplish it?

But we also have our role to play. This will not happen automatically, because it involves our freedom. It is precisely our own self-consciousness which has to be transformed. And our part in the work is difficult; very difficult, in fact. It is also true that not the least of the difficulties is the human body, with its subconscious and unconscious tendencies and habits. That is why so many are tempted to call the task impossible and to look for some other environment in which the transformation will somehow magically take place of itself. But nothing in God's self-expression in the world so far has come easily, instantaneously, or from extrinsic causes. Everything has developed slowly, often with failures along the way, and from its own interior potentiality.

God has chosen to manifest Himself in the finite in this way, says Aurobindo. Let us therefore not be weaklings, or revolt against the world with violence and impatience, but unite ourselves with the divine will and cooperate in the great drama. Let us call on Shakti, Divine Energy, to sustain us in the struggle to bring to birth the next phase of the divine manifestation. It is admittedly difficult, but

it is not impossible. There is even empirical evidence in
the lives of some among us that advances on this road
have been made. Since there is evolution, Aurobindo concludes, we need not escape the world, and since the world
is God's own self-expression, we must not abandon it if
we would be true to our divine vocation.

THE CASE AGAINST MAYAVADA

When we compare Aurobindo with Sankara, we have to
admit that Aurobindo is not a philosopher's philosopher.
He does not engage in the logical or metaphysical sub-
tleties which characterize the work of Sankara. He does
not even follow Sankara himself carefully. As we remarked
before, he seems to have missed the point that for Sankara
the perceiver is just as unreal as the perceived. Also, he
tends to ignore the fact that Sankara grants that within
the realm of the phenomenal consciousness there is a public world where all the usual perceptions, judgments, and
values are valid.

It is true, of course, that when Sankara is pressed as
to what is "really real," he holds that only the unitary
Brahman qualifies. The multiple world is no longer visible
to the consciousness awakened to Brahman. But this is not
so unlike what Aurobindo himself holds. In Ignorance
man sees the world as composed of separated entities. In
Knowledge he sees that really they are all one; in fact,
there is only one Being, and these many beings are merely
differentiations within it. The doctrinal difference would
seem to be that Sankara holds that any type of multiplicity
whatsoever is false, whereas Aurobindo holds that there
is genuine multiplicity harmoniously contained within the
unity.

Aurobindo correctly calls Sankara to task for not being clear about the status and value of the individual. If there is no multiplicity whatever in the state of Knowledge, what has happened to the individual? Was there just one "individual" all along? Would not this doctrine be solipsism? Or did the apparent individual turn out to be unreal? In that case, who was saved, who liberated? Sankara does not give satisfactory answers to these questions. He is obviously concerned for the salvation of the individual man, but his metaphysical position does not seem to allow this man sufficient reality to be worthy of this concern.

Could we not say that Aurobindo himself is indulging in "mental logic" in criticizing Sankara in this way? Is it not possible that the apparent individual, one among many as seen in Ignorance, finds himself as the true individual, perfectly united with all the other apparent individuals and with the Absolute in such a way that each of them experiences continuity of his individual being and consciousness but also unbroken unity of the one Brahman? However, Sankara himself seems not to have urged this view, but only to have insisted that multiplicity and unity are contradictory. If his arguments are restricted to mental logic, Aurobindo is justified in refuting him by mental logic.

The real difference between the two, finally, and the one which moves Aurobindo to debate with Mayavada, is a difference of attitude toward life. Sankara's attitude toward the phenomenal world of individuals and ordinary perceptions and actions, is one of tolerance at best. His ideal is to lose consciousness of it forever. This is what hurts Aurobindo. Even though it is possible to achieve Sankara's ideal—Aurobindo himself had reached that state of consciousness—Aurobindo does not believe that this is a worthy ideal for mankind. It fails both man and God, he feels, and makes the whole marvelous creation pointless. This may not be a sophisticated technical criticism of a great metaphysical structure, but perhaps it is important for this very reason. It offers an integral human judgment on a purely intellectual and speculative theory, and recalls philosophy to its role within the whole context of human life.

Aurobindo is, in this way, unremittingly realistic. Whatever is *there,* in any sense, we must accept and absorb into our picture of reality. Even if the world is phenomenal, the *fact* that it is phenomenal is a real fact and has to be given its eternal place in the whole. A place in the whole means a place in God's purpose, for Aurobindo. His conclusion from this point is that if God chooses to manifest Himself phenomenally, devotion to God dictates that we cooperate in this manifestation, not try to escape it.

Here we can see how deeply committed to a theistic position Aurobindo is. The will of God is the whole of reality for him, and surrender to, or cooperation with, the will of God is man's highest destiny. Phenomenal world and individual man have evidently been willed by God or we would not perceive them, even in Ignorance. Therefore, they have some divine purpose and destiny. Our duty is to seek that purpose and work for that destiny. Mayavada, Aurobindo feels, does not consider the whole picture of being from (so to speak) God's point of view in an attitude of humble acceptance of the divine will, but looks at the situation strictly from man's standpoint, with a view to releasing him from discomfort into personal bliss as soon as possible. The Christian impatience to obtain immediate participation in the divine life after a brief span on earth, spent mostly on the vital and mental levels,

Aurobindo considers equally shortsighted and self-centered. These points, we feel, offer a novel angle of vision on these questions, and while they may be somewhat overdrawn in their criticism, they bear consideration.

THE MARKS OF A SOUND THEORY

Aurobindo may not be a professional philosopher, but he has undertaken to construct a metaphysical system, and it is therefore appropriate to examine it as to its consistency, elegance, verifiability, and fruitfulness.

One of the interesting points to consider in terms of the question of consistency is Aurobindo's notion of Matter. Is it matter as it has been conceived in the West? Is it really "equally real" with Spirit in Aurobindo's system? Does it remain "matter" after all the transformations Aurobindo prophesies for it?

It is difficult for any system, scientific or philosophical, to define matter, and Aurobindo does not do it clearly. For him it is the lowest level of the manifest world, the least conscious. All the higher levels are involved in it but it manifests the least of the divine glory of any stratum. It is the final result of the movement of separation which began in the Overmind. Here Aurobindo's concept makes a connection with the Western scholastic definition of matter as being characterized by having "parts outside of parts." In a way, Aurobindo's "matter" is at the opposite pole from "spirit," as it is in the West, because he constructs his levels of being as a hierarchy between them. But it is not an absolutely different kind of substance from spirit, as it is in the West. For Aurobindo there is only one substance, Brahman. Brahman is Spirit, and therefore even Matter is a modality of Spirit.

Can this Matter be equally real with Spirit, then? Insofar as it is actually of the substance of Spirit, it is necessarily equally real. But because it is at the bottom of Aurobindo's scale of being, there is also a sense in which its whole reality is derived, whereas Spirit's is inherent. The claim to equal status with Spirit thus is a little misleading, it seems.

After the transformation, when Matter has been taken up into Supermind and made a perfect instrumentality for divine self-expression, will it still be matter? If matter is "that which offers resistance to change in its condition of rest or motion," perhaps not, for Aurobindo's conception of transfigured Matter seems to be that it offers no resistance to the will of the Supermind. He even says that he expects to accomplish by direct spiritual means effects in matter which formerly required physical forces. This would seem to indicate that even the inertia which defines matter in the scientific sense is no longer present. Matter, in Aurobindo's own sense, however, remains. It is that level of being which is the base for all other formulations and is of itself the least manifest. We may conclude, then, that while not perfectly clear, Aurobindo seems to be fairly consistent in his treatment of matter.

The transformation of matter is only one part of the transformation of the world and the question of consistency can be enlarged to include the whole. How much "transformation" can a being undergo and still be itself? If the world has to be changed to the extent that Aurobindo requires in order to fulfill its destiny, in what sense can he say that it is still "this" world? Aurobindo, because he thinks in terms of evolution, identifies beings by continuity of existence rather than by changelessness of essence. If there is continuous transformation of the being without a radical break, then it is the same being. If the evolutionary factor is ignored, and the critic compares the world in its present state with the world in its perfected state, he could very well say they are two different worlds and Aurobindo is not consistent in referring to both as simply "the world."

But because Aurobindo makes the evolutionary factor intrinsic to the world, he can admit whatever changes are needed to bring this world up to the divine standard and still maintain that it is the "same" world. Furthermore, he is justified in valuing "this" world and working with it, because it—and it alone—is going to become that perfect world. The evolutionary factor thus makes all the difference between an attitude of respecting and working for this world and an attitude of simply using and then discarding this world because a completely new one is expected. It is quite consistent for him, therefore, to speak of the world as real and valuable, yet expect it to be greatly transformed.

Elegance in a theory presupposes consistency. But, in addition, a theory to be elegant must hold without distortion a diversity of known facts within the unity of a single principle. The mark of elegance so defined, when applied to a theory about the real world, includes the mark of verifiability. Certainly, Aurobindo's system attempts to hold the widest possible diversity of facts within its principle, even the entire universe of our experience. Its single principle is that the Divine Real has three poises, transcendent, universal, and individual, of which the latter two are undergoing the continuous transformation of evolution. So far as diversity can be reduced to simplicity, it seems to meet the test. But does its representation of reality escape distortion?

Probably the most questionable element in Aurobindo's system, and the one on which he most seems to distort our experience in order to make it fit the theory, is his treatment of evil. He feels that by making God Himself the victim of what we call evil, he has somehow broken the back of the classical "problem of evil" which contrasted the good, powerful God with helpless, suffering man. Aurobindo's view should, theoretically, eliminate the contrast, because it identifies the powerful God and the suffering man by making the latter the "individual poise" of Brahman. However, there is still some distinction, even in Aurobindo's scheme. The Supermind acts from above on man (in his present sense of identity) and Aurobindo refers frequently to God's "grace" toward man. If there is sufficient distinction to permit these actions, then there is sufficient distinction to permit the question Why does the God of grace, or the Supermind, permit this useless, senseless suffering? Aurobindo tries to argue that it is not useless or senseless. Pain has its purposes in the evolution of Nature. This can be admitted to some extent, but it does not cover all instances of evil.

Another of Aurobindo's arguments is that what seems to us evil or painful is not necessarily so; it is only in the Ignorance that we experience things this way. However, his own argument with the Mayavadin can now be turned against him: the fact that it *seems* so to us is a real seeming and *this* is evil. Despite Aurobindo's efforts, the problem of evil remains.

His most helpful contribution in this regard is his insistence that man is not so helpless in the face of evil as he appears. Supported by the divine forces of evolution, he can advance toward the conquest of evil in his world. Powerful remedies are already available in the untapped realms of consciousness and can be brought down into our world by yoga. It will be remembered that it was in order to gain divine power to overthrow the evils from which his nation suffered that Sri Aurobindo first took up the practice of yoga. It is the continuation and expansion of this project that actually constitutes his whole career, of which the philosophy is only the intellectual expression.

Perhaps Aurobindo's attitude of optimism and his belief that his program is concretely practicable may seem a distortion of our experience. Is it not his expectation that the Gnostic Being will evolve on earth, and the divine life as he describes it be lived here, somewhat fantastic? The answer to this question seems to depend on how far one's faith and imagination can stretch. There is no a priori reason that we can discover why this should be impossible. The moral evidence for it at this moment in history certainly seems slight. But evolution is a slow process, patient of many setbacks. It has nevertheless come this far, and when we sufficiently appreciate what a marvel even our present world is, perhaps we can believe that it is capable of persevering to the end and being saved.

As for verifying Aurobindo's tenets, beyond what has already been done in examining the arguments, they can be verified only in practice. This is congenial to the ancient tradition of Indian thought which Aurobindo is eager to revive, and is reasonable in itself. Every theory about the universe implies a program of action. One way to test the theory is to try the action.

The notions of universal evolution and of God present in the world have stimulated the imaginations of many in recent years. The possibility of uniting secular values, so evident in the modern world, with the sacred values of a long tradition has renewed hope and religious interest in many people. But the promise of this vista needs to be made concrete, to be translated into daily life so that it can be realized.

Aurobindo has tried to show a way in which this can be done. The suggestions he has made deserve a thoughtful consideration and even practical trial of their claim to validity and fruitfulness. In his own ashram in Pondicherry his principles are being tried in practice. The latest project of the Ashram, supported by the Indian Government and by UNESCO, has been the foundation of an international city, Auroville, which will attempt to build an ultramodern technical civic life on an explicitly spiritual foundation.

Perhaps there is a helpful suggestion to other cultures in this. We in the West have separated our intellectual philosophical life too much from the practical life of the person and the society, just as we have separated institutionalized religious life from the natural life of the spirit. One final conclusion we might draw from this study of the teaching of Sri Aurobindo is that these areas need to be reunited and a concerted effort made to attain an integral life.

Bibliography

Primary Sources

Sri Aurobindo. *A Practical Guide to the Integral Yoga.*
Pondicherry: Sri Aurobindo Ashram Press, 1965.*
(Extracts compiled from the writings of Sri Auro-
bindo and the Mother, first published in 1955.)

————. *Essays on the Gita.* 1950. (1st edition, Ramaswamy
Shashtrulu & Sons, Madras, 1922; reprint of the first
chapters that appeared under the same title in the
Arya, Vol. III and IV from August 1916 to July
1918. 2nd edition, Arya Publishing House, Calcutta,
1926, with the title *Essays on the Gita, First Series.*
Essays on the Gita, Second Series: 1st edition, Arya
Publishing House, Calcutta, 1928; reprinted from
the *Arya,* Vol. V and VI from August 1918 to July
1920. The text was revised at the time of the second
edition in 1942.) **

————. *Messages of Sri Aurobindo and the Mother,* Second
Series. 1952.

————. *On the Veda.* 1964. (Contents originally published
as: *The Secret of the Veda, Arya,* August 1914 to
July 1916; *Selected Hymns, Arya,* August 1914 to

---

* Unless otherwise indicated, all works cited are published by the Sri
Aurobindo Ashram Press.
** Information on original editions taken from A.B. Purani, *The Life
of Sri Aurobindo,* Appendix, pp. 329–43.

July 1915; *Hymns of the Atris, Arya,* August 1915 to December 1917; *Other Hymns, Arya,* August 1915 to January 1920. The chapter "The Origins of Aryan Speech," found among the author's MSS, here published [posthumously] for the first time.)

————. *On Yoga* I (*The Synthesis of Yoga*), 1957. ([1st edition, 1955.] Part I, "The Yoga of Divine Works," was first published by the Sri Aurobindo Library, Madras, 1948, and consisted of reprints, very much enlarged, of the first twelve chapters appearing under this title in the *Arya* from January 1915 to November 1915. It is here included with the addition of chapter XIII [incomplete]. Part II, "The Yoga of Integral Knowledge," [revised] and succeeding parts are also taken from *Arya,* August 1914 to January 1921.)

————. *On Yoga* II. 1958. (Collected letters on yoga, including those in "Bases of Yoga" [Calcutta: Arya Publishing House, 1936], "Lights on Yoga" [Howrah: Sri Aurobindo Library, 1935], "The Riddle of This World" [Calcutta: Arya Publishing House, 1933], and "More Lights on Yoga" [Pondicherry: Sri Aurobindo Ashram, 1948].)

————. *Speeches and Writings.* 1952. (The collected speeches were first published in 1922 and included speeches made between 1908 and 1910 and first published in *Bande Mataram* and *The Karmayogin.*)

————. *Sri Aurobindo on Himself and on the Mother.* 1953. (Collection of letters and notes written by Sri Aurobindo on different occasions, concerning his life, his activities, and his spiritual experiences. The notes for the aid of his biographers date from 1943–46, while the excerpts from letters cover roughly the period 1930–1950.)

————. *The Human Cycle.* New York: The Sri Aurobindo Library, 1950. (These chapters originally appeared under the title *The Psychology of Social Develop-*

ment in *Arya* from August 1916 to July 1918.)

——. *The Ideal of Human Unity.* New York: Dutton, 1950. (First appeared in *Arya,* September 1915 to July 1918, revised prior to World War II, brought up to date of publication by addition of an Introduction.)

——. *The Ideal of the Karmayogin.* 1950. (1st edition not traceable; reprinted at Chandernagore and Calcutta. The twelve articles included in it were originally written in the *Karmayogin* in 1909–10 [Nos. 1–38]. The last two articles in it are by Sister Nivedita.)

——. *The Life Divine.* 1960.* (First published as two volumes in three parts, Calcutta: Arya Publishing House, Vol. I, 1939, Vol. II, 1940. Vol. I: the first twenty-seven chapters are reprinted with some additions from *Arya,* August 1914 to October 1916; chapter 28 added. Vol. II: nineteen of the chapters reprinted from *Arya,* rearranged; chapters 1, 2, 6, 10, 19, 25, 26, and 28 are new.)

N.B.: There are various recent editions of this work whose paginations do not agree. The edition used here is Volume III of the Sri Aurobindo Center of Education Collection.

——. *The Mother.* 8th ed. 1956. (1st edition, Calcutta: Arya Sahitya Bhavan, 1928.)

——. *The Riddle of This World.* 1951. (1st edition, Calcutta: Arya Publishing House, 1933.)

——. *The Supramental Manifestation.* 1952. (Reprint of articles appearing in the *Bulletin of Physical Education* in 1949–50.)

——. *The Yoga and Its Objects.* 1964. (1st edition, Chandernagore: Pravartak Publishing House, 1921.)

——. *Thoughts and Aphorisms.* 1959. (1st edition, 1958. The original version, only a portion of which was revised by the author and subsequently published as a separate book under the title, *Thoughts and*

Glimpses. That portion is excluded from this collection.)

——. *Thoughts and Glimpses.* 1964. (First published in *Arya.* 1st edition, 1920.)

Secondary Sources

Bolle, Kees W. *The Persistence of Religion.* Leiden: Brill, 1965.

Bose, A. C. *Hymns from the Vedas.* New York: Asia Publishing House, 1966.

Chaudhuri, Haridas. "Has Sri Aurobindo Refuted Mayavada?" in *Indian Philosophical Congress* (Silver Jubilee Commemorative Volume), 1950.

——. *Sri Aurobindo: The Prophet of Life Divine.* 2nd ed. 1960.

——. *The Philosophy of Integralism.* Calcutta: Sri Aurobindo Pathamandir, 1954.

—— and Spiegelberg, Frederic, eds. *The Integral Philosophy of Sri Aurobindo.* London: Allen & Unwin, 1960.

Dasgupta, Surendranath. *A History of Indian Philosophy.* 5 vols. Cambridge: The University Press, 1922–55.

Diwakar, R. R. *Mahayogi Sri Aurobindo.* Bombay: Bharatiya Vidya Bhavan, 1962.

Gokhale, B. G. *Indian Thought through the Ages*: A Study of Some Dominant Concepts. London: Asia Publishing House, 1961.

Gupta, N. K. *The Coming Race.* Madras: Sri Aurobindo Library, 1944.

Hiriyanna, M. *Outlines of Indian Philosophy.* London: Allen & Unwin, 1964.

Maitra, S. K. *An Introduction to the Philosophy of Sri Aurobindo.* Calcutta: Culture, 1941.

——. *The Meeting of the East and the West in the Philosophy of Sri Aurobindo.* 1956.

Mitra, Sisirkumar. *Sri Aurobindo and the New World.* 1957.

———. *The Vision of India.* New York: Laico, 1949.

Modi, P. M. *A Critique of the Brahma-Sutra.* Bhavagar: privately printed, 1943.

Patanjali. *Yoga Sutras.* Translated and with an Introduction by Swami Prabhavananda and Christopher Isherwood, as *How to Know God.* Hollywood: Vedanta Press, 1953.

Purani, A. B. *The Life of Sri Aurobindo.* 2nd ed. 1960.

Radhakrishnan, S. *Indian Philosophy.* 2 vols. London: Allen & Unwin, 1923.

———. *The Principal Upanishads.* London: Allen & Unwin, 1953.

——— and Moore, C. A., eds. *A Source Book in Indian Philosophy.* Princeton: Princeton University Press, 1957.

Raju, P. T. *Idealistic Thought of India.* London: Allen & Unwin, 1953.

Reyna, Ruth. *The Concept of Maya from the Vedas to the 20th Century.* Bombay: Asia Publishing House, 1962.

Roy, Dilip Kumar. *Sri Aurobindo Came to Me.* n.d.

Sankara. *Commentary on the Vedanta Sutras.* Translated by George Thibaut as *The Vedanta Sutras of Badarayana, with the commentary by Sankara.* 2 parts. New York: Dover, 1962.

———. *Vivekachudamani.* Translated by Swami Madhavananda. Calcutta: Advaita Ashrama, 1957.

Sastry, T. V. Kapali. *Lights on the Fundamentals.* Madras: Sri Aurobindo Library, 1950.

———. *Sri Aurobindo: Lights on the Teachings.* Madras: Sri Aurobindo Library, 1948.

Satprem. *Sri Aurobindo, or The Adventure of Consciousness.* New York: India Library Society, 1964.

Sethna, K. D. *The Indian Spirit and the World's Future.* 1953.

Sri Aurobindo and His Ashram. Official publication of the Ashram. 1964.

Index

27, 255–56, 264. *See also* Being

Realization: as bringing into being, 38, 138, 201, 223; of God, 196, 236; as knowledge, 22, 210; self-, 218, 235; as spiritual experience, 27, 29, 43, 46, 61, 202, 203; supramental, 38, 181; transcendent, 212, 243. *See also* Spiritual experience

Rebirth, 230

Reconciliation, 46–47, 49, 89, 247, 255, 257; example of, 52, 54, 98, 176; as harmony, 73; as overcoming distinction, 50; by yoga, 138. *See also* Integration; Method, Aurobindo's

Reflexion, 129

Religion, 29 n.19, 62. *See also* Christianity; Hinduism

Renunciation, 182, 203, 206, 212–13, 222, 242

Richard, Mira, 35, 35 n.13. *See also* Mother

Richard, Paul, 22 n.5

Rita, 83–84, 189

Rishis, 33, 190

Roy, Dilip Kumar, 23 n.5; 28 n.17

Sachchidananda, 67, 67 n.6, 92, 121–22, 126, 127, 134, 147, 254; as God, 224; evolution of, 68, 133, 235; as Higher Maya, 69; and Ignorance, 114, 116, 120; and Lower Maya, 96; manifest, 89, 131, 140, 151, 225; and Supermind, 85, 94

Sacrifice, 145, 249. *See also* Detachment

Sadhana, 24, 24 n.8, 25, 28, 35, 213

Salvation (deliverance), 25, 56, 253; collective, 249, 251; in Mayavada, 45, 174, 209, 265; of Nature, 231; obstacle to, 262; post-mortem, 217; reality of, 174, 191. *See also* Liberation

Samadhi, 27, 27 n.16, 118, 180

Samhitas, 189

Sanatana Dharma, 29 n.19

Sankara, 42, 56, 89, 152, 154, 160–67, 172, 175, 177, 180, 181, 183, 186–87, 213, 239, 264–65

Sankhya, 58

Sannyasa, 39

Sastry, T. V. Kapali, 15, 187 n.79, 192, 227–28

Sat, 57

Satprem, 32, 33, 251; quoted, 29 n.19

Satya, 189

Sayana, 188

Science, 74–75

Self, 37, 112, 144, 197, 199, 201, 221, 234, 254; as Brahman, 159, 161, 163, 195; cosmic, 94, 97; gnostic, 148; as God, 241; infinite, 139, 222; One, 108, 241, 252; real (true), 66, 107, 112, 113, 141, 161, 174, 177, 237; -realization, 27 n.16; according to Sankara, 46, 167, 184; secret (hidden), 134, 197, 237; of Supermind, 87, 92; supreme, 178, 210, 242; of things, 67, 158

Separation, 42, 80; and evil, 64–65, 124–26; and evolution, 73; and Ignorance, 108, 110–11, 264; and the individual, 49, 76, 238–39, 262; and logic, 52; and Matter, 74–75; and Mind, 50, 71–72, 71 n.10; and Overmind, 93, 267

Sethna, K. D., 15, 207, 214

Sevenfold chord of Being, 95–96

Shakti, 48, 49 n.2, 59, 61, 77, 165, 227, 254, 263. *See also* Mother, Divine

Shaw, G. B., 253

Shiva, 49

Siddhi, 38; Day of, 35–40

Sin, 215 n.2

Society, 205, 211–12; and the person, 272. *See also* Collective; Community

Sorokin, P., quoted, 13

Soul, 122, 126, 136, 139, 201, 238, 243, 246; transcendent, 243; ultimate state of, 247

Space, 38, 76, 111

Spengler, Oswald, 229–30